APPLICATIO DIGITAL MARKETING

FOR SUCCESS IN BUSINESS

Abhishek Das

An IIFT Alumni, Google Certified Digital Marketing Expert

bpb

BPB PUBLICATIONS

Distributors:

BPB PUBLICATIONS
20, Ansari Road, Darya Ganj
New Delhi-110002
Ph: 23254990/23254991

COMPUTER BOOK CENTRE
12, Shrungar Shopping Centre,
M.G.Road, BENGALURU–560001
Ph: 25587923/25584641

MICRO MEDIA
Shop No. 5, Mahendra Chambers, 150 DN
Rd. Next to Capital Cinema, V.T. (C.S.T.)
Station, MUMBAI-400 001
Ph: 22078296/22078297

BPB BOOK CENTRE
376 Old Lajpat Rai Market,
Delhi-110006
Ph: 23861747

DECCAN AGENCIES
4-3-329, Bank Street,
Hyderabad-500195
Ph: 24756967/24756400

Published by Manish Jain for BPB Publications, 20, Ansari Road, Darya Ganj, New Delhi-110002 and Printed by Repro India Pvt Ltd, Mumbai

Table of Contents

Preface

As we are moving forward in this current digital era, we emphasize on those techniques which are more efficient and economic. This book offers a variety of digital marketing tools, technique, application methodologies, their complexity, efficiency and many more aspects. It also focuses on concept for digital marketing which drives our business and its day-to-day operations effectively.

Keeping in mind the changing scenario in business environment, Authors are confident to explain digital marketing tools and techniques, applied methodologies which may prove as a first step for a beginner.

The book will describe:

- Digital Marketing Applications concept and techniques.
- Value Chain of Digital Marketing Process and Operations.
- Why Digital Marketing is useful for each and every Business.
- Basis picture of what will a business miss out on if they don't market their products/services online.
- Technological edge for a venture when they implement digital marketing well in their firm. Branding with the help of Digital Marketing Tools.
- Financial payment methods to help determine annual budget for Digital Marketers.
- Determine a bid strategy based on your goals.
- Social Media Advertisement Platforms.
- What are some of the best ways to integrate email marketing with social media participation? Digital marketing and measurement model.
- How do you use Web Analytics effectively to make most out of it for your business?
- Future Evolution of Digital Marketing and Role of WordPress in it.
- **Digital Marketing:** A Great Tool for Market research.
- **Copywrites:** An Art or Science
- **Copyright:** A Globally Practiced Method to Prevent Plagiarism and Control Data Duplicity.
- How a Business Can Convert its Visitors into Qualified Business Leads Using CRM/AI. How an Entrepreneur setup an Online Store for Their Online Business (Including- Business Case-I & II)

Although the content has been supervised by many senior educationists, there may be some shortcomings. As human is prone to errors, authors wish to forgive the mistakes and we welcome your suggestions and criticism if any! The authors will try their best to incorporate such valuable suggestions in the subsequent editions of this book.

ABHISHEK DAS

Acknowledgements

First and foremost, I would like to thank God. I could never have done this without the faith I have in you, the Almighty.

Secondly, I would also like to thank my parents for their throughout support and faith in me. I could never have done this without you.

I would extend my gratitude to BPB Publication for bringing out the book in its present form.

A great thanks to my family and friends, without their support i wouldn't be able to complete this task.

"Parents are always been the boost up part behind a rising sun".

ABHISHEK DAS

x

Chapter 1: Digital Marketing Applications

1.1 Introduction

Digital Marketing (also known as data led marketing) is an umbrella concept for marketing of diversified products or services using technological tools primarily on the internet, but also includes mobile devices, display advertisement and many other digital medium. Digital Marketing consists of various tools and methods showcased in the picture below.

Digital marketing being an umbrella term covers all the above aspects displayed in the image, further elaborated below.

1.2 Search engine optimization (SEO)

Search engine optimization, or SEO, attempts to improve a website's organic search rankings in Google's search engine homepage by increasing the visibility of the website contents relevant to the searchers. Search engines regularly update their algorithms to penalize poor quality sites that try to game their rankings and reward websites backed by rich and relevant quality content embedded into it, helps businesses moving to the right target audience for advertisers. Many Digital Marketing firms offer SEO paid services seeing its future potential as a smart business.

1.3 Website Design

Briefly, website design means planning, creation and updating of websites. Website design also involves information architecture, website structure, user interface, navigation ergonomics, website layout, colours, contrasts, fonts and imagery (photography) as well as icons design.

All these website elements combined together form websites. Often, the meaning of "design" is perceived solely as a visual aspect. In reality, website design includes more abstract elements such as usability, ergonomics, layout traditions, user habits, navigation logic and other things that simplify the using of websites and help to find information faster.

Sometimes the technical side of website design is emphasized in the definition of design. Surely, the modern website building involves server side scripting like PHP, ASP, MySQL and CGI, websites' visual side is defined with html and CSS, user experience is enhanced with dynamic JavaScript and AJAX. When talking to people with poor technical knowledge, instead of speaking about technical details, we concentrate on functionalities, e. g. to what extent it is possible to update a website through content management system and which features are visible to users.

In classical terms, design describes the visual appearance of a website. Traditional approach involves contrast, colouring, balance, emphasis, rhythm, style of graphical elements (lines, shapes, texture, colour and direction), and use of icons, background textures and general atmosphere of overall website design.

All these elements are combined with the fundamental principles of design in order to create a superb result that meets the goals set for the website.

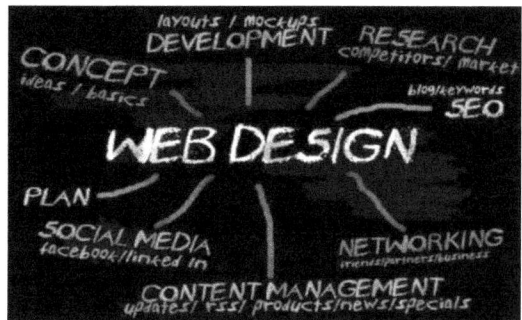

Apart from the above mentioned web designing techniques to enhance the look and feel factor of the webpage, there are many other technical aspects involved into it, like web analytics, payment gateway, flash, graphics, sound effects can also be embedded depending on the nature of the business to empower the website as revenue generating tool for your business.

1.4 Blogs

Platforms like BlogSpot create an online platform for companies and clients to connect online and promote contents, also helpful to exchange knowledge, Companies that recognize the need for information, originality/ and accessibility employ blogs to make their products popular and unique/ and ultimately reach out to consumers who are savvy to social media. Blogs allow a product or company to provide longer descriptions of products or services can include testimonials and can link to and from other social network and blog pages. Blogs can be updated frequently and are promotional techniques for keeping customers and also for acquiring followers and subscribers who can then be directed to social network pages. Online communities can enable a business to reach the clients of other businesses using the platform. To allow firms to measure their standing in the corporate world, sites enable employees to place evaluations of their companies. Some businesses opt out of integrating social media platforms into their traditional marketing regimen. There are also specific corporate standards that apply when interacting online. To maintain an advantage in a business-consumer relationship, businesses have to be aware of four key assets that consumers maintain: information, involvement, community, and control. For example look at equitymaster an equity research firm promotes their research products and services through and informative blog to attract more people for buying their subscriptions.

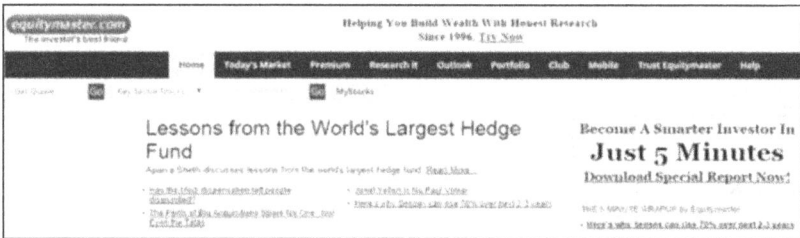

One can develop a blog to promote customized content, share knowledge or skills with the users on google/any other online platform. It's one of the simplest form to promote yourself as an individual showcasing your talent and skills to reach mass and attract them to either avail your service or bagging innovative business proposals from investors or business community looking to invest in new ventures to maximize their profitability. As sample a personal promoted blog screenshot has been shared to make you understand, how an independent blog gather interest and audience later revenue. Here an induvial has tried to share how a delicious recipe can keep you healthy and ensure essential nutrients you require in your daily life.

1.5 Web/Link Dictionaries

A web directory or link dictionary is an online list or catalogue of websites. That is, it is a directory on the World Wide Web of (all or part of) the World Wide Web. Historically, directories typically listed entries on people or businesses, and their contact information; such directories are still in use today.

As a local business, attracting new customers can be a major challenge. Quickly disappearing are the days when people go to the Yellow Pages to find local businesses. Today, people are turning to the internet as a way to find trusted business recommendations.

One way local businesses can get found is through inclusion in online directories. Adding a listing to these online directories is easy, but if you only list in a few, you're really missing a huge opportunity to get found by online searchers.

Some examples of such online/link directories are-

1. Google
2. Yellow Pages
3. Yahoo!
4. Sulekha
5. Facebook
6. Just Dial
7. LinkedIn
8. Trip Advisor

Please find below some of the business directory services offered by various service providers.

1.6 Search Engine Marketing (SEM)

Search engine marketing, or SEM, is designed to increase a website's visibility in search engine results pages especially during any google search. Search engines provide sponsored results and organic (non-sponsored) results based on a web searcher's query. Search engines often employ visual cues to differentiate sponsored results from organic results. Search engine marketing includes all of an advertiser's actions to make a website's listing more prominent for topical keywords. Such unique keywords help that particular advertisement to filter billions of searches and appear on top based on relevance. Look at the advertisements below appearing on a page during any search made relevant for the subject to reach to a particular target audience/set of viewers.

1.7 Video Marketing

YouTube is another popular avenue for any advertisers interested in giving a visual understanding of the product features through colourful videos. Advertisements are done in a way to suit the target audience. The type of language used in the commercials and the ideas used to promote the product reflect the audience›s style and taste. Also, the ads on this platform are usually in sync with the content of the video requested; this is another advantage YouTube brings for advertisers. Certain ads are presented with certain videos since the content is relevant. Promotional opportunities such as sponsoring a video is also possible on YouTube, «for example, a user who searches for a video on Cardio training may be presented with a sponsored video from a fitness company in results along with other videos on YouTube. YouTube also enable publishers to earn money through its YouTube Partner Program. Companies can pay YouTube for a special "channel" which promotes the company's products or services. It's an effective tool to go viral since whoever comes on YouTube to view any sort of content, can be entertaining, study material, movies, songs, cartoons, animated videos an online ad will automatically appears before you start watching the actual show on YouTube.

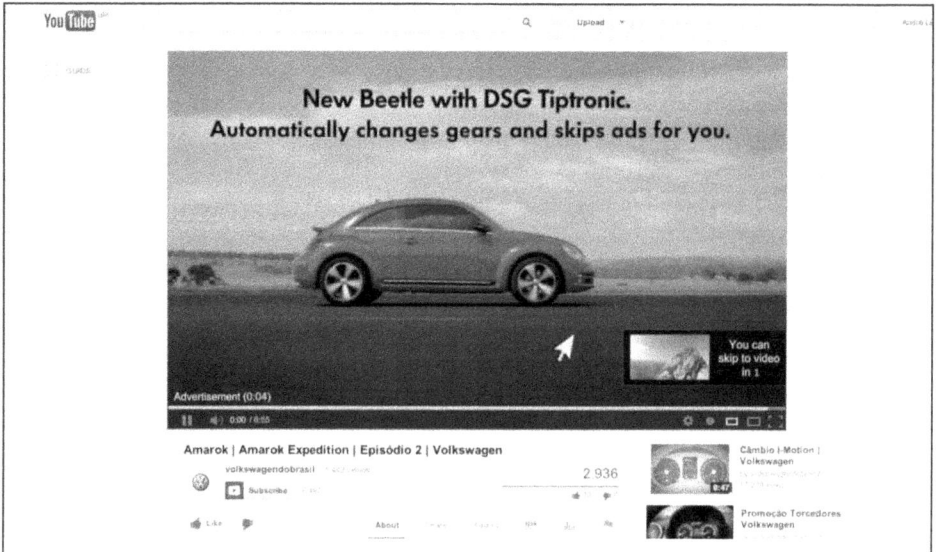

1.8 Email Marketing

Email marketing in comparison to other forms of digital marketing tools is considered cheap. It is also a way to rapidly communicate a message such as their value proposition to existing or potential customers. Yet this channel of communication may be perceived by recipients to be bothersome and irritating especially to new or potential customers, therefore the success of email marketing is reliant on the language and visual appeal applied. In terms of visual appeal, there are indications that using graphics/visuals that are relevant to the message which is attempting to be sent, yet less visual graphics to be applied with initial emails are more effective in-turn creating a relatively personal feel to the email. In terms of language, the style is the main factor in determining how captivating the email is. Using casual tone invokes a warmer and gentle and inviting feel to the email in comparison to a formal style. For combinations, it's suggested that to maximize effectiveness, using no graphics/visual alongside casual language. In contrast using no visual appeal and a formal language style is seen as the least effective method initially, but way forward once your brand becomes known to your recipients your graphics appeals to the customer for further information extraction.

Look at the below appended emailer sent by Amazon to promote their newly arrived products in amazon. They simply extract your email id through various affiliated vendors to send you promotional emailers to enhance product awareness and brand visibility consequently. Users with their diverse need in their daily life love to be informed, therefore they keep on browsing, comparing and purchasing products to fulfill their daily need through these platforms like Amazon, Flipkart, Healthkart for their diverse need.

1.9 Social Media Marketing

The term 'Digital Marketing' has a number of marketing tools/components embedded as it supports different channels used in and among these, comes the Social Media. When we use social media channels (Facebook, Twitter, LinkedIn, Instagram, Google+, etc.) to market a product or service, the strategy is called Social Media Marketing. It is a procedure wherein strategies are made and executed to draw in traffic for a website or to gain attention of buyers over the web using different social media platforms.

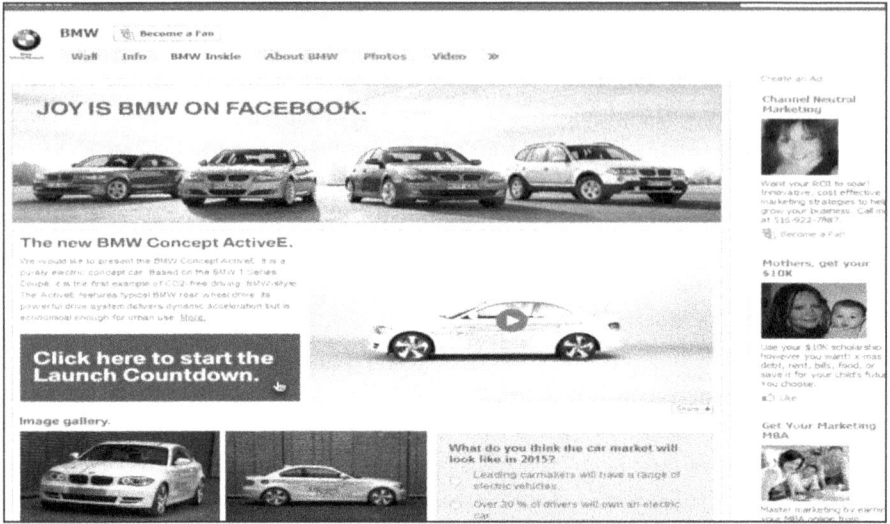

1.10 Content Marketing

Content is a form of marketing focused on creating, publishing and distributing content for a targeted audience online. It is often used by businesses in order to:

- Attract attention and generate leads
- Expand their customer base
- Generate or Increase online sales
- Increase brand awareness or credibility
- Engage an online community of users

Content marketing means attracting and transforming prospects into customers by creating and sharing valuable free content. The purpose of content marketing is to help the company to create sustainable brand loyalty and provide valuable information to consumers, as well as create willingness to purchase products from the company in the future. This relatively new form of marketing usually does not involve direct sales. Instead, it builds trust and rapport with the audience.

Unlike other forms of online marketing, content marketing relies on anticipating and meeting an existing customer need for information, as opposed to creating demand for a new need. As James O'Brien of Contently wrote on Mashable, "The idea central to content marketing is that a brand must give something valuable to get something valuable in return. Instead of the commercial, be the show. Instead of the banner advertisement, just to be the feature story. For content marketing, continuous delivery of large amounts of content is required, preferably within a content marketing strategy.

When businesses pursue content marketing, the main focus should be the needs of the prospect or customer. Once a business has identified the customer's need, information can be presented in a variety of formats, including news, video, white papers, e-books, infographics, email newsletters, case studies, podcasts, how-to guides, question and answer articles, photos, blogs, etc. Most of these formats belong to the digital channel.

Digital content marketing is a management process that uses digital products through different electronic channels to identify, forecast and satisfy the content requirements of a particular audience. It must be consistently updated and added to in order to influence the behaviour of customers.

Especially for content advertisement via various media either through affiliation or space purchase, companies always are focused on certain ideas, events and build customized/specialized contents to hit viewers mind for a particular timeframe and gain maximum volume out of that period as much as possible for them to do.

Digital marketing is also referred as "online marketing", "internet marketing" or "web marketing" as well. The term Digital marketing has gained popularity in overtime in technological advance developed countries like USA, UK and also in developing economies like India, china and Bangladesh. In counties like USA the term online marketing is still prevalent. In few European countries like Italy the term web marketing is prevalent; otherwise globally including UK the term digital marketing has become the most common and popular.

Digital Marketing has seen a revolution during 1990s and 2000s when most of the brands and businesses started their branding and marketing using digital technologies and tolls wisely. Since Digital marketing platforms are emerging as the next Marketing revolution almost all the corporate houses has predominantly started incorporating Digital Marketing as an effective component into their overall marketing strategy. As people are increasingly using digital devices more instead of taking out time from their busy daily schedule and visit physical shops, digital marketing campaigns are becoming more effective and efficient day by day.

Certain features offered by digital marketing which contributes in brand awareness via "ease of Access" and allowing consumers to get engaged with customer service team of a business via " Interaction through chat/mail" has enabled organizations to gain customer confidence and empowered customers to share their feedback directly to the organization. Therefore the communication gap between producers and end users are narrowing down drastically.

Users with an access to the internet can use many such digital mediums like Facebook, YouTube, Whatsapp and email etc. to establish and immediate interaction with the concern departments. Through digital media it can create a multi-communication channel where information can be quickly exchanged across the globe.

Digital Marketing techniques such as search engine optimization (SEO), search engine marketing (SEM), content marketing, influencer marketing, product campaign marketing, content automation, e-commerce, social media marketing, display advertisement, email direct marketing etc... Digital marketing has progressed enough and extends to non-internet channels as well that provides digital media, through mobile devices (SMS & MMS) etc. we will discuss later this topic later in the proceeding chapters.

Marketers always try to create hype through periodic dialogues and schemes to attract customer's attention and stand under limelight.

1.11 Some Examples of Value Chain of Digital Marketing Process and Operations

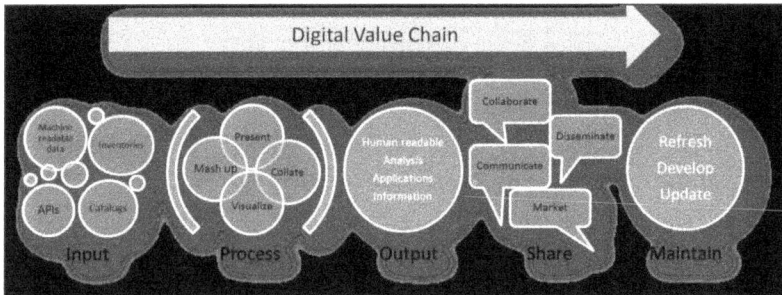

Sectorial Digital Marketing Strategies (Pharma Industry)

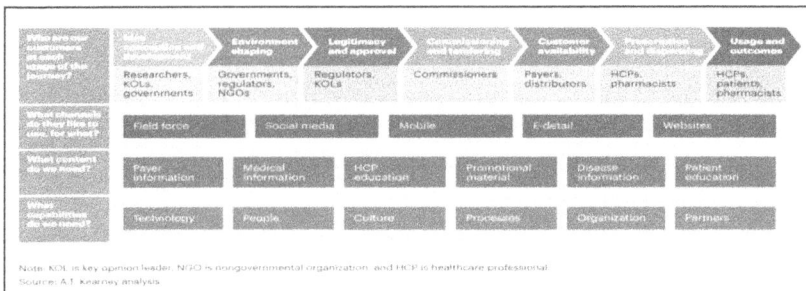

Sectorial Digital Marketing Strategies (Real Estate Industry)

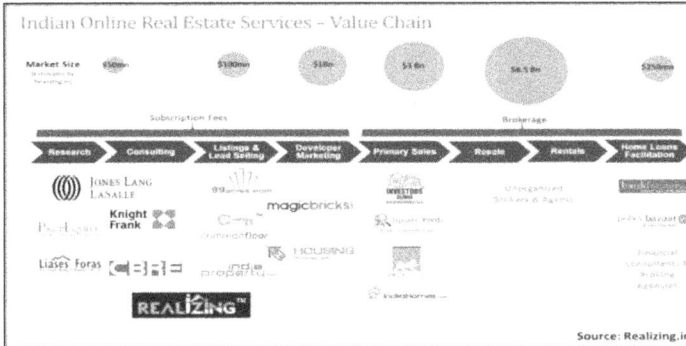

Sectorial Digital Marketing Strategies (BFSI Industry)

We see more than 30 areas emerging as new norms in banking.

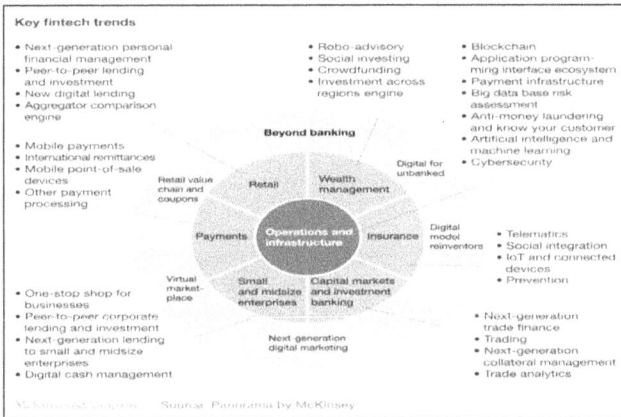

Sectorial Digital Marketing Strategies (Automobile Industry)

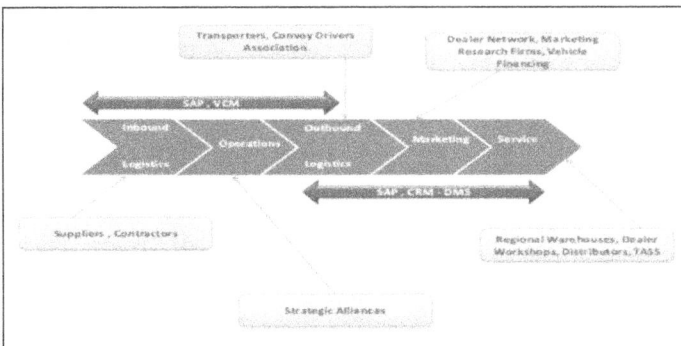

Value Chain & Value System of Tata Motors

Digital Transformation and Industry 4.0 Revolution Models

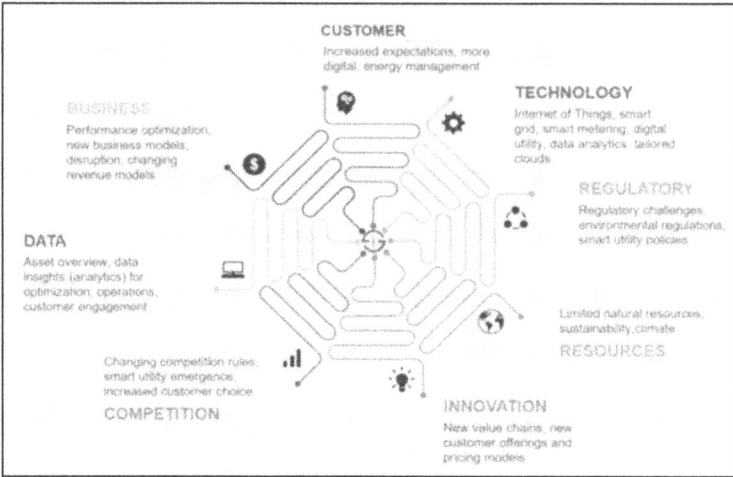

Utility Industry Transformation

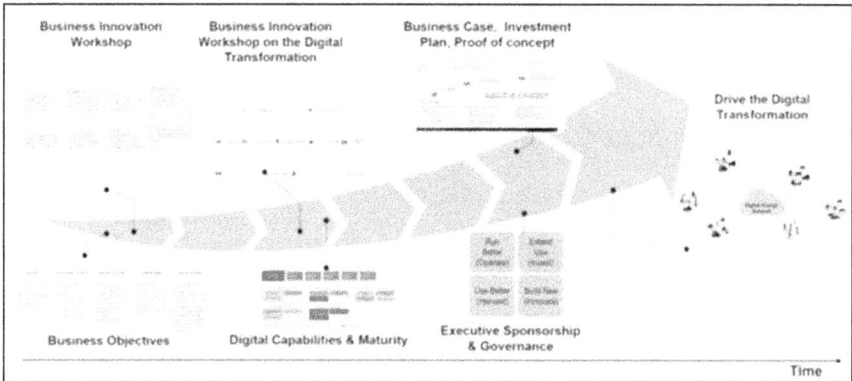

Start of the Journey towards the Transformation of a
Digital Enterprise for Oil & Gas

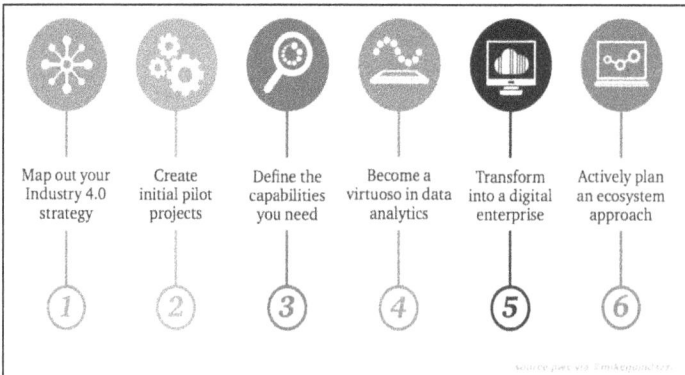

Blueprint for Digital Success

1.12 Why Digital Marketing is useful for Each and Every Business?

It's Cost-Effective

Digital marketing is far more cost-effective than traditional marketing. Over 59% Marketers claim to have saved considerably using digital marketing techniques & tools, making it less surprising to know that over 28% Business Owners are allocating Budget for Digital in their marketing strategies.

It Focuses on Conversions

Whatever digital marketing tools and techniques you may use, the success of the efforts is quantified by the total number of conversions or sales, thus making it very result-oriented.

Increase in Return on Investment (ROI)

Higher conversion rate means more sales which in turn mean higher revenue. Companies using Digital Marketing strategies have 3 times better return on Investment than those who don't. Not only these companies using digital marketing have 3.3 times but also better chances of expanding their business too.

Digital Marketing Ensures Sustainable Growth

Even a business website attracts a lot of traffic but if it fails to convert it, then that business will eventually cease to exist. Digital Marketing overcomes this obstacle by charting out a sustainable growth plan by converting the traffic into conversions.

1.13 As Organizations Seek to Integrate the Massive Flow of Digital Data into their Brand Strategy, they Face a Triple Challenge to Stay Ahead

With Google now processing over 40,000 search queries every second - a staggering 3.5 billion requests a day – data creation has exceeded imaginable levels. Managed well, this onslaught of information can be used to unlock fresh insights, build better policies and create new sources of economic value. These potential successes, however, depend on companies' ability to respond to the new challenges associated with digital integration. To remain competitive, organisations – large companies, governments, political parties and associations – need to address the question of how they incorporate this digital tsunami into their value creation process.

Who's taking care of your digital data?

The cyber revolution requires digital integration, not digital acquisition. Yet, many companies still choose to outsource data listening and analytics capabilities and rely on external partners who specialise in gathering online data, to provide weekly or monthly updates about the changing digital landscape. At times, collaborators within the company may get access to dashboards that track on-line content, but usually they lack the time, training and perspective that would allow them to successfully leverage digital data. Of even greater concern, companies don't even ask themselves where or how they want to create novel value in the first place.

Understanding digital intelligence

The gap between what digital intelligence involves and what brand leaders think it means stems from two major misunderstandings on the very nature of digital data.

The first misunderstanding concerns the rhythm of digital information: this new data is continuous and real-time, from search to geo localisation to social media and e-commerce data. If we look at companies as social bodies, then digital data represents the new lifeblood that flows outside of them from key stakeholders including consumers, competitors and collaborators. Thus it is vital that companies become more agile in their response to the digital momentum. Corporations' lack of integration, and their tendency to rely on infrequent updates from outside partners, is at odds with the fluid and ever-changing nature of digital data flow. This does not mean that outsourcing or thorough analyses of stocks of data is bad – in fact these are necessary to understand what's happening in the long-term or have access to superior analytics capabilities; but the reality is, these companies often lack technical or strategic perspectives to put digital data into perspective.

Smart data rather than big data

The second misunderstanding is that digital intelligence is not so much about quantity but rather about the quality of information. Unfortunately the now popular buzzword "big data" emphasises and overvalues the magnitude of data. Successful digital listening relies less on how much information is heard and more on the quality of one's listening approach and the extent to which this fits with what the brand aims to achieve.

Brands need to think about the kind of value they aim to create before tuning their listening strategy appropriately. As an analogy, consider a cocktail party and how often it is more useful to direct your ears towards a particular conversation to get meaningful information, as opposed to trying to capture the overall sum of conversations around you. In short, digital intelligence is more about smart data than big data.

This requires brands to be proactive, and not just reactive, regarding the kind of value they aim to create.

1.14 13 challenges to successful digital integration

To successfully integrate digital intelligence into their processes, brands need to meet three key challenges: an operational challenge (how to know what to listen to); an organisational challenge (how to share in real time the digital information collected within the organisation); and a strategic challenge (how to systematically use digital insights in the process of creating value).

1. **The first challenge:** operational - seems easy to overcome. To work on it brands need to first think about how to link the desired outcomes (what are the objectives?) with relevant data sources (what type of media platforms or type of data are being accessed?). In some cases, geo-localised data will appear to be of primary importance. In other cases, when focusing on brand perceptions, social media mentions could outweigh other sources. Or, in cases where brands aim to predict whether a trend will garner more interest in the future, relying on search data may be the key.

    It is only after these objectives and sources have been identified that organisations should develop an external or internal system to synthesise the insights gathered.

2. **The second challenge:** organisational – involves deciding which parties within the organisation will have access to this data; the terms of their access (such as frequency or training in digital listening); and how the data and insights will be shared within the relevant teams (such as the brand team).

    It is at this point that organisations often succumb to the temptation to rely solely on an external provider. However it is now more than ever, that internal input is most vital. Only frequent discussions among company collaborators across different ranks and functions coupled with external intelligence will fully reveal the potential of the data, and yield relevant analyses through the multiplicity of viewpoints and data interpretation.

    In service industries such as banking or tourism, giving access to monitoring tools to individual leaders running businesses (e.g. Brand managers) is critical to help them track performance on a daily basis and address potential concerns. In fact, a few major brands in hoteling already track their hotels' e-reputation, make their listening platform available to the hotel's managers, and include each hotel's online reputation scores as a part of the staff's remuneration.

3. The third challenge: strategic – involves recognising how each insight brings value to a specific domain of value creation (for instance, identifying whether an insight is particularly useful for the branding strategy or the development of a new product or a staff recruitment policy).

Decision-makers in the C-suite must pay particular attention to how they integrate these insights into their decision-making process. A good example of this is L'Oréal Paris which, having discovered momentum on the web indicating increasing interest for a particular hairstyle in 2011, decided to closely monitor the development of consumers' interest for this hairstyle. This led to the development of a new hair dye solution targeting this need as well as the integration of their new insights at different points on their value chain, from branding to positioning and to product development. As one example of a more thorough process of bottom-up digital brand building, L'Oréal Paris decided to choose as the brand name for their new product the very term consumers used in their organic searches for the hairstyle (i.e., "ombre").

Leveraging digital data to create agile companies

In a world where the digital revolution transforms markets and rapidly changes the competitive landscape, the ability to integrate digital intelligence gives companies a significant edge in understanding and anticipating market movements. As the cyber world becomes ever more inundated with information, it is time for brands to integrate digital intelligence into their operational, organisational and strategic decisions, to foster the degree of agility that will give them a sustainable competitive advantage in the decades ahead.

1.15 What will a Business miss out on if they don't Market their Products/Services Online?

There is no single Brand that would say that we don't want more visibility or that we don't want more sales. Don't you agree? Brands that are online have seen an immense growth in building Brand Recognition, Engagement with its Customers and obviously Sales by using the right Marketing Tools and Techniques. Digital Marketing helps these brands to target the right customers, to reach them where they are in the online ecosystem and to convert them into Buyers and also to sustain them for a long period of time- converting them into Brand Loyalists.

1.16 Utility and Advantages of Digital Marketing

In an ever complex retail business environment fresh customer engagement is becoming essential everyday but challenging. Retailers therefore are trying shift from a linear marketing approach of one-way communication to a value exchange model of mutual dialogue and benefit-sharing between producer and consumer exchanges are more non-linier in nature.

In today's competitive world many social media platforms are well utilized as digital marketing channels such as Facebook, Whatsapp, LinkedIn, Instagram, YouTube and many more. Social media and online communities allow individuals to easily create content and publish the same on public for their participation. This process creates mass awareness and can boost your business multiple times. Apart from revenue sourcing one can take this as a branding opportunity. Such campaigns can directly accumulate public opinion and experiences through reviews and product feedback to the business.

Many public surveys conducted globally at very low cost can find consumers and help to make shopping decisions and fetch you new businesses periodically. Also can enable analytics to find right set of target audience for your business may tell you purchased similar products in last six months or one year.

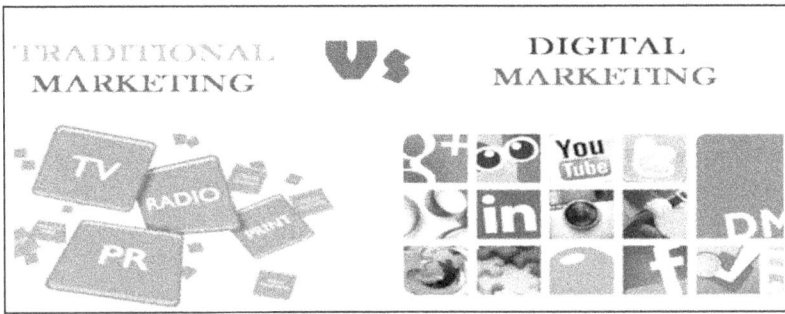

Omni channel strategy

Omni channel strategy also known as multi-communication channel is becoming increasingly important for enterprises who must adapt the changing business environment and changing expectation of the customer. The "endless aisle" within the retail space can lead consumers to purchase products online that fit their needs while retailers do not have to carry the inventory within the physical location of the store because of the intervention of logistic players within this value chain. Internet based retailers are also implementing physical stores to display best of their products to give consumers touch and feel factor.

Please find below a sample diagram of Omni channel marketing strategy:

Omni-Channel Experience

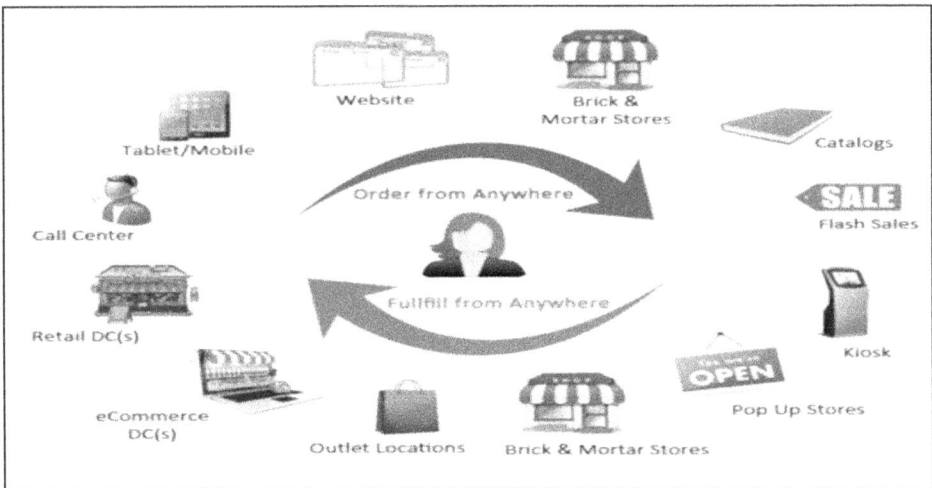

An Omni-channel approach not only benefits consumers but also benefits business bottom line due to low operations cost. Research suggests that customers spend more than double when purchasing through an Omni-channel retailer compared to a single-channel retailer, and are often more loyal. This could be due to the ease of purchase and the wider availability of products across all channels using a single customer relationship unique number.

Customers do often research online and then buying in stores and also browsing in stores and then searching for other options online. Online customer research into products is particularly popular or lower-priced items including groceries and makeup. Consumers are increasingly using the Internet to get product information, compare prices, and search for deals and promotions. Moreover due to the multiple sellers' offers customers get the optimum price benefit hence they are slowly but steadily inclining towards online purchases rather than visiting stores and buying stuffs regularly.

There are a number of ways brands can use digital marketing to benefit their brands, like positive word of mouth communications and peer-to-peer dialogue or might be influencing reviews are often have a greater effect on customers mind and their buying decisions consequently.

The use of social media interaction allows brands to receive both positive and negative feedback from their customers as well as determining what media platforms work well for them, therefore such customer feedback towards product development or continuous product improvement through updated versions brings prosperity to the business houses. The potential reach of social media is indicated by the fact that in 2015, each month the Facebook platform had more than 126 million average unique users and YouTube had over 97 million average unique users indicates how helpful your brand promotion can be through these digital media platforms.

One of the prime objectives of digital marketing is to continuously starve for new customers and keep on engaging them to bring them on-board. In such context a key objective of digital marketing is to engaging digital marketing customers and allowing them to interact with the brand through servicing and delivery of digital media. Information is easy to access at a fast rate through the use of digital communications. Users with access to the Internet can use many digital mediums, such as Facebook, YouTube, Forums, and Email etc.

Through Digital communications it creates a Multi-communication channel where information can be quickly exchanged around the world by anyone without any face to face interaction or social segregation since face to face interaction is mostly not possible in between producers and end-users.

1.17 Competitive Advantages of Digital Marketing

Businesses can create competitive advantage through various means by using internet based digital marketing platforms. To reach the maximum potential customers, firms use social media as its main tool to bag channel of information. Through this a business can create a system in which they are able to pinpoint behavioral patterns of customers and their needs using data analytics and search patterns. Creating a social media business page on Facebook or Instagram will further increase traction and relationship between new consumers and existing consumers as well as consistent brand reinforcement therefore improving brand awareness resulting in a possible rise for consumers up the Brand Awareness Pyramid. Although there may be inconstancy with product images which may damage this overall exercise to a greater extent, therefore it's always advisable to be truthful and genuine to the customer when you're selling your goods or services online and be highly cautious on avoiding my misinterpretation led mistrust way forward. The primary benefit of digital marketing over traditional marketing method is the cost benefit for a firm keen for branding and new customer acquisition through viral brand promotions.

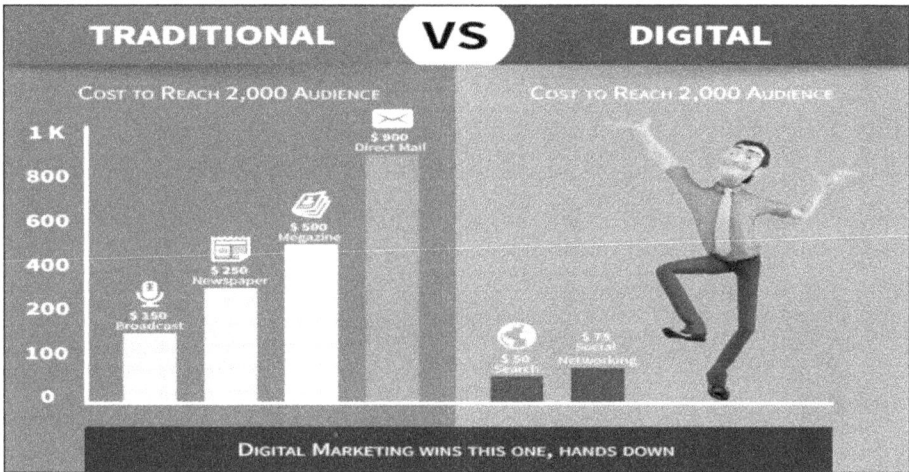

Maintaining a healthy social media relationship with customers requires a business to be consistent in interactions and prudent in terms of product quality and after sales services which is renowned as Customer Services; firms can feedbacks received from the customer for further betterment of their overall performance and quality aspects. Due to the massive user volume globally, effective use of digital marketing can result in relatively lowered costs in relation to traditional means of marketing; led to increased topline revenue with controlled costs.

Brand awareness has been proven to work more effective in countries that are high in uncertainty avoidance, also these countries that have uncertainty avoidance, social media marketing works effectively there. Yet brands must be careful not to viral on the use of this type of marketing to avoid any sort of misapplications that could negatively harness the actual brand image. Brands that represent themselves in an anthropomorphizing manner are more likely to succeed in situations where a brand is marketing to this demographic. Since social media usage can enhance the knowledge of the users and thus decrease the risk of uncertainty of the brand and their respective product line.

Let us look at the diagram which distinguish traditional marketing channels with new age digital marketing channels-

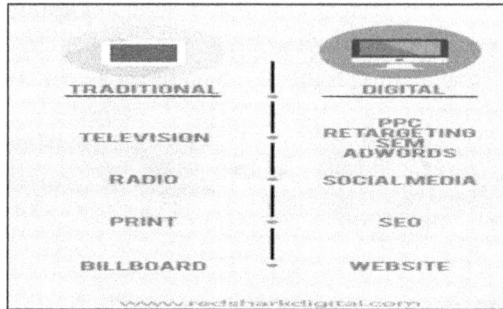

New let us look at the competitive advantages and benefits of digital marketing from the operational prospective and actionable-

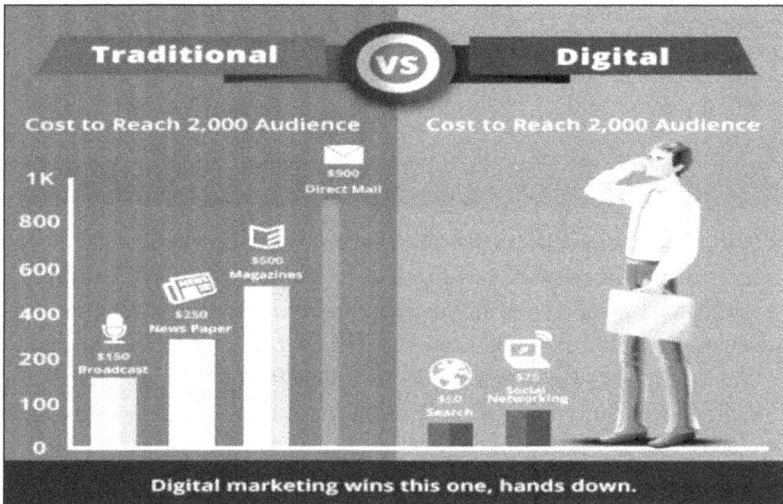

1.18 Key Benefits of Mobile Marketing- A synopsis

Mobile Marketing

Mobile marketing is multi-channel online marketing technique focused on reaching out to a specific audience through their smart phone, tablets etc. Mobile marketing can provide time and location specific customers to promote targeted goods, services.

SMS Marketing

We can see marketing through cell phones' SMS (Short Message Service) became increasingly popular in India at present, because as people are getting busy with their work schedule day by day they are avoiding checking emails regularly but one thing they can't ignore is their smartphone. Therefore the new age marketers has identified the opportunity there itself and planned to outreach audience via mobile device only. A research says on an average, SMS messages are read within four minutes, making them highly convertible and even more profitable for the marketers following this channel of marketing. Over the past few years SMS marketing has become a legitimate and popular advertising channel in some parts of the country especially in the rural clusters where not much public internet or cyber cafes are available yet.

Western Europe and some other countries, mobile SPAM messages (SMS sent to mobile subscribers without legitimate and explicit opt-in consent from the subscriber) remain an issue in many other parts of the world, partly due to the carriers selling their member databases to third parties. In India, however, government's efforts of creating National Do Not Call Registry have helped cell phone users to stop SMS advertisements by sending a simple SMS or calling 1909. SMS has become the one of the most popular branch of the Mobile Marketing industry with several 100 million advertising SMS sent out every month in India alone.

SMS marketing services typically run off a short codes like VM-155400, VM-ICICIB, VM- AxisBk, AM- AIRBNK etc., now if you can interpret well and analyze this unique short codes smartly you will be able to identify the marketers, for instance, VM-155400 stands for Vodafone Mobile followed by few numeric values means it's their direct promotions, on the other hand VM- ICICIB stands for Vodafone Mobile doing a third party ICICI Bank promotion affiliated with them for similar marketing techniques, similarly AM- AIRBNK code suggests it's an advertisement done by Airtel Mobile for their very own Airtel Payment Bank. But sending text messages to an email address is another methodology (though this method is not supported by the carriers). Short codes are 5 or 6 digit numbers that have been assigned by all the mobile operators in a given country especially for the use of brand campaign and other consumer services. Due to the high price quote of short codes generally priced in between INR 5000– INR 10000 a month, many small businesses opt to share a short code in order to reduce monthly costs. The mobile operators vet every short code application before provisioning and monitor the service to make sure it does not diverge from its original service description. Another alternative to sending messages by short code or email is to do so through one's own dedicated phone number.

In case of any doubts the mobile operators offer an opt out option to the consumers and the ability for the consumer to opt out of the service at any time by sending the word STOP via SMS or clicking on a hyperlink appended below the message generally. Mobile operators in any promotion/marketing activity wherever a financial transaction is involved send an OTP (One time password expires within next 15 mins. Or can be used once only) to verify the authenticity of the user and transaction as well.

Please refer to the pictures below showcase an OTP message template for two way verification process of a service provider-

App-based marketing

Due to the strong growth in the usage of smartphones, app usage has also grown significantly; better to say multi-times over the last 10 years. Therefore, mobile marketers have identified the opportunities lies in this space and increasingly taken advantage of smartphone apps as a marketing resource. Marketers aim to optimize the visibility of all the apps in a single store known as Google play store, available and pre-installed in each and every smartphone runs on android operating platform which create a massive awareness among users and will maximize the number of downloads. This practice is called App Store Optimization (ASO) which is being run on a predefined algorithm developed by android developers in various updated versions we see periodically.

There is a lot of competition in this field as well. However, just like other services, it is not easy anymore to rule the mobile application market easily, for example you as a user have options to use swiggy and food panda in a single store where both of them have similar business model and almost same services. Most companies have acknowledged the potential of Mobile Apps to increase the interaction between a company and its target customers. With the fast progress and growth of the smartphone market, high-quality Mobile app development **is essential to obtain a strong position in a mobile app store**. Moreover a research says instead of steep competition in the mobile app space quality of product, user experience and quality of service given an edge to the winner to tap the maximum market share.

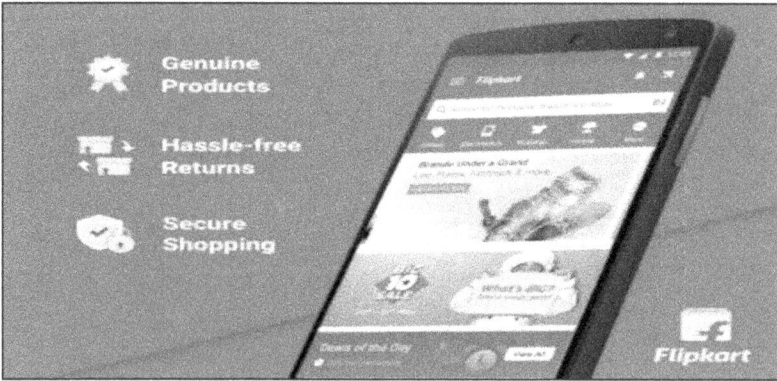

Apps are now a days being integrated with company website to also promote it and aware customers about their presence in app store. It's a complementary method where the similar products and offerings can be viewed in a computer screen as well in your hand held devices as well at the same time. Similarly in order to attract more customers and business volume firms plan app based shopping festival to ensure people download and use their mobile app as much as possible to create multi-channel revenue model.

Smart companies like Flipkart, Swiggy, Snapdeal keeps on launching app-based marketing schemes periodically to ensure people must come on to their platform, download it from app store, use it, experience and buy it only from apps they have built, such activities makes their digital marketing strategies segregated and create multi-modal revenue stream for the company.

Payment Gateway/Mobile Wallets

Whatever we do in the digital marketing front, we do it to generate revenue and profit finally. Therefore payment gateway or mobile wallets are the newest addition to the entire set of tools we use for our marketing purpose. This method ease all type of transactions related to your business. Many brands like PayTm, Mobikwik, BillDesk etc. has emerged in the Indian market developed such products and providing options both to the business and customers to make frequent small payments at their ease irrespective of devices you use. Most of the firms are just integrating this mechanism with their website to get money online from the customers directly. Now it's a win-win deal for all three entities involved in a transaction (Buyer, Seller, Service Provider) where buyer can make quick payment effortlessly, sellers has no trouble to encash the revenue and realize the payment in minimum possible TAT and gateway developer enjoy a small percentage of commission in each of these transactions to survive their own business model as well. This mechanism is widely famous across the globe now and makes life easier for all the stakeholders involved in a business transaction.

In-game mobile marketing

There are essentially three major trends in mobile gaming right now: interactive real-time 3D games, massive multi-player games and social networking games. This means a trend towards more complex and more sophisticated yet richer game play. On the other side, there are the so-called casual games, i.e. games that are very simple and very easy to play. Most mobile games today are such casual games and this will probably stay so for quite a while to come.

Brands are now delivering promotional messages within mobile games or sponsoring entire games to drive consumer engagement. This is known as mobile advergaming or ad-funded mobile game.

In in-game mobile marketing, advertisers pay to have their name or products featured in the mobile games. For instance, racing games can feature real cars made by Ford or Chevy. Advertisers have been both creative and aggressive in their attempts to integrate ads organically in the mobile games.

Although investment in mobile marketing strategies like advergaming is slightly more expensive than what is intended for a mobile app, a good strategy can make the brand derive substantial revenue. Games that use advergaming make the users remember better the brand involved. This memorization increases virility of the content so that the users tend to recommend them to their friends and acquaintances, and share them via social networks. In many cases we found many brand collaborate with the game developer, sponsor their codes and finally embed their brand in the game so that whenever user access the game with the help of internet or even offline for that matter, the customized content attached with the game will automatically pop-up immediately to attract viewers.

Look at this picture where a soccer game developer has embedded Adidas and EM sports inbuilt into the game to ensure visibility of the users.

One can include/promote many characters through games which people like to explore and play with.

1.19 Technological Edge for a Venture

The first and foremost advantage of technology in venture is to get optimum operational efficiency and cost effectiveness. Apart from these two major aspect technology helps entrepreneurs to manage business resources efficiently, it can be human resource or equipment required to run the show.

When we are talking about technological edge of a venture, let's compare an online business with an offline business with the help of a case to understand its various aspects in a better way. Let's assume business model of Big Basket (An online Grocery store) vs. business model of Reliance Fresh (A traditional hyper retailer) in retail consumer space.

Costs of Establishment of a Traditional Retail Store

Monthly Retail Lease

In major cities, a storefront location will cost you between INR. 250-275 per square feet a month. The average retail shop is around 1,000 square feet (remember you'll need non-public and storage space), so leasing costs at the lower end of the commercial real estate market will run around INR. 2, 75,000 in per month, therefore INR. 33, 00,000/year. There is usually a minimum lease period of 1 year and sometimes 3 years minimum. So in worst case scenario your ideal establishment cost can go up to INR. 1 crore initially during incubation stage.

Upfront Investment

You will also have to renovate the retail space to suit your business- create a sign, buy shop fittings and equipment etc. This can cost INR. 10, 00,000 for a 1000 sqft. Store. Let's go with a moderate figure of INR. 7, 50,000 for renovation, sign creation, lease closing costs and equipment costs.

Staff

Unless you have family members who are skilled and willing to work for nothing, you're going to need at least ten staff members to cover the entire retail store operations, starting from stacking and segregate items to cash counter management during the operations hours of 9:00 am – 9:00 pm at least in Indian context, seven days per week. Minimum wage in the province of such a staff is 8000/month. Let's say you pay 80,000/month towards gross salary of your staffs only.

OPEX

OPEX includes your electricity cost, infrastructure maintenance cost of the store, day to day repairing cost and equipment maintenances cost. All put together in an ideal scenario for such commercial activities should stand at INR. 1,00,000/month.

Total Cost: INR. 40, 00,000 initial investment and then INR. 1, 80,000 monthly costs, comes to a hefty total of INR. 21, 60,000 per year

Costs of an Online E-Commerce Store:

- **Web Development Costs:** A custom e-commerce website costs around INR. 2, 00,000 to 3, 00,000. This includes complete shopping cart functionality, blog, social media and payment gateway integration, reviews and ratings features, and full analytics tracking to track visitors and sales.

- **Web Hosting Costs:** This is your business, so find a reliable company to host on high-speed servers. This will cost around INR. 5,000/month.

- **No Sales Staff Costs:** However, instead of paying INR. 80, 000 per month to sales staff and hoping traffic will walk in the door, you can invest some of that money in highly-targeted pay-per-click (PPC) advertising to drive online traffic to your website. Let's say you're willing to spend INR. 5000 per month towards PPC, SEM and SEO services. The delivery boys engaged in an online business supply chain can either be outsourced on profit sharing basis or can be developed from scratch against a negligible cost over the period of time, therefore you can easily avoid any fixed cost and enjoy variable payment method, means if you gain desired profit then you are sharing a percentage of it with the vendor mutually decided beforehand.

- **Technical and Marketing Support:** If you are very technical and know all about digital marketing, you can do it all yourself. If not, you will need technical assistance for your website because you'll be making changes to features, content, and images as you tweak the website for better results. You should also hire someone who can run online marketing for you. Budget INR. 20,000 per month (max) for technical and marketing support. If you don't want to deal with orders and shipping, you can spend some of this budget on an order fulfillment service at a fraction of what it would cost to pay sales staff working in 10 hours a day in a store. They will charge per order fulfilled and some minimum monthly amount.

- **More Measurable Results:** The biggest advantage of marketing an online e-commerce website is that you can track the ROI you get from every marketing dollar spent. Compare this to traditional marketing, which is difficult to track and even more difficult to analyze. A good online marketing resource can manage an ongoing PPC campaign for you and provide insights on how to improve results.

- **Operations Cost:** Mostly e-commerce is smart enough to negotiate to a negligible delivery cost with logistics partners if they themselves are not doing it. In most of the cases such e-commerce firms develop their own supply chain to ensure cost effectiveness along with efficient TAT to ensure favorable customer feedback. In this said business model warehouse might be required for your centralized storage and later use it as the distribution point. Now this is not at all an expensive affair at all because most of the companies prefer to establish such warehouse in remote corner of the city/state can cost you about INR. 15, 000 per month, which comes to INR. 1, 80, 000 per year in your cost book.

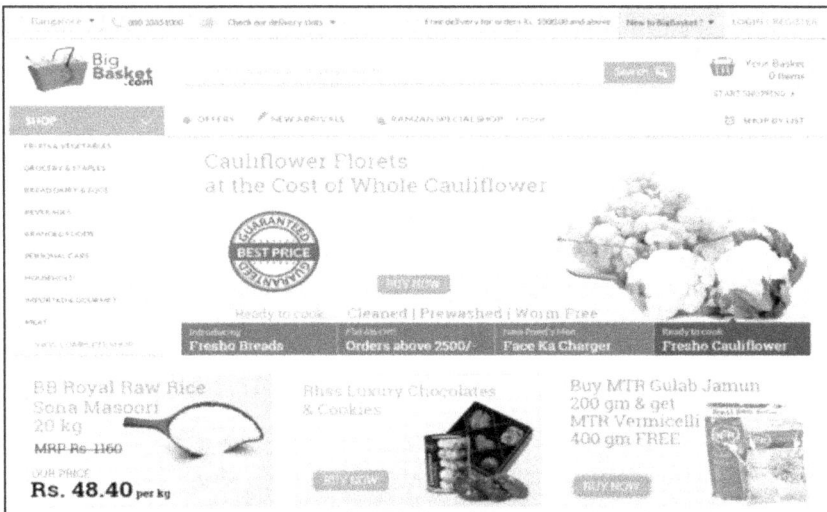

❖ *Total Cost:* INR. 3, 00,000 initial investment and INR. 45,000 per month as operational cost can be accounted for on your cost sheet, therefore it comes to INR. 5, 40, 000 as yearly cost. If you are not doing your own shipping and handling ads in whatever a service charges which is very nominal to handle order fulfilment. You can budget 3%-5% profit sharing on this account.

Minimize Risk

Depending on the products you want to sell, one of these options could be preferable. Regardless of whether you go with e-commerce, traditional retail, or both, you still need set aside budget to promote the business.

Start-up costs are significantly lower for an E-commerce website and there's no lock-in to a long-term lease. More importantly for new businesses, an online business model provides a relatively inexpensive, less risky, and easier testing ground to fine-tune your business model. Once you've found online success and a customer base, you will have more confidence to expand into retail locations and/or a larger e-commerce system as your customer base increases.

1.20 Advantages and Disadvantages of Digital Marketing

Advantages

Cost

The low costs of electronic communication reduce the cost of displaying online advertisements compared to offline ads. Online advertising, and in particular social media, provides a low-cost means for advertisers to engage with large established communities. Advertising online offers better returns than in other media.

Measurability

Online advertisers can collect data on their ads' effectiveness, such as the size of the potential audience or actual audience response, how a visitor reached their advertisement, whether the advertisement resulted in a sale, and whether an ad actually loaded within a visitor's view. This helps online advertisers improve their ad campaigns over time.

Formatting

Advertisers have a wide variety of ways of presenting their promotional messages, including the ability to convey images, video, audio, and links. Unlike many offline ads, online ads also can be interactive. For example; some ads let users input queries or let users follow the advertiser on social media. Online ads can even incorporate games.

Targeting

Publishers can offer advertisers the ability to reach customizable and narrow market segments for targeted advertising. Online advertising may use geo-targeting to display relevant advertisements to the user's geography. Advertisers can customize each individual ad to a particular user based on the user's previous preferences. Advertisers can also track whether a visitor has already seen a particular ad in order to reduce unwanted repetitive exposures and provide adequate time gaps between exposures.

Coverage

Online advertising can reach nearly every global market, and online advertising influences offline sales.

Speed

Once ad design is complete, online ads can be deployed immediately. The delivery of online ads does not need to be linked to the publisher's publication schedule. Furthermore, online advertisers can modify or replace ad copy more rapidly than their offline counterparts.

Apart from these pointers few more are stated below.

- Digital Marketing is an effective communication aspect for the companies to target a large number of potential consumers at the same time.

- Digital Marketing enables direct advertising and creates awareness about a product or brand.

- Digital Marketing makes advertisements more accessible to the target customers at any time or any place.

- Digital Marketing enables the companies to make advertisements internationally and expand their customer reach to other countries across the geographical boundaries.

- With the development of new technologies and use of internet in business, the brands may take a great advantage to increase the reach of customers and communicate to its clients successfully.

- Due to the popularity and capabilities of digital marketing, customers have become more convenient to shop online at any time (24/7 basis) whether the shops are over or across the borders. Digital Marketing has opened-up an opportunity for the companies and retailers to direct its customers to an outlet of the online store.

- Big brands and even small commercial stores are reaping benefits of digital marketing. Digital Marketing is leveraging advantages that old school traditional marketing strategies cannot offer in that easy manner. Credit goes to digital marketing. Huge corporate houses and all size businesses, now have a bigger impact in the way consumers interact with their brands online.

- You must check our special analysis which provides you 7 digital marketing benefits and you could create a base for your digital knowledge as well.

- Consequently, you can master the skill set of digital marketing and use it for your own business. If not, at least make a strong career out of it.

7 Key Advantages of Digital Marketing

You should not miss out on reading these 7 digital marketing benefits.

Digital marketing allows you to enhance your marketing plans and evolves your competitive strength even if you don't have huge budgets to spend. Money which was spent on traditional marketing can evolve your competitive strength in your industry through digital marketing.

With digital marketing, your business can:

1. **Users connect to online content:** Did you know? 72% of professional digital marketers think well-designed content has more effect on customers than an advertisement in a magazine. Nearly 69% digital marketing experts content on social media superior to direct mail and public relation events. That is one of the key benefits of digital marketing; you can connect to your customers. Consequently for that, maintaining a dominant social media presence is very crucial for both customer engagement and marketing trends.

2. **Track customers' entire journey:** Analytics is a key module in digital marketing. Through analytics, you can track your customer's actions on your website.

    Right from visiting to page, which part of the website is being viewed, their decisions and preferences of products, every moment can be tracked. Learn more about how to increase your sales exponentially through remarketing.

3. **Conversion optimization:** That term sounds too technical correct?

    Just read this small paragraph and you shall understand this digital marketing term thoroughly.

    Tracking allows you to know more about customer's journey; right from the first click to the leaving of website. Digital marketing allows you to test and optimize your website for conversion. It's not a onetime activity; it is an on-going process. Brands like Amazon and Flipkart have been doing this for quite a long time.

    You can learn tracking for free with our ultimate free guide for tracking on Facebook.

4. **Connect with mobile customers:** What's the point of a website if that's not mobile friendly? With the AMP feature famous in the market has boosted the amount of searches through phone.

    Nearly 82% of mobile searchers use their phones to check on prospective in-store purchases. It's a brilliant opportunity for business owners to shift their focus on digital marketing and make mobile user friendly interfaces.

5. **Realize higher ROI and revenue:** When you set your own business or work for an existing one, your focus will be on returns on what you invest. May it be time, may it be labour, and may it be money.

    Gradually when you increase your digital reach out, you can increase your revenue in a predictable way. On comparison with traditional marketing, digital marketing allows you real time results.

Real time data allows you to predict results and you can exactly know what kind of digital marketing practice yield you the highest revenue.

6. **Analyse and adapt easily:** By now you might have realised 'real time' has been frequently used in the digital industry. That is because; digital marketing provides real, timely data, which you can observe. You can adapt to trends and the actions that your targeted audience are taking.

Digital marketing is so instant that don't have to rely on a sample data set or make any educated guesses. All you need to do is plan, execute, and adapt on the go based on true performance data.

7. **Become more competitive:** First of all, who said that digital marketing is a monopolistic area to invest? It is damn competitive. Right from a huge brand to a local vendor, everyone competes in their limits on this digital platform. And that's how businesses will work in future as well. If you as an entrepreneur or a marketer are not a part of this digital marketing game, you are way behind. Probably, it is going to be more competitive in the future, ensure your business is competitive by employing a smart digital marketing strategy.

Reach out to more customers with Digital Marketing

It is needless to say that the benefits are plentiful. Hence, you should surely evolve from traditional marketing to digital.

Subscribe to our blog updates to know more how you can apply digital marketing to your existing business. If not, at least you can make the highest paying career out of it.

Conclusion

In conclusion, there are many more benefits of digital marketing. 7 Especially relevant benefits are enlisted here. After all this while, digital marketing has enhanced as a field. It is really imperative as well a crucial to reap benefits of digital marketing.

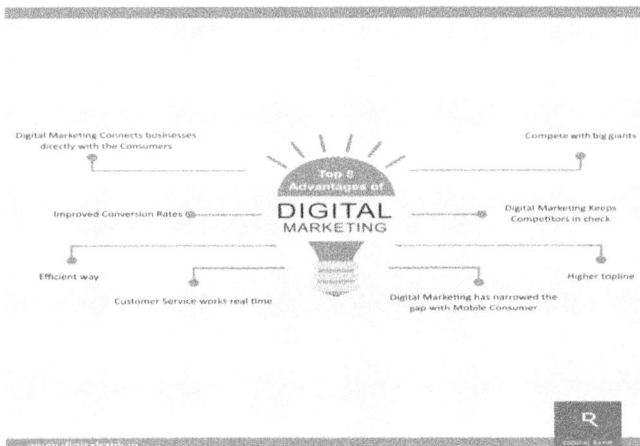

Let's imagine your business is ready with a new product or service for sale. But how will you know your potential customers?

For a business to thrive, the newly launched product or service must be known to potential buyers.

Your business should be known among the targeted audience. You should, anyhow, communicate with your customers readily available; you have to use marketing strategies to create product or service awareness.

This is what digital marketing does. It educates the people about your product on the internet. It can be considered as the process of attracting targeted audiences online that will make a difference between a successfully thriving business and a failed one.

Once your business is known to prospects, it increases your chances that customers will make a purchase.

New customers start to spread the words among their friends and family about the product or service you recently launched. Your sales will steadily increase as the word spreads.

Without employing the strategies, the sales may never happen. And, without sales, a company cannot succeed. As simple as that!

The present and future of a business rest on a solid reputation. When a business reaches the high expectations of the public, its reputation stands on firmer ground. Digital marketing builds brand name recognition!

Digital marketing is an asset for small scale business. It gives small business a chance to compete against various major businesses in a same field and direction. A right and accurate strategy for digital marketing can put a small business in the same box as bigger businesses, in a short duration of time.

Digital marketing is necessary for your business, but it can be an expensive investment if you don't know what you're doing, what strategy you should strictly follow and who your target audience are. Though your business build product is of excellent quality, but advertisement and marketing strategy would suffer!

To promote a business there are two ways of marketing one is Traditional Marketing which includes Print Media, TV commercials, etc.

The second one is Digital Marketing which includes:

- **Content Marketing:** It is creating and distributing valuable and relevant content to allure and retain a customer to drive profitable customer action.
- **Video Marketing:** In this type of marketing, business creates a short video (maybe long) regarding a product. Video marketing is the more preferred type of marketing than content marketing these days.
- **E-mail Marketing:** In this, business directs a commercial message to an individual or an organization using email.

- **Search Engine Optimization:** It is the strategy used to obtain a high-ranking place in the search results page of a search engine (SERP) to increase the number of visitors to a website.

- **Social Media Marketing:** It is one of the approaches to gain web traffic with the help of social media websites. The goal is to spread the content on social media websites to gain attention.

- **Local listing:** Register your business with sites like Google, Bing, and Yahoo. This will give your quality back links and will improve online presence. This increase referral traffic to your website. It is a free way to engage your potential customers.

It is hard to imagine future of a business without digital marketing these days. If you are owning a business (of any size), you should equally focus on the digital marketing of your business.

Disadvantages

Security Concerns

According to many investigation based research report, the current state of online advertising endangers the security and privacy of users. Since every online services you use ask you to login with your credentials before any service is rendered to the customers, during this process one must realize that they are basically sharing all their personal information like Address, Mobile Number, even PAN number in some occasion with the businesses which might be misused way forward can raise many security concerns. We've commonly heard about the word "phishing" which is a perfect example of security concern for online users.

Banner Blindness

Eye-tracking studies have shown that Internet users often ignore web page zones likely to contain display ads (sometimes called "banner blindness"), and this problem is worse online than in offline media. On the other hand, studies suggest that even those ads "ignored" by the users may influence the user subconsciously.

Fraud on the Advertiser

There are numerous ways that advertisers can be overcharged for their advertising. For example, click fraud occurs when a publisher or third parties click (manually or through automated means) on a CPC ad with no legitimate buying intent For example, click fraud can occur when a competitor clicks on ads to deplete its rival's advertising budget, or when publishers attempt to manufacture revenue.

Click fraud is especially associated with pornography sites. In 2011, certain scamming porn websites launched dozens of hidden pages on each visitor's computer, forcing the visitor's computer to click on hundreds of paid links without the visitor's knowledge

As with offline publications, online impression fraud can occur when publishers overstate the number of ad impressions they have delivered to their advertisers. To combat impression fraud, several publishing and advertising industry associations are developing ways to count online impressions credibly.

Technological Variations

Heterogeneous Clients

Because users have different operating systems, web browsers and computer hardware (including mobile devices and different screen sizes), online ads may appear to users differently from how the advertiser intended, or the ads may not display properly at all. A 2012 comScore study revealed that, on an average, 35% of ads were not «in-view» when rendered; meaning they never had an opportunity to be seen. Rich media ads create even greater compatibility problems, as some developers may use competing (and exclusive) software to render the ads (e.g. Comparison of HTML 5 and/or Flash).

Furthermore, advertisers may encounter legal problems if legally required information doesn't actually display to users, even if that failure is due to technological heterogeneity. In India, the concern ministry and consumer forum of India has released a set of guidelines indicating that it's the advertisers' responsibility to ensure the ads display any required disclosures or disclaimers, irrespective of the users' technology.

Ad Blocking

Ad blocking, or ad filtering, means the ads do not appear to the user because the user uses technology to screen out ads. Many browsers block unsolicited pop-up ads by default. Other software programs or browser add-ons may also block the loading of ads, or block elements on a page with behaviours characteristic of ads (e.g. HTML auto play of both audio and video). Approximately 10% of all online page views come from browsers with ad-blocking software installed, and some publishers have 30%+ of their visitors using ad-blockers.

Anti-targeting Technologies

Some web browsers offer privacy modes where users can hide information about themselves from publishers and advertisers. Among other consequences, advertisers can't use cookies to serve targeted ads to private browsers. Most major browsers have incorporated Do Not Track options into their browser headers, but the regulations currently are only enforced by the honour system.

Privacy Concerns

The collection of user information by publishers and advertisers has raised consumer concerns about their privacy. Sixty percent of Internet users would use Do Not Track technology to block all collection of information if given an opportunity. Over half of all Google and Facebook users are concerned about their privacy when using Google and Facebook, according to *Gallup*.

Many consumers have reservations about online behavioural targeting. By tracking users' online activities, advertisers are able to understand consumers quite well.

Advertisers often use technology, such as web bugs and respawning cookies, to maximizing their abilities to track consumers. According to a 2011 survey conducted by Harris Interactive, over half of Internet users had a negative impression of online behavioural advertising, and forty percent feared that their personally-identifiable information had been shared with advertisers without their consent. Consumers can be especially troubled by advertisers targeting them based on sensitive information, such as financial or health status. Furthermore, some advertisers attach the MAC address of users' devices to their 'demographic profiles' so they can be retargeted (regardless of the accuracy of the profile) even if the user clears their cookies and browsing history.

Trustworthiness of Advertisers

Scammers can take advantage of consumers' difficulties verifying an online persona's identity, leading to artifices like phishing (where scam emails look identical to those from a well-known brand owner) and confidence schemes like the Nigerian «419» scam. The Internet Crime Complaint Centre received 289,874 complaints in 2012, totalling over half a billion dollars in losses, most of which originated with scam ads, where it was very difficult to track their device IP address in order to track them.

Consumers also face malware risks, i.e. malvertising, when interacting with online advertising. Cisco's 2013 Annual Security Report revealed that clicking on ads was 182 times more likely to install a virus on a user's computer than surfing the Internet for porn. For example, in August 2014 Yahoo's advertising network reportedly saw cases of infection of a variant of Crypto locker ransomware.

Spam

The Internet's low cost of disseminating advertising contributes to spam, especially by large-scale spammers. Numerous efforts have been undertaken to combat spam, ranging from blacklists to regulatory-required labelling to content filters, but most of those efforts have adverse collateral effects, such as mistaken filtering. We all are aware of what SPAM is all about since we everyday see our mailbox flooded with SPAM mails, instead on inbuilt filtration process used by mail service providers like Google, Yahoo! It's almost impossible to restrict all the irrelevant content to hit your inbox on regular basis.

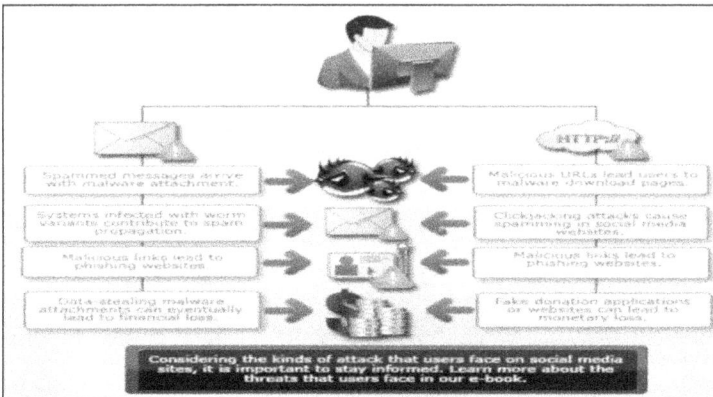

Digital Marketing is an expansion tool for the businesses, facing some limitations and hindrances. Some of these limitations have been identified and discussed below:

Digital marketing is closely reliant on the internet. In some areas, internet facility may not be accessible to the consumers or with poor internet connections.

As digital marketing is highly dependent on the internet, so the marketers may find it hard to make their advertisements more comprehensive and start a conversation with their consumers about the company brand image or products.

Digital Marketing has a drawback when a customer searches for a specific product of a specific company on the internet, many competing goods, and services having same marketing strategies appear on the customer's home page. This conflicts the customer and provides an alternative option to choose a cheaper product of the better quality of other company. As a result, some customers lack trust on a lot of advertisements that appear on websites or social media and consider it frauds or look like a dishonest brand.

Another drawback of digital marketing is that even a person or group of persons can harm the image of a recognized brand through '**Doppelganger**'. Anti-brand activists, bloggers, and opinion leaders spread the term 'Doppelganger' to disapprove the image of a certain brand.

Another practical drawback of Digital Marketing is that it is only beneficial for consumer goods. The industrial goods and pharmaceutical products cannot be marketed using digital channels.

Hands down, the biggest problem with digital marketing is the proliferation of "internet marketers" who are absolutely saturating all things digital with what really amounts to intelligent spamming.

This creates an incredible amount of competition and fewer and fewer opportunities for newcomers.

Everybody and their brother wants to become an affiliate marketer, lead gen expert, SEO provider, content marketer, email marketer, or Amazon drop-shipper… OR, they want to sell you a course on how to become an affiliate marketer, lead gen expert, SEO provider, content marketer, email marketer or Amazon drop-shipper.

The disadvantages, then. One, if you want to become a "digital marketer" (whatever that means), you will have to deal with intense competition and a high learning curve that is constantly changing. Oh, and lots and lots of lousy and incorrect help and advice from hordes of wannabes.

Second, if you have a legitimate product or service—in other words, a real business—that you'd like to market online or on Facebook, Twitter, etc., you have to find some way to be visible in an absolute morass of spam and slime balls.

1.21 Summary & Conclusion

From the above case study we've learned how the business community has changed over the last 10 years. This transformation happened due to the fast changing dynamics in the market and continuous change in customer needs and preferences. Earlier consumer used to go to the market, roam around, chose the right product according to his/her need, bargain and them buy it finally. As the years have gone past, people become more active in managing multitasks, professional minded and believe in ease of shopping and save their precious time which they can utilize in some other priority area in their list.

It is also evident that slowly but steady these online businesses are slowly capturing the consumer market share over a period of time. Researchers have identified the opportunities during the change in the consumer behavior and came up with many innovative business ideas with the help of disruptive technologies to get an additional edge over their competitors.

While the case replicates the fixed cost (CAPEX+OPEX) of an offline business for an entire year stands at INR. 61, 60, 000 an online competition has a cost advantage due to its moderate fixed cost of INR. 8, 40, 000 for the same period of operations. Now by analyzing this business situation one can save INR. 53, 40, 000 straight away and utilize the same fund for procurement and marketing purposes to acquire new fresh customers every day. Such activities will ensure more on-board customer databank with an online firm will help them to grow multi folded over the years to come.

Now when we are discussing about online businesses and pretending their benefit one should keep in their mind is that online businesses are not meant for any and every products consumed by the customer. Whenever it comes to the business of premium or high value products like Rolex Watches, Designer Jwellery, Armani Outfits its always advisable to go for offline/showroom operations, because people can afford to make purchase of daily requirements through online shopping because of its tiny monitory value therefore low risk but won't prefer to buy high value products online because whenever customers think to spend big money behind a certain products or a set of products, they always prefer to visit the store, feel the ambiance, taste the quality, judge the brand equity and then buy to ensure they get desired worth of quality materials against their hard earned money.

For a start-up led by an entrepreneur or a group of entrepreneurs must control their establishment and operational cost because they can never predict/judge their topline revenue right at their starting phase. It's therefore always advisable to embed technologies to get the cost benefit and also enjoy its automated efficiency right from their incubation stage. It will help them to burn limited money and earn maximum possible revenue way forward. In case a start-up can acquire good amount of customer and can reach traction then they can easily maximize their profitability due to controlled bottom-line, In case they fail to do so, still they will have limited loss which might be well budgeted at the starting because of well forecasted cost implications led by controlled bottom-line operations.

Apart from the above written case to prove an edge on cost aspect of digital marketing, there are multiple other beneficiary methods of Digital Marketing we can discuss in this chapter.

- **Pay-per-sale or PPS** (sometimes referred to as cost-per-sale or CPS) is an online advertisement pricing system where the publisher or website owner is paid on the basis of the number of sales that are directly generated by an advertisement. It is a variant of the CPA (cost per action) model, where the advertiser pays the publisher and/or website owner in proportion to the number of actions committed by the readers or visitors to the website.

  In many cases, it is impractical to track all the sales generated by an advertisement. However, it is more easily tracked for full online transactions such as selling songs directly on the internet. Unique identifiers, which can be stored in cookies or included in the URL, are used to track the movement of the prospective buyer to ensure that all such sales are attributed to the advertisement in question.

- **Telephone Call Tracking, pay-per-sale:** Some companies handle transactions "offline," meaning sales driven by online traffic are closed via inbound telephone calls or in person rather than online. In these cases, a cookie-based rotating system of telephone numbers can be used to accurately trace a phone call to the source online visitor. This way, a phone call that converts into business can be traced to the keyword search term that drove the phone call. As a result, bids on the source traffic can be appropriately adjusted and managed.

- **Pay-per-Sale Search Engine Marketing** is a variant of pay-per-sale, whereby the traffic source is largely search engine traffic such as that from Google's AdWords "pay-per-click" system. The business model means that merchants no longer bear the cost of "pay-per-click"; instead, the "pay-per-sale" provider takes on the risk of conversion.

  CPS belongs to the larger family of CPA, which is different from Cost Per Impression in which advertisers pay every time their advertisement is displayed, irrespective of whether the display created any action on the part of reader or visitor to the website or not.

- **Affiliate Networks** usually offer the "pay-per-sale" business model and have done so since inception. However, there is typically an upfront set-up fee, as well as monthly minimum charges for the advertiser, in addition to relatively stringent requirements around entry into the network to begin with. The industry has four core players: the merchant (also known as retailer or brand), the network, the publisher (also known as 'the affiliate'), and the customer. Typically, affiliate networks such as Value Click or Commission Junction will connect merchants (advertisers) with publishers, or owners of sites, which can send traffic to the merchants' sites in exchange for a bounty, or commission for each sale delivered

- **Affiliate marketing** is a type of performance-based marketing in which a business rewards one or more affiliates for each visitor or customer brought by the affiliate's own marketing efforts. The industry has four core players: the merchant (also known as 'retailer' or 'brand'), the network (that contains offers for the affiliate to choose from and also takes care of the payments), the publisher (also known as 'the affiliate'), and the customer. The market has grown in complexity, resulting in the emergence of a secondary tier of players, including affiliate management agencies, super-affiliates and specialized third party vendors.

Affiliate marketing overlaps with other Internet marketing methods to some degree, because affiliates often use regular advertising methods. Those methods include organic search engine optimization (SEO), paid search engine marketing (PPC - Pay per Click), e-mail marketing, content marketing and in some sense display advertising. On the other hand, affiliates sometimes use less orthodox techniques, such as publishing reviews of products or services offered by a partner.

Affiliate marketing is commonly confused with referral marketing, as both forms of marketing use third parties to drive sales to the retailer. However, both are distinct forms of marketing and the main difference between them is that affiliate marketing relies purely on financial motivations to drive sales while referral marketing relies on trust and personal relationships to drive sales.

Affiliate marketing is frequently overlooked by advertisers. While search engines, e-mail, and syndication capture much of the attention of online retailers, affiliate marketing carries a much lower profile. Still, affiliates continue to play a significant role in e-retailers' marketing strategies.

- **Online advertising:** Online advertising also called online marketing or Internet advertising or web advertising is a form of marketing and advertising which uses the Internet to deliver promotional marketing messages to consumers. Consumers view online advertising as an unwanted distraction with few benefits and have increasingly turned to ad blocking for a variety of reasons.

It includes email marketing, search engine marketing (SEM), social media marketing, many types of display advertising (including web banner advertising), and mobile advertising. Like other advertising media, online advertising frequently involves both a publisher, who integrates advertisements into its online content, and an advertiser, who provides the advertisements to be displayed on the publisher's content. Other potential participants include advertising agencies that help generate and place the ad copy, an ad server which technologically delivers the ad and tracks statistics, and advertising affiliates who do independent promotional work for the advertiser.

A research study revealed that in 2011, Internet advertising revenues in the United States surpassed those of cable television and nearly exceeded those of broadcast television. In 2013, Internet advertising revenues in the United States totalled $42.8 billion, a 17% increase over the $36.57 billion in revenues in 2012. U.S. internet ad revenue hit a historic high of $20.1 billion for the first half of 2013, up 18% over the same period in 2012. Online advertising is widely used across virtually all industry sectors. In India also online advertisement has witnessed multi-folded growth during last one decade.

Many common online advertising practices are controversial and increasingly subject to regulation. Online ad revenues may not adequately replace other publishers' revenue streams. Declining ad revenue has led some publishers to hide their content behind paywalls.

❑❑

Chapter 2: Display Advertising

2.1 Introduction

Display advertising conveys its advertising message visually using text, logos, animations, videos, photographs, or other graphics. Display advertisers frequently target users with particular traits to increase the ads' effect. Online advertisers (typically through their advertisement servers) often use cookies, which are unique identifiers of specific computers, to decide which ads to serve to a particular consumer. Cookies can track whether a user left a page without buying anything, so the advertiser can later retarget the user with ads from the site the user visited.

As advertisers collect data across multiple external websites about a users online activity, they can create a detailed profile of the users interests to deliver even more targeted advertising. This aggregation of data is called behavioural targeting. Advertisers can also target their audience by using contextual to deliver display ads related to the content of the web page where the ads appear, Retargeting, behavioural targeting, and contextual advertising all are designed to increase an advertiser's return on investment, or ROI, over untargeted ads.

Advertisers may also deliver ads based on a users suspected geography through retargeting. A users IP address communicates some geographic information (at minimum, the user's country or general region). The geographic information from an IP can be supplemented and refined with other proxies or information to narrow the range of possible locations. For example, with mobile devices, advertisers can sometimes use a phone's GPS receiver or the location of nearby mobile towers. Cookies and other persistent data on a user's machine may provide help narrowing a user's location further.

2.2 Web Banner Advertising

Web banners or banner ads typically are graphical ads displayed within a web page. Many banner ads are delivered by a central ad server.

Banner ads can use rich media to incorporate video, audio, animations, buttons, forms, or other interactive elements using Java applets, HTML5, Adobe Flash, and other programs.

Frame ad (traditional banner) Frame ads were the first form of web banners. The colloquial usage of "banner ads" often refers to traditional frame ads. Website publishers incorporate frame ads by setting aside a particular space on the web page. The Interactive Advertising Bureau's Ad Unit Guidelines proposes standardized pixel dimensions for ad units.

2.3 Pop-ups/Pop-under

A pop-up ad is displayed in a new web browser window that opens above a website visitor's initial browser window. A pop-under ad opens a new browser window under a website visitor's initial browser window. Pop-under ads and similar technologies are now advised against by online authorities such as Google, who state that they "do not condone this practice.

A floating ad, or overlay ad, is a type of rich media advertisement that appears superimposed over the requested website's content. Floating ads may disappear or become less obtrusive after a preset time period.

2.4 Expanding Ad

An expanding ad is a rich media frame ad that changes dimensions upon a predefined condition, such as a pre-set amount of time a visitor spends on a webpage, the user's click on the ad, or the user's mouse movement over the ad. Expanding ads allow advertisers to fit more information into a restricted ad space.

2.5 Trick banners

A trick banner is a banner ad where the ad copy imitates some screen element users commonly encounter, such as an operating system message or popular application message, to induce ad clicks. Trick banners typically do not mention the advertiser in the initial ad, and thus they are a form of bait-and-switch. Trick banners commonly attract a higher-than-average click-through rate, but tricked users may resent the advertiser for deceiving them.

2.6 News Feed Ads

"News Feed Ads", also called "Sponsored Stories", "Boosted Posts", typically exist on social media platforms that offer a steady stream of information updates news feed) in regulated formats (i.e. in similar sized small boxes with a uniform style). Those advertisements are intertwined with non-promoted news that the users are reading through. Those advertisements can be of any content, such as promoting a website, a fan page, an app, or a product.

Some examples are: Facebook's "Sponsored Stories", LinkedIn's "Sponsored Updates", and Twitter's "Promoted Tweets".

This display ads format falls into its own category because unlike banner ads which are quite distinguishable, News Feed Ads' format blends well into non-paid news updates. This format of online advertisement yields much higher click-through rates than traditional display ads.

2.7 Branding with the help of Digital Marketing Tools

Businesses focused on expanding their reach to more customers will want to pay attention to the increase in volume of visitors, as well as the quality of those interactions. Traditional measures of volume include number of visitors to a page and number of emails collected, while time spent on page and click-through to other pages/ photos are good indicators for engagement.

● Number of visitors to a page

● Time spent on the page

● Click-through across pages/ photos

● Number of emails collected

Brand Health Metrics

Businesses want to measure the impact that their messages have impact on consumers. Brand health refers to the positive or negative feedback that a company gets. It also measures how important a brand is for consumers. With this companies want to find out if brand reputation influences their customers to make a purchase.

Measures in this Part Comprise

● Word of mouth (WoM) is the number of times a brand has been talked versus its competitors (conversations and feedbacks). Outside the digital world, WoM stands for the space and frequency a brand advertisement is placed on traditional media.

● Sentiment is when the brand has positive, negative or neutral feedback. Any and every brand intent to generate as many positive WoM/feedback is possible to collect.

● Brand Influence refers to the number of times a post, comment or tweet is shared on different platforms. It shows the strength of a brand over its competitors to engage customers globally.

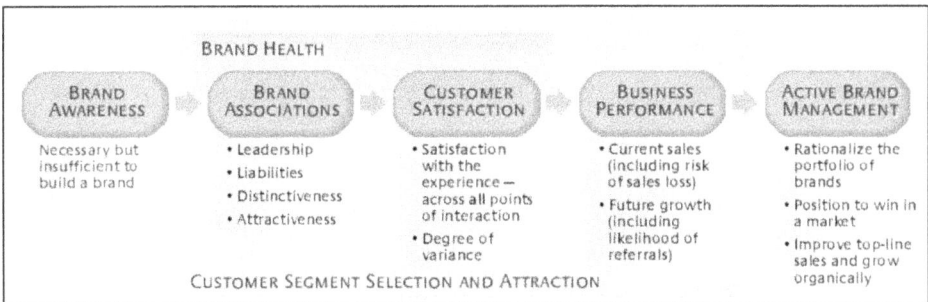

BRAND HEALTH

BRAND AWARENESS	BRAND ASSOCIATIONS	CUSTOMER SATISFACTION	BUSINESS PERFORMANCE	ACTIVE BRAND MANAGEMENT
Necessary but insufficient to build a brand	• Leadership • Liabilities • Distinctiveness • Attractiveness	• Satisfaction with the experience – across all points of interaction • Degree of variance	• Current sales (including risk of sales loss) • Future growth (including likelihood of referrals)	• Rationalize the portfolio of brands • Position to win in a market • Improve top-line sales and grow organically

CUSTOMER SEGMENT SELECTION AND ATTRACTION

2.8 Diversified User Base

For businesses hoping to reach not only more - but also to new customers online, they should pay attention to the demographics of new visitors, as evidenced by cookies that can be installed, different sources of traffic, different online behaviours, and/or different buying habits of online visitors.

● Demographics of visitors

- Sources of traffic (i.e., SEO, social media, referral, direct)
- Differences in buying patterns and user-behavior of visitors

2.9 Sales

Businesses are always keen and focused on increasing sales through content marketing, it should look at traditional e-commerce metrics including click-through-rate from a product-page to check-out and completion rates at the check-out. Altogether, these form a conversion funnel. Moreover, to better understand customers' buying habits, they should look at other engagement metrics like time spent per page, number of product-page visits per user, and re-engagement.

- Conversion through the sales process (the process from sign-up to check-out), including click-through-rates at each stage of the conversion funnel
- Time spent on the page
- Re-engagement (i.e., % of return visitors)
- Click-through across product pages/emailers

Please find below the picture replicating how digital marketing can help increasing your sales number over the period of time gradually.

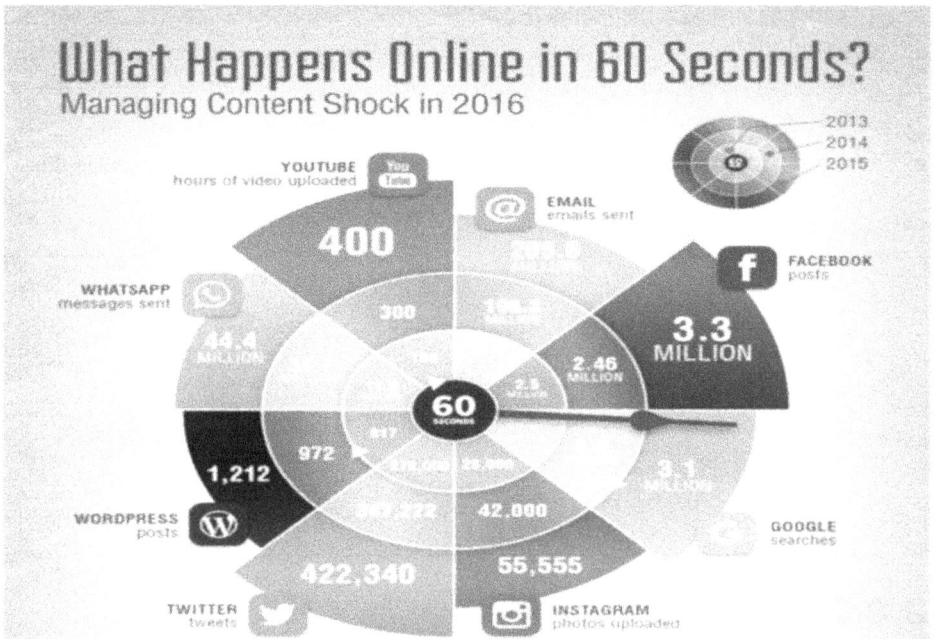

What Happens Online in 60 Seconds?
Managing Content Shock in 2016

2013
2014
2015

YOUTUBE
hours of video uploaded
400

EMAIL
emails sent

FACEBOOK
posts

WHATSAPP
messages sent
44.4 MILLION
300

3.3 MILLION

2.46 MILLION

60 SECONDS

2.5

972

1,212

WORDPRESS
posts

42.000

3.1 MILLION

GOOGLE
searches

422,340

55,555

TWITTER
tweets

INSTAGRAM
photos uploaded

Look at how the entire cycle from marketing to sales conversion take place through this diagram appended below.

Digital Marketing Sales Funnel

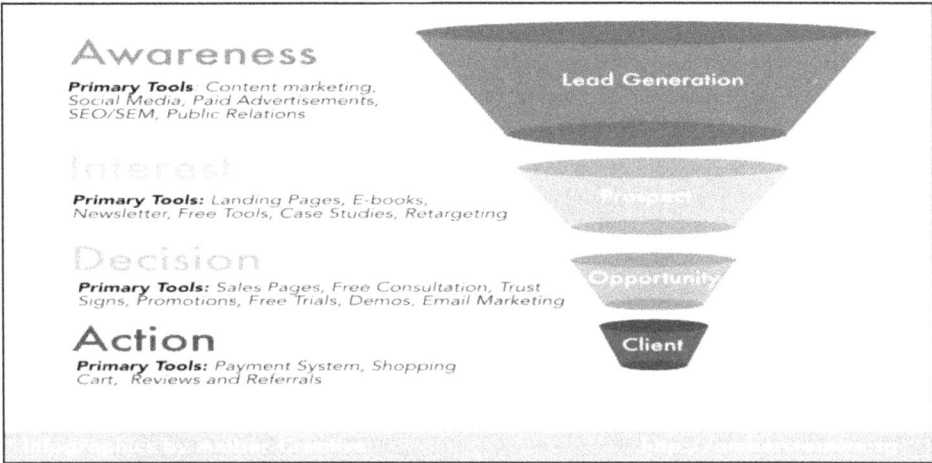

Awareness

Primary Tools: Content marketing,
Social Media, Paid Advertisements,
SEO/SEM, Public Relations

Interest

Primary Tools: Landing Pages, E-books,
Newsletter, Free Tools, Case Studies, Retargeting

Decision

Primary Tools: Sales Pages, Free Consultation, Trust
Signs, Promotions, Free Trials, Demos, Email Marketing

Action

Primary Tools: Payment System, Shopping
Cart, Reviews and Referrals

Lead Generation

Prospect

Opportunity

Client

2.10 Innovation Metrics

Companies want to analyse if their social media campaigns are generating commentary among consumers. This helps them to come up with ways to improve their product and service. This involves "high level of brand engagement and builds brand loyalty".

Examples:

● When a company makes a post through their social media platforms and shares its ideas, consumers can be influenced or motivated to share their opinions.

● Trend spotting refers to the latest consumers' comments about a brand, product or service that must be targeted. Some tools can be provided by Google Trends, Trends map (Twitter) and other sites that report what is in everybody's mouths worldwide.

An Innovation Matrix

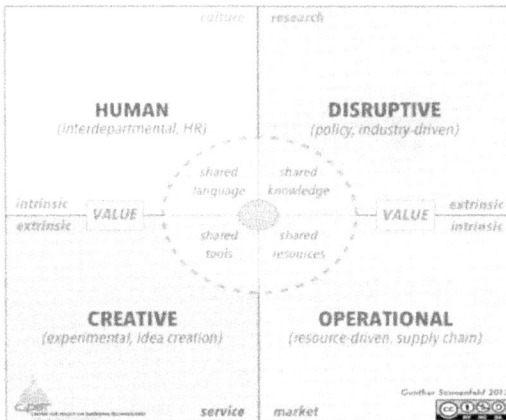

2.11 Online Classified Advertising

Online classified advertising is advertising posted online in a categorical listing of specific products or services. Examples include online job boards, online real estate listings, automotive listings, online yellow pages, and online auction-based listings. Just Dial and eBay are two prominent providers of online classified listings in Indian context. OLX is an excellent example of a platform showcase online classified advertisements as per users desire.

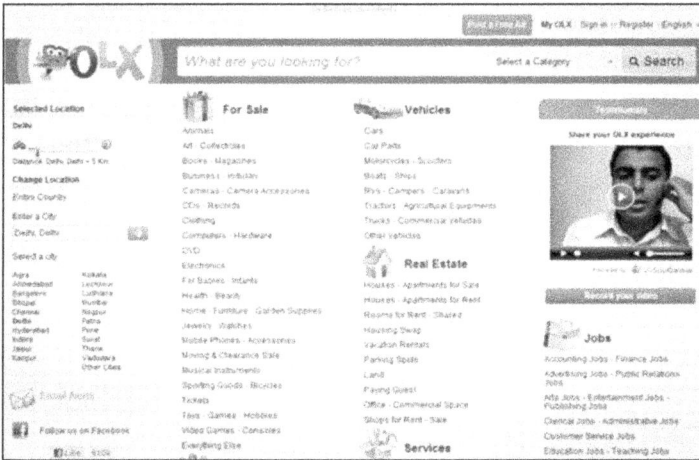

2.12 Adware

Adware is software that, once installed, automatically displays advertisements on a user›s computer. The ads may appear in the software itself, integrated into web pages visited by the user, or in pop-ups/pop-under. Adware installed without the user's permission is a type of malware. It's an unexpected pop up suddenly appears on your screen with certain eye catchy contents.

2.13 Affiliate Marketing

Affiliate marketing occurs when advertisers organize third parties to generate potential customers for them. Third-party affiliates receive payment based on sales generated through their promotion. Affiliate marketers generate traffic to offers from affiliate networks, and when the desired action is taken by the visitor, the affiliate earns a commission. These desired actions can be an email submission, a phone call, filling out an online form, or an online order being completed. Look at an example of third party affiliate marketing display marked in red arrow below on a webpage you're browsing for certain usage.

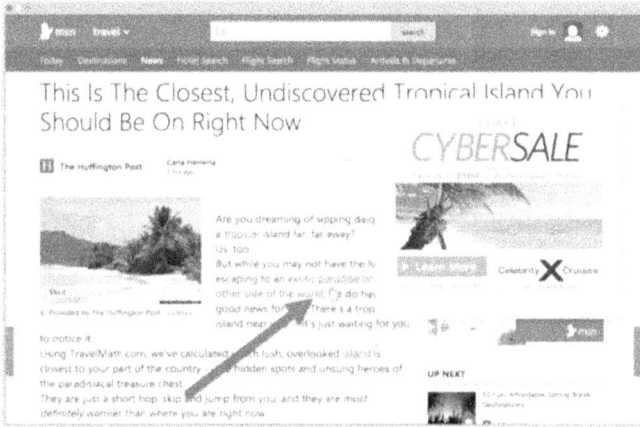

2.14 Content Marketing

Content marketing was though discussed earlier still a method which is a marketing tool that involves the creation and sharing of media and publishing content in order to acquire and retain customers. This information can be presented in a variety of formats, including blogs, news, video, white papers, e-books, infographics, case studies, how-to guides and more. Now look at an example of visual content marketing example on Coca-Cola's official webpage.

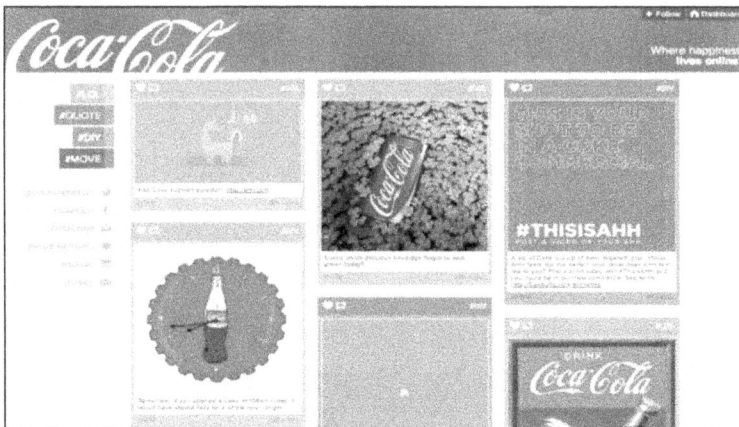

Considering that most marketing involves some form of published media, it is almost (though not entirely) redundant to call 'content marketing' anything other than simply 'marketing'. There are, of course, other forms of marketing (in-person marketing, telephone-based marketing, word of mouth marketing, etc.) where the label is more useful for identifying the type of marketing. However, even these are usually merely presenting content that they are marketing as information in a way that is different from traditional print, radio, TV, film, email, or web media.

2.15 Online Marketing Platform

Online marketing platform (OMP) is an integrated web-based platform that combines the benefits of a business directory, local search engine, search engine optimisation (SEO) tool, customer relationship management (CRM) package and content management system (CMS). EBay and Amazon are widely used as online marketing and logistics management platforms.

On Facebook, Twitter, YouTube, LinkedIn, and other Social Media, retail online marketing is also used. Online business marketing platforms such as Just Dial, Sulekha, Yellow Pages, Grotal and Lecanto have been able to engage a good volume of customers to their listing page/online marketing platform.

Unlike television marketing in which BARC India, TAM Media Research Ratings can be relied upon for viewing metrics, online advertisers do not have an independent party to verify viewing claims made by the big online platforms.

There are multiple online marketing platforms available for you to grow your business as showcased in the pictures appended above, now it completely depends on your strategy and budget, that what would you use, when and how you will utilize these platforms to maximize your profit.

2.16 Financial Payment Methods to help Determine Annual Budget for Digital Marketers

CPM (Cost Per Mile)

Cost per mile, often abbreviated to CPM, means that advertisers pay for every thousand displays of their message to potential customers (mille is the Latin word for thousand).

In the online context, ad displays are usually called "impressions." Definitions of an "impression" vary among publishers, and some impressions may not be charged because they don't represent a new exposure to an actual customer. Advertisers can use technologies such as web bugs to verify if an impression are actually delivered.

Publishers use a variety of techniques to increase page views, such as dividing content across multiple pages, repurposing someone else›s content, using sensational titles, or publishing tabloid or controversial content.

CPM advertising is susceptible to «impression fraud,» and advertisers who want visitors to their sites may not find per-impression payments a good proxy for the results they desire.

CPC (Cost Per Click)

CPC (Cost per Click) or PPC (Pay per click) means advertisers pay each time a user clicks on the ad. CPC advertising works well when advertisers want visitors to their sites, but it's a less accurate measurement for advertisers looking to build brand awareness. CPC's market share has grown each year since its introduction, eclipsing CPM to dominate two-thirds of all online advertising compensation methods.

Like impressions, not all recorded clicks are valuable to advertisers. Gold Spot Media reported that up to 50% of clicks on static mobile banner ads are accidental and resulted in redirected visitors leaving the new site immediately.

CPE (Cost Per Engagement)

Cost per engagement aims to track not just that an ad unit loaded on the page (i.e., an impression was served), but also that the viewer actually saw and/or interacted with the advertisement.

CPV (Cost Per View)

Cost per view video advertising. Both Google and YouTube endorsed this standardized CPV metric to the IAB's (Interactive Advertising Bureau) Digital Video Committee, and it's garnering a notable amount of industry support. CPV is the primary benchmark used in YouTube Advertising Campaigns, as part of Google's AdWords platform.

CPI (Cost Per Install)

The CPI compensation method is specific to mobile applications and mobile advertising. In CPI ad campaigns brands are charged a fixed of bid rate only when the application was installed.

Attribution of Ad Value

In marketing, "attribution" is the measurement of effectiveness of particular ads in a consumer's ultimate decision to purchase. Multiple ad impressions may lead to a consumer "click" or other action. A single action may lead to revenue being paid to multiple ad space sellers.

Other Performance-based Compensation

CPA (Cost per Action or Cost per Acquisition) or PPP (Pay per Performance) advertising means the advertiser pays for the number of users who perform a desired activity, such as completing a purchase or filling out a registration form. Performance-based compensation can also incorporate revenue sharing, where publishers earn a percentage of the advertiser's profits made as a result of the ad. Performance-based compensation shifts the risk of failed advertising onto publishers.

Fixed Cost

Fixed cost compensation means advertisers pay a fixed cost for delivery of ads online, usually over a specified time period, irrespective of the ad's visibility or users' response to it. One example is CPD (cost per day) where advertisers pay a fixed cost for publishing an ad for a day irrespective of impressions served or clicks.

2.17 Determine a Bid Strategy Based on Your Goals

AdWords offers several bid strategies that are tailored to different types of campaigns. Depending on which networks your campaign is targeting, and whether you want to focus on getting clicks, impressions, conversions, or **view** you can determine which strategy is best for you. In this article, we'll describe how to use your advertising goals to choose your bid strategy.

Consider Your Goals

Each bid strategy is suited for different kinds of campaigns and advertising goals. For the purposes of bidding, you'll want to consider four basic types of goals, along with your current campaign settings.

- **If you want customers to take a direct action on your site,** and you're using conversion tracking, then it may be best to focus on conversions. AdWords Smart Bidding lets you do that.

- **If you want to generate traffic to your website**, focusing on clicks could be ideal for you. Cost-per-click (CPC) bidding may be right for your campaign.

- **If you want to increase brand awareness**—not drive traffic to your site— focusing on impressions may be your strategy. You can use cost per thousand viewable impressions (vCPM) bidding to put your message in front of customers. You can also use a Target Search Page Location or Target Outranking Share strategy to maximize visibility.

- **If you run video ads and want to increase views or interactions with your ads**, you can use cost-per-view (CPV) or CPM or cost-per-thousand (CPM) bidding.

- **If you run video ads and your goal is to increase product or brand consideration** you can use cost-per-view (CPV).

2.18 Focus on Conversions with Smart Bidding

If you want to focus on conversions, consider using AdWords Smart Bidding to take much of the heavy lifting and guesswork out of setting bids. Smart Bidding is a set of automated bid strategies that uses machine learning to optimize for conversions or conversion value in each and every auction—a feature known as "auction-time bidding." It also factors in a wide range of auction-time signals such as device, location, time of day, language, and operating system to capture the unique context of every search.

Below are the four Smart Bidding strategies you can use.

- **Target CPA (cost-per-acquisition)**: If you want to optimize for conversions, you can use Target CPA to help increase conversions while targeting a specific cost-per-acquisition (CPA). Learn more About Target CPA bidding.

- **Target ROAS (return-on-AD-spend)**: If you want to optimize for conversion value, you can use Target ROAS to help increase conversion value while targeting a specific return-on-ad-spend (ROAS). Learn more About Target ROAS bidding.

- **Maximize Conversions**: If you want to optimize for conversions, but just want to spend your entire budget instead of targeting a specific CPA, you can use Maximize Conversions. Learn more About Maximize Conversions bidding.

- **Enhanced cost-per-click (ECPC)**: If you want to automatically adjust your manual bids to try to maximize conversions, you can use ECPC. It's an optional feature you can use with Manual CPC bidding. Learn more About ECPC.

2.19 Focus on Clicks with CPC Bidding

If you're focusing on gaining clicks to generate traffic to your website, there are two cost-per-click bid strategies to consider:

- **Maximize Clicks**: This is an automated bid strategy. It's the simplest way to bid for clicks. All you have to do is set a daily budget, and the AdWords system automatically manages your bids to bring you the most clicks possible within your budget. Learn more About Maximize Clicks bidding.

- **Manual CPC bidding**: This lets you manage your maximum CPC bids yourself. You can set different bids for each ad group in your campaign, or for individual keywords or placements. If you've found that certain keywords or placements are more profitable, you can use manual bidding to allocate more of your advertising budget to those keywords or placements. Learn more About Manual CPC bidding.

Maximize Clicks could be a good option for you if the following describes your campaign:

- You have an advertising budget you'd like to reach consistently.

- You don't want to spend time monitoring and updating individual cost-per-click (CPC) bids, and you're willing to let the AdWords system update CPC bids automatically.

- You're mainly interested in increasing website traffic.

- You're new to AdWords or don't know exactly how much to bid for particular keywords or placements.

Maximize Clicks isn't a good choice for you if your advertising goals include maintaining a specific ad position or cost per conversion. It isn't possible to set individual CPC bids with Maximize Clicks, but you can set a maximum CPC bid for your entire campaign.

Example

You have a website that sells a variety of art supplies, and your main goal is to bring more customers to your site. You have a set amount that you want to spend on advertising each month, and there isn't a particular product you want to emphasize most. Maximize Clicks lets you decide the overall amount of your budget, then we'll find you the most customers based on that.

With Manual CPC bidding, you can fine-tune your maximum CPC bids to help control the cost and volume of clicks on your ads. Manual CPC bidding could be a good choice for you if your campaign fits this description:

- You'd like to control maximum CPC bids for individual ad groups, keywords, or placements.

- You're mainly interested in increasing website traffic, not necessarily brand awareness.

- You don't need to reach a target budget every month. (If you do need to reach a target budget, Maximize Clicks may be a better choice.)

- Your campaign targets the Search Network, the Display Network, or both.

If you're not sure which keywords or placements are most profitable, or if you don't have time to devote to managing manual bids, Maximize Clicks is probably a better fit for you.

Example

Although your website sells a wide range of art supplies, you're most interested in selling paint brushes. With Manual CPC bidding, even if your ad group has 15 keywords, you can choose to set a higher bid for only the keyword "paint brushes," which will apply whenever that keyword triggers your ad.

2.20 Focus on Impressions

If you want to focus on impressions, you can try one of the following bid strategies to help maximize visibility.

- **Target Search Page Location**: This is an automated bid strategy that automatically sets your bids to help increase the chances that your ads appear at the top of the page, or on the first page of search results. Learn more About Target Search Page Location bidding.

- **Target Outranking Share**: This is an automated bid strategy that lets you choose a domain you want to outrank so that your ad is displayed above that domain's ads, or shows when that domain's ad does not. You can set how often you want to outrank that domain, and AdWords automatically sets your Search bids to help meet that target. Learn more About Target Outranking Share bidding.

- **Cost-per-thousand Impressions (CPM):** With this bid strategy, you'll pay based on the number of impressions (times your ads are shown) that you receive on YouTube or the Google Display Network.

- **Cost-per-thousand Viewable Impressions (vCPM)**: This is a manual bidding strategy you can use if your ads are designed to increase awareness, but not necessarily generate clicks or traffic. It lets you set the highest amount you want to pay for each 1,000 viewable ad impressions on the Google Display Network. vCPM bidding probably isn't for you if the goal of your campaign is a direct response from customers, like buying a product or filling out a form. Learn more about vCPM bidding.

Here are some cases in which we'd recommend manual vCPM bidding:

- Your ads are designed to increase awareness, but not necessarily generate clicks or traffic.

- You prefer the traditional industry metrics of vCPM (cost-per-thousand viewable impressions) campaigns.

- You're targeting particular **placements**, not just keywords. (Combined with placement targeting, bidding for impressions can help ensure your ads appear to a specific audience that will be interested in your ads.)

- You're mainly interested in increasing brand awareness. Image ads and other multimedia formats often serve that purpose best, and these ad formats run on the Display Network.

- Your message is in the ad itself, so you don't need people to click through to your site. This may apply to events (such as a television premiere) or political advertising.

Manual vCPM bidding probably isn't for you if the goal of your campaign is a direct response from customers, like buying a product or filling out a form.

Example

You're giving a free concert in Paris, and want to get as many music lovers to come as possible. You're running a campaign with vibrant image ads that share the date, time, and location of the event -- everything a music fan needs to know to show up. As long as people see your ad, they'll know your whole message. Viewable CPM bidding can help you get it in front of as many eyes as possible.

Focus on views or interactions (for video ads only)

If you run video ads, you can use cost-per-view (CPV) bidding. With CPV bidding, you'll pay for video views and other video interactions, such as clicks on the calls-to-action overlay (CTAs), cards, and companion banners. You just enter the highest price you want to pay for a view while setting up your True View video campaign. If you're new to automated bidding in AdWords, read about automated bidding first. To use Smart Bidding, you need to have conversion tracking enabled. Learn how to Set up conversion tracking.

Why use AdWords Smart Bidding with AdWords Smart Bidding, you get 4 key benefits that help you save time and improve performance.

1. **Advanced machine learning:** In bidding, machine learning algorithms train on data at a vast scale to help you make more accurate predictions across your account about how different bid amounts might impact conversions or conversion value. These algorithms factor in a wider range of parameters that impact performance than a single person or team could compute.

2. **Wide range of contextual signals:** With auction-time bidding, you can factor in a wide range of signals into your bid optimizations. Signals are identifiable attributes about a person or their context at the time of a particular auction. This includes attributes like device and location, which are available as manual bid adjustments, plus additional signals and signal combinations exclusive to AdWords Smart Bidding. See a list of several of these important signals below.

2.21 Device

Description: AdWords can optimize bids for Target CPA or Target ROAS strategies based on whether someone is on a mobile, desktop, or tablet device.

Example: For a car dealership, bids may be adjusted if a person is searching on a mobile device and therefore more likely to book an appointment at a nearby location.

Physical Location

Description: AdWords can optimize bids based on the specific location (down to the city) someone is located in, even if the advertiser's implemented location targeting isn't as specific.

Example: For a bank, even if the advertiser's location targeting is set to New York State, bids may be adjusted if a person searches for "new checking account" from a city with higher branch penetration where they're more likely to apply for an account.

Location Intent

Description: AdWords can optimize bids based on someone's location intent in addition to their physical location.

Example: For a travel provider, bids may be adjusted if someone is actively researching a vacation destination you offer (e.g. "Sikkim vacations in august"), even if they're not physically located near there.

Weekday & Time of Day

Description: AdWords can optimize bids based on someone's local time of day and day of week in their time zone.

Example: For a restaurant, bids may be adjusted if someone searches at 8 PM on a Thursday when people are more likely to make a reservation for the weekend, compared to 8 AM on a Monday.

Remarketing List

Description: AdWords can optimize Search and Display bids based on which remarketing list someone belongs to (coming soon for Shopping), and can also account for how recently a user was added to that list. Search also takes into account each list a user is on, for a given campaign or ad group.

Example: For an online clothing retailer, bids may be adjusted if a person has already browsed a product during a previous site visit, and whether they added it to a shopping cart last week, when they're more likely to want to buy it soon, versus last month.

Ad Characteristics

Description: AdWords can optimize bids based on which version of an ad will be shown, including whether it's for a mobile app.

Example: For a telecom company, bids may be adjusted if the ad shown is the "Latest Deals" creative or the "Flexible Plans" creative, or if it points to the mobile site or app, based on which variation has a higher likelihood of converting. For Display campaigns, bids take into account which ad sizes and formats are more likely to convert.

Interface Language

Description: AdWords can optimize bids based on someone's language preferences.

Example: For a Spanish language learning site, bids may be adjusted for the query, "learn a new language" if a person's language preference is set to English instead of Spanish, where they're less likely to purchase a new tutorial.

Browser

Description: AdWords can optimize bids based on the browser someone is using.

Example: For a health foods company, bids may be adjusted if a person searches from Chrome, which has resulted in a higher conversion likelihood for that business in the past, compared to other browsers.

Operating System

Description: AdWords can optimize bids based on the operating system someone is using.

Example: For a gaming app developer, bids may be adjusted if a person searches for "puzzle game" on Google Play from an Android device that has been upgraded to the latest OS version, which is more likely to result in an app install, compared to an older OS version.

Demographics (Search and Display)

Description: AdWords can optimize bids based on age and gender. For Display campaigns, bids can also be optimized for interests.

Example: For a toy retailer, bids may be adjusted if someone has been identified as likely being a parent and is more likely to convert on a Display ad promoting a new line of educational toys.

Actual search query (Search and Shopping)

Description: AdWords can optimize bids based on the text of the query that triggered the ad, not just the matching keyword.

Example: For a shoe retailer, bids may be adjusted if a person's search query is "leather boots" and they're more likely to buy a new pair compared to a search for "boot repairs," even if both queries broad match to the keyword "boots".

Search Network Partner (Search only)

Description: AdWords can optimize bids based on which search partner site the ad appears on.

Example: For a consumer packaged goods brand, bids may be adjusted if a query is coming from a more relevant search on an e-commerce site, which has higher conversion likelihood, compared to a news site.

Web Placement (Display only)

Description: AdWords can optimize bids based on which site placement the ad appears on.

Example: For a consumer packaged goods brand, bids may be adjusted if the ad appears on a popular, high-traffic site, which has higher conversion likelihood.

Site Behaviour (Display only)

Description: AdWords can optimize bids based on someone's activity on your site, including number of pages viewed, value of products browsed, how far through the conversion process they progressed, and other sites previously visited.

Example: For a furniture brand, bids may be adjusted if a person has browsed several couches priced at a higher value compared to lamps that have a lower price point.

Product Attributes (Shopping only)

Description: AdWords can optimize bids based on similar attributes across products such as price, condition, brand, and product category.

Example: For a retailer selling outdoor gear, bids may be adjusted if you add a new tent to your product data that is similar to other tents that have high conversion likelihood.

Mobile App Ratings (coming soon)

Description: AdWords can optimize bids based on the strength and quantity of an app's reviews.

Example: For a fitness brand, bids may be adjusted if an app has many excellent reviews and is more likely to result in an install.

Price Competitiveness (Coming Soon for Shopping)

Description: AdWords can optimize bids based on how your product price compares to other advertisers who are participating in the same auctions that you are.

Example: For a cookware retailer, bids may be adjusted if you're offering a strong deal on a knife set compared to other advertisers.

Seasonality (Coming Soon for Shopping)

Description: AdWords can optimize bids based on seasonal performance trends during different times of year.

Example: For an electronics retailer, bids may be adjusted if a person is searching for a new television during the holiday season, which typically sees higher conversion likelihood.

❑❑

Chapter 3: Social Media Advertisement Platforms

3.1 Facebook

Facebook probably doesn't need much of an introduction – launched in 2004; the social network now is the largest social media platform with more than 1.7 billion monthly active users worldwide. The company today is more than just a social network – Facebook acquired messaging app WhatsApp and started its own successful messenger. They also bought photo-sharing platform Instagram and the virtual reality company Oculus VR. Since most Facebook users log into the site every day and engage with other users, brands and content, the platform knows a lot about their users. For advertisers Facebook is one of the most attractive online channels, because it lets them utilize their rich user data to target very specific audiences. And since most companies and brands are already present on Facebook, ads are a great way to build a following and boost engagement for the content they share.

Facebook has in recent years become a popular channel for advertising, alongside traditional forms such as television, radio, and print. With over 1 billion active users, and 50% of those users logging into their accounts every day, it is an important communication platform that businesses can utilize and optimize to promote their brand and drive traffic to their websites. There are three commonly used strategies to increase advertising reach on Facebook.

Improving the effectiveness of posts, achieved by adjusting the length and timing of posts to influence the number of likes and comments it receives. This will help the post reach a greater number of Facebook users, ultimately increasing its reach.

Increasing network size, achieved by analysing user behaviour to determine how often to post and what type of content to post.

Buying more reach, achieved by paying Facebook to advertise a post, What Facebook ads look like Here you have four different choices – you can create an ad that features a single image, a single video, or multiple images that are displayed either in a carousel format or as a slideshow. Single Image Single Video/Slideshow Carousel etc.

Improving effectiveness and increasing network size are organic approaches while buying more reach is a paid approach which does not require any further action. Most businesses will attempt an "organic" approach to gaining a significant following before considering a paid approach. Because Facebook requires a login, it is important that posts are public to ensure they will reach the widest possible audience. Posts that have been heavily shared and interacted with by users are displayed as 'highlighted posts' at the top of newsfeeds. In order to achieve this status, the posts need to be engaging, interesting, or useful. This can be achieved by being spontaneous, asking questions, addressing current events and issues, and optimizing trending hashtags and keywords. The more engagement a post receives, the further it will spread and the more likely it is to feature on first in search results.

Another organic approach to Facebook optimization is cross-linking different social platforms. By posting links to websites or social media sites in the profile 'about' section, it is possible to direct traffic and ultimately increase search engine optimization. Another option is to share links to relevant videos and blog posts. Facebook Connect is a functionality that launched in 2008 to allow Facebook users to sign up to different websites, enter competitions, and access exclusive promotions by logging in with their existing Facebook account details. This is beneficial to users as they don't have to create a new login every time they want to sign up to a website, but also beneficial to businesses as Facebook users become more likely to share their content. Often the two are interlinked, where in order to access parts of a website, a user has to like or share certain things on their personal profile or invite a number of friends to like a page. This can lead to greater traffic flow to a website as it reaches a wider audience. Businesses have more opportunities to reach their target markets if they choose a paid approach to SMO. When Facebook users create an account, they are urged to fill out their personal details such as gender, age, location, education, current and previous employers, religious and political views, interests, and personal preferences such as movie and music tastes. Facebook then takes this information and allows advertisers to use it to determine how to best market themselves to users that they know will be interested in their product. This can also be known as micro-targeting. If a user clicks on a link to like a page, it will show up on their profile and newsfeed. This then feeds back into organic social media optimization, as friends of the user will see this and be encouraged to click on the page themselves. Although advertisers are buying mass reach, they are attracting a customer base with a genuine interest in their product. Once a customer base has been established through a paid approach, businesses will often run promotions and competitions to attract more organic followers

The amount of businesses that use Facebook to advertise also holds significant relevance. Currently there are 3 million businesses that advertise on Facebook. This makes Facebook the world's largest platform for social media advertising. What also holds importance is the amount of money leading businesses is spending on Facebook advertising alone. Proctor and Gamble spend $60 million every year on Facebook advertising. Other advertisers on Facebook include Microsoft; with a yearly spend of £35 million, Amazon, Nestle and American Express all with yearly expenditures above £25 million per year.

Furthermore the amount of small businesses advertising on Facebook is of relevance. This number has grown rapidly over the upcoming years and demonstrates how important social media advertising actually is. Currently 70% of the UK's small businesses use Facebook advertising. This is a substantial amount of advertisers. Almost half of the world's small businesses use social media marketing product of some sort. This demonstrates the impact that social media has had on the current digital marketing era.

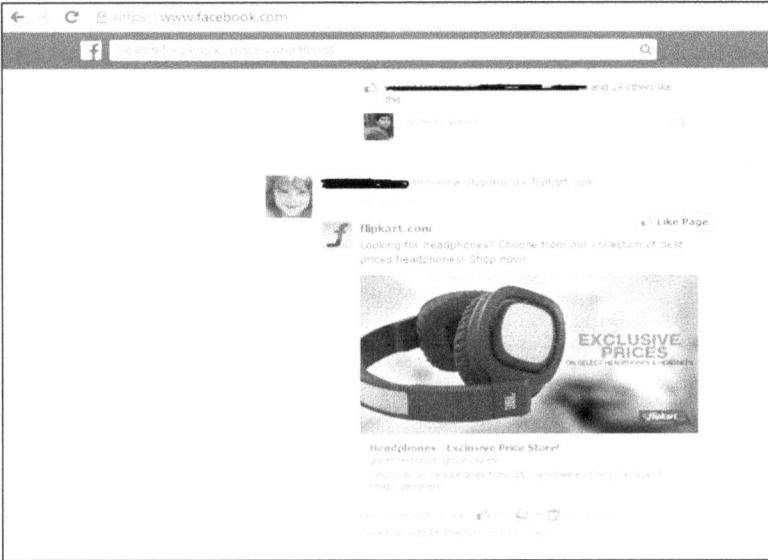

Facebook also offers a new, more immersive ad experience on mobile. They call it Facebook Canvas. Canvas looks like a normal mobile news feed ad, but once a user taps to open the ad, he or she is taken to a full screen experience (videos, images, text, products) that the advertiser can customize.

To learn more about Facebook Canvas, go to canvas.facebook.com. Here is an example of how cruise company Holland America Line used Facebook Canvas to advertise a Caribbean getaway: What objectives can I meet with my Facebook ads?

You can optimize ads on Facebook based on what specific objective your campaign has. Generally, Facebook distinguishes three different kinds of objectives that follow the traditional user journey from awareness to conversion:

1. **Raising awareness:** This includes campaigns to raise brand awareness, local awareness and to maximize reach.

2. **Consideration:** These are ads that drive traffic to your website, boost the engagement of your posts, increase app downloads or video views and help you collect customer data (leads) to use in follow-up campaigns.

3. **Conversion:** These are ads that increase the conversion on your website or online shopping, advertise specific products to users who have interacted with your shop before, or get people to visit your local store.

These campaign objectives require you to add a few lines of code to your website, which will then implement the Facebook pixel on your site. To learn how to create a Facebook pixel and how to add it to the code of your website, have a look here. If you want to track the actions that happen inside your mobile app as a result of your ads, your developer should implement a piece of code called App Events. Point them to Facebook's developer site to learn more.

Based on past user behavior data, Facebook will show your ad to those people in your target audience who are most likely to perform the action you want them to.

What targeting options does Facebook offer?

Facebook offers a variety of targeting options that you can combine to build a specific audience:

Location	Target users by country, state, city, zip code, or the area around your physical business.
Demographics	Target users by age, gender, education, and the languages they speak.
Interests	Target users by interests, based on profile information, pages, groups or content they engage with. You can choose from hundreds of categories like sports, movies, music, games, or shopping. You can also target users who like specific pages.
Behaviors	Target users based on what Facebook knows about user behavior, such as the way they shop, the phone they use, or if they plan to buy a house or a car.
Connections	Target users who like your page or app and their friends.
Custom	Target existing customers based on data (e.g., emails, phone numbers) you provide. You can also create Lookalike Audiences – people who are similar to your existing customers.

What is the minimum budget to advertise on Facebook?

When you set up your daily budget on Facebook, the minimum daily budget depends on what your ad set gets charged for.

The ad set gets charged for	Min. daily budget
Impressions	INR. 80
Clicks, likes, video views, post engagement	INR. 500
Offer claims, app installs and other low-frequency events	INR. 400

If you want to set up a lifetime budget instead, i.e., a total budget for the duration of the campaign, your minimum budget is calculated by multiplying the minimum daily budget by the number of days the campaign lasts.

Case Studies

Cupcake' Bake Shop in Berkeley, California wanted to grow its business both with consumers and businesses in the area. The company targeted its ad to people aged 18–55, living within 5 miles of the shop who were interested in weddings, flowers and cupcakes. Over the course of one year the campaign generated 4.5X more sales than print advertising.

NBA team Orlando Magicwanted to promote single-game ticket sales and decided to reach their existing database of customers and website users using

Facebook's "Custom Audience" targeting. In addition they reached local basketball fans by targeting people in Orlando aged 18 and older with interests in live events, Orlando Magic or basketball. The campaign led to a 84% higher return on the money spent ('ad spend') than all other advertising channels.

Gaming company King wanted to increase downloads of their mobile app game Candy Crush Saga. The company tested both ads featuring a single image and ads using Facebook's carousel format with multiple images. The test showed that the carousel ad led to 1.4X more Android app installs and lowered the advertising costs per install by 32%

Twitter

Twitter, also known as the "SMS of the Internet", was founded in 2006 and now has more than 300 million registered monthly active users who post and read messages with up to 140 characters. Users can add links, photos and videos to their tweets, include hashtags to help others find their message, and run polls within a tweet.

For advertisers, Twitter offers a variety of ad types that can be tailored to different campaign objectives, from increasing website visits and sales to creating a bigger following for a company's Twitter account. Twitter also offers rich options to target a specific audience, including demographic, interest and behaviour targeting.

What ad Types does Twitter offer?

Twitter organizes its different ad types by campaign objective: i.e., the action an advertiser wants a user to perform. Depending on which campaign objective you choose, the ad will be displayed in a different format, which Twitter calls "Cards." For detailed technical specifications of the different card types, take a look at Twitter's documentation. Here is an overview of the different campaign objectives you can choose from, and what the ads look like to the user:

Tweet Engagement

Promote a new or existing tweet to your target audience. You pay for engagement with the tweet, e.g., clicks, retweets, likes, follows and replies. If you prefer to maximize brand awareness and care less about engagement, you can book an Awareness campaign. Here you pay for the number of impressions (CPM). You can attach up to four images to your tweet. If you do this, only 116 characters are available for your Tweet, as 24 characters are used for the images.

Twitter allows companies to promote their products in short messages known as tweets limited to 140 characters which appear on followers' Home timelines Tweets can contain text, Hashtag, photo, video, Animated GIF, Emoji, or links to the product's website and other social media profiles, etc. Twitter is also used by companies to provide customer service. Some companies make support available 24/7 and answer promptly, thus improving brand loyalty and appreciation.

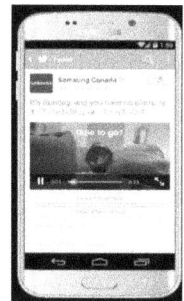

Video Views

Embed a video in a tweet and promote it to your desired audience. Your videos will auto-play muted on scroll, encouraging users to tap or click to open the tweet and watch. Twitter will show your ad as a "Video Card" that consists of your ad copy (max. 140 characters), a video, a video title (max. 70 characters), and a video description (max. 200 characters). You pay for video views, which Twitter defines as follows: "A view occurs when a video is at least 50% in-view on the user's device and has been watched for at least 2 seconds, or the user clicks to watch the video in full screen." Promoted tweet with video

Grow your Followers

If you want to promote your Twitter account and grow your follower base, this is the ad type for you. Twitter suggests to your target audience that they follow your account, and also indicates whether any of their followers follow your account. These ads show up in the user feed and in the "Who to follow" sidebar on Desktop. You pay for every follower the ad generates.

Website Visits

Drive your audience to your website using this campaign type. Twitter will display your message in a "Website Card" that consists of your ad copy (max. 116 characters), an image and a website title/description (max. 70 characters). You will pay for website link clicks.

Website Conversions

This ad type makes use of the "Website Card" shown above, but optimizes campaigns for conversions such as purchases or downloads on your website. Advertisers have to integrate the Twitter website tag on their site, so Twitter can track conversion. User data about interests and intent helps Twitter optimize the campaign delivery. Although the objective is conversion, you still pay for website link clicks.

App Installs and Re-engagements

If your campaign objective is to generate downloads of your mobile app or motivate people to open it again, this could be a great ad type for you. This promoted tweet is shown as an "App Card" which consists of an ad copy (116 characters), an image, the app name, price and rating (pulled from the app store), and a call to action button. You can choose to either pay for app link clicks or app installs.

Lead Generation

With the lead generation campaign type, you can create promoted tweets that aim to collect the user's email address, so you can follow up with a newsletter or offer. The Lead Generation Card includes your ad copy (116 characters), a Call to Action button (20 characters), a short description (50 characters) and an image. If a user clicks the Call to Action button, Twitter will submit the name and email associated with the user's Twitter account and show a customizable message (100 characters). You pay for the number of leads generated.

Location	Target users by country, state, region, metro area, or ZIP code.
Gender	You can target only male or only female users or both. Twitter infers genders from information users share as they use Twitter, e.g., their profile names.
Languages	By default, Twitter delivers campaigns to all languages, so make sure to target only people who understand your message.
Devices, Platforms and Carriers	Target users who use specific mobile devices (e.g. iOS, Android, Blackberry) and mobile phone carriers (e.g. AT&T, Verizon) to access Twitter. You can also target users based on when they first used Twitter on a new device or carrier.
Interest	Target users based on 25 interest categories that expand into 350 subtopics, from Automotive to Travel. Twitter identifies user interests based on what content users engage with and what usernames they follow.
Followers	Provide Twitter with a list of usernames and your ad will reach users who have similar interests as those who follow any of the accounts you have listed.
Keyword	Reach users based on the keywords of their search queries, recent Tweets, and Tweets they recently engaged with. For each keyword, you can define whether you want to target users with exact keyword matching, broad matching (i.e., Twitter will also target related keywords) or negative matching (i.e., Twitter won't target users who match for this keyword).
Behavior	To target users based on their online and offline behavior (e.g., product or shopping preferences), Twitter utilizes user data that third-party data providers have shared with them.
Tailored Audiences	With tailored audiences, you can target existing customers, leads or website visitors. To do this, you have to upload a list of emails, Twitter IDs or mobile advertising IDs. Alternatively, you can put a code snippet on your website so Twitter can identify your website visitors. You can either focus a campaign on a tailored audience, or exclude the tailored audience if you prefer to reach only new prospects.

What is the minimum budget to advertise on Twitter?

Twitter requires you to set up a maximum daily budget for your campaigns, after which Twitter will stop distributing your ad. Optionally, you can also set a maximum budget for the duration of the whole campaign. The cost of an action (defined by campaign type, as explained earlier) depends on how much other advertisers, who compete with you for the same audience, bid. Unlike Facebook and Instagram, Twitter does not ask you to commit a minimum budget.

Case Study

L'Oréal Paris Australia wanted to drive traffic and engagement from exclusive TV content around red carpet events, using Twitter. To do this, the brand used Promoted

Tweets, a Promoted Trend and a Twitter Amplify campaign that directed users to L'Oréal's get the Look Website.

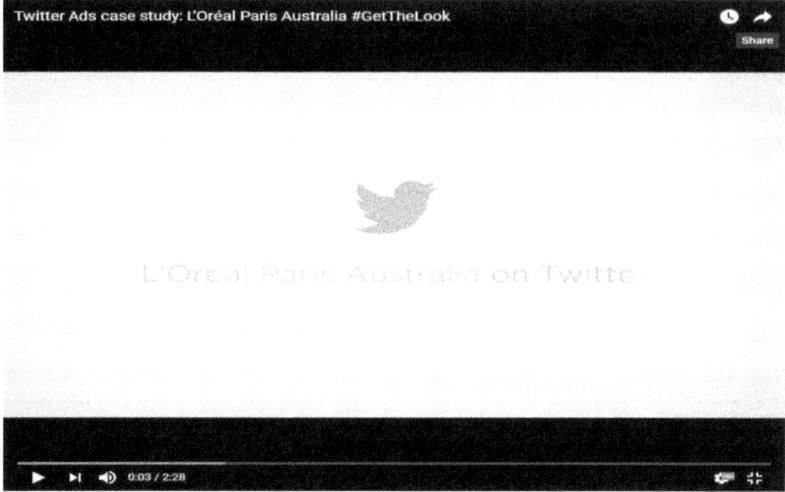

Google+

Google+, in addition to providing pages and some features of Facebook, is also able to integrate with the Google search engine. Other Google products are also integrated, such as Google AdWords and Google Maps. With the development of Google Personalized Search and other location-based search services, Google+ allows for targeted advertising methods, navigation services, and other forms of location-based marketing and promotion. Google+ can also be beneficial for other digital marketing campaigns, as well as social media marketing. Google+ authorship was known to have a significant benefit on a website's search engine optimization, before the relationship was removed by Google. Google+ is one of the fastest growing social media networks and can benefit almost any business.

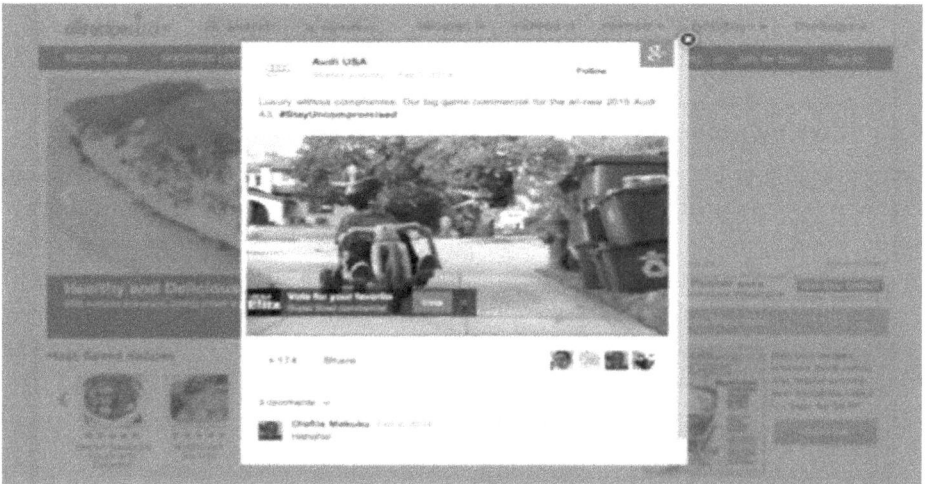

3.2 LinkedIn

LinkedIn is the largest professional social network in the world with more than 460 million registered accounts. Of these, about 106 million users visit the site at least once a month. In addition to allowing users to connect with each other and search for business contacts, LinkedIn offers group features, company pages, and job listings. They also have a publishing platform on which invited thought leaders, influencers, and all other registered users can publish posts.

From an advertising standpoint, LinkedIn can be a great platform for two purposes: To promote employers, their jobs and stories, and to advertise products and services that are of interest to a professional audience.

What ad types does LinkedIn offer?

LinkedIn offers two types of ads – Sponsored Content and Text Ads. These ad types can be booked via LinkedIn's self-service platform, called Campaign Manager. In addition, larger advertisers can book display ads and promotional messages, called Sponsored InMail, via the LinkedIn Ad Sales team. If you want to learn more about these options

Sponsored Content

LinkedIn's Sponsored Content Ad allows you to publish a promotional update on users' newsfeeds, alongside all the updates from their regular connections. The update is marked as 'Sponsored,' but other than that it looks and behaves exactly like a normal update. Your update can include an image, video, infographic, PDF, SlideShare or link to a blog post or landing page.

To set up a Sponsored Content Ad, you need to have access to a Company Page or a Showcase Page, or create a new one. Your content will be shared in the name of this company or brand. With a click on the user name or icon, people can visit the respective page and follow your updates. Your Sponsored Content Ad can either promote an existing update from your page or an update you create specifically for your campaign. LinkedIn gives you various targeting options to reach your desired audience, which we will cover later.

LinkedIn, a professional business-related networking site, allows companies to create professional profiles for themselves as well as their business to network and meet others. Through the use of widgets, members can promote their various social networking activities, such as Twitter stream or blog entries of their product pages, onto their LinkedIn profile page. LinkedIn provides its members the opportunity to generate sales leads and business partners. Members can use "Company Pages" similar to Facebook pages to create an area that will allow business owners to promote their products or services and be able to interact with their customers. Due to spread of spam mail sent to job seeker, leading companies prefer to use LinkedIn for employee's recruitment instead using different a job portal. Additionally, companies have voiced a preference for the amount of information that can be gleaned from a LinkedIn profile, versus a limited email.

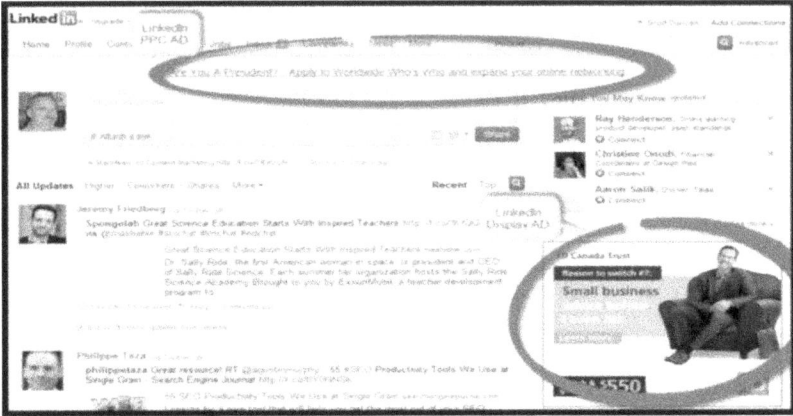

What targeting options does LinkedIn offer?

LinkedIn lets you target users based on their demographics, education, professional experience, and group memberships:

Demographics	Target users by age, gender and location.
Education	Target users by schools, degrees and field of study.
Experience	Target users by job function and title, seniority, skills, company name, company industry and company size.
Groups	Target users by the groups they belong to on LinkedIn.

What is the minimum budget to advertise on LinkedIn?

You can set up your Sponsored Content and Text Ad campaigns both as a click (CPC) or impression (CPM) based campaigns. The minimum daily budget for both ad types is INR. 700.

With both campaign types, the LinkedIn Campaign Manager will show you a suggested bid range based on what other advertisers are bidding for the same audience. The minimum CPC or CPM bid for Text Ads is INR. 140. For Sponsored Content, the minimum bid depends on your target audience.

3.3 WhatsApp

WhatsApp is an excellent method of mass marketing by sharing your content to individuals in your contacts or might be in groups where up to 279 members can participate. WhatsApp joined Facebook in 2014, but continues to operate as a separate app with a laser focus on building a messaging service that works fast and reliably anywhere in the world. WhatsApp started as an

alternative to SMS. Whatsapp now supports sending and receiving a variety of media including text, photos, videos, documents, and location, as well as voice calls. Whatsapp messages and calls are secured with end-to-end encryption, meaning that no third party including WhatsApp can read or listen to them. Whatsapp has a customer base of 1 billion people in over 180 countries. It is used to send personalised promotional messages to individual customers. It has plenty of advantages over SMS that includes ability to track how Message Broadcast Performs using blue tick option in Whatsapp. It allows sending messages to Do Not Disturb (DND) customers. Whatsapp is also used to send a series of bulk messages to their targeted customers using broadcast option. Companies started using this to a large extent because it is a cost effective promotional option and quick to spread a message. Still, Whatsapp doesn't allow businesses to place ads in their app.

3.4 Instagram

Instagram is an online and mobile social network for photo- and video-sharing with more than 500 million monthly active users worldwide. Users can share photos and videos publicly and privately on the Instagram app and through other social networking platforms such as Twitter, Tumblr or Facebook. Instagram started out with photos that were square shaped but now is open to pictures in any aspect ratio as well as videos with up to 60 seconds.

For Advertisers, Instagram is a fantastic platform to tell a company's story in a visual and engaging way. Successful campaigns do not sell products or advertise big discounts but bring products or brand's authentic heart and soul to life. Advertisers have to carefully balance the information and the inspiration value of their campaigns to encourage the community to like and share their ads.

Since Instagram was acquired by Facebook in 2012, the advertising platforms merged and most of the advertising and targeting options are the same for both platforms. Similar to Facebook ads, to run ads on Instagram, you'll need a Facebook Page for the brand or product you are promoting.

What ad types does Instagram offer?

Similar to what we have seen for Facebook, we can classify Instagram's ad options based on what the ads look like and what objectives they have. All Instagram ads will be placed in the user feed, both in the browser and the app version.

In May 2014, Instagram had over 200 million users. The user engagement rate of Instagram was 15 times higher than of Facebook and 25 times higher than that of Twitter. Latest studies estimate that 95% of prestige brands have an active presence on Instagram and include it in their marketing mix. When it comes to brands and businesses, Instagram's goal is to help companies to reach their respective audiences through captivating imagery in a rich, visual environment. Moreover, Instagram provides a platform where user and company can communicate publicly and directly, making itself an ideal platform for companies to connect with their current and potential customers.

Many brands are now heavily using this mobile app to boost their marketing strategy. Instagram can be used to gain the necessary momentum needed to capture the attention of the market segment that has an interest in the product offering or services. As Instagram is supported by Apple and android system, it can be easily accessed by smartphone users. Moreover, it can be accessed by the Internet as well. Thus, the marketers see it as a potential platform to expand their brands exposure to the public, especially the younger target group. On top of this, marketers do not only use social media for traditional Internet advertising, but they also encourage users to create attention for a certain brand. This generally creates an opportunity for greater brand exposure. Furthermore, marketers are also using the platform to drive social shopping and inspire people to collect and share pictures of their favourite products. Many big names have already jumped on board: Starbucks, MTV, Nike, Marc Jacobs, and Red Bull are a few examples of multinationals that adopted the mobile photo app early. Fashion blogger koovs fashion, India, goes by @koovsfashion or #koovsxyou on Instagram, collaborated with garments manufacturers to do a piece on how brands are using Instagram to market their products, and how makers make money from it. Bernstein, who currently has one and a half million followers on Instagram, and whose «outfit of the day» photos on Snapchat get tens of thousands of screenshots, explained that for a lot of her sponsored posts, she must feature the brand in a certain amount of posts, and often cannot wear a competitor›s product in the same picture. According to Harper›s Bazaar, industry estimates say that brands are spending more than $1 billion per year on consumer-generated advertising. Founder of Instagram Kevin Systrom even went to Paris Fashion week, going to couture shows and meeting with designers to learn more about how style bloggers, editors, and designers are currently dominating much of the content on his application.

Instagram has proven itself a powerful platform for marketers to reach their customers and prospects through sharing pictures and brief messages. According to a study by Simply Measured, 71% of the world›s largest brands are now using Instagram as a marketing channel. For companies, Instagram can be used as a tool to connect and communicate with current and potential customers. The company can present a more personal picture of their brand, and by doing so the company conveys a better and true picture of itself. The idea of Instagram pictures lies on on-the-go, a sense that the event is happening right now and that adds another layer to the personal and accurate picture of the company. In fact, Thomas Rankin, co-founder and CEO of the program Dash Hudson, stated that when he approves a blogger›s Instagram post before it is posted on the behalf of a brand his company represents, his only negative feedback is if it looks too posed. «It›s not an editorial photo,» he explained, «We›re not trying to be a magazine. We›re trying to create a moment. Another option Instagram provides the

opportunity for companies to reflect a true picture of the brand from the perspective of the customers, for instance, using the user-generated contents thought the hashtags encouragement. Other than the filters and hashtags functions, the Instagram›s 15-second videos and the recently added ability to send private messages between users have opened new opportunities for brands to connect with customers in a new extent, further promoting effective marketing on Instagram.

What objectives can I meet with my Instagram ad? For self-service customers, Instagram offers a range of different objectives for which you can optimize your campaign. Similar to Facebook, Instagram will show your ad to the people in your target audience who are most likely to take the action you want them to take. The campaign objectives you can choose from are:

● Brand awareness

● Reach

● Traffic (for clicks to your website or to the app store page of your app)

● App installs

● Engagement (with your posts)

● Video views

● Conversions (on your website or app)

This campaign objective requires you to implement the Facebook pixel on your site. To learn how to create a Facebook pixel and how to add it to the code of your website, have a look here. If you want to track the actions that happen inside your mobile app as a result of your ads, your developer should implement a piece of code called App Events. Point them to this site to learn more.

What targeting options does Instagram offer?

Instagram offers the same targeting options as Facebook. You can combine them to build a specific audience:

Location	Target users by country, state, city, zip code, or the area around your physical business.
Demographics	Target users by age, gender, education, and the languages they speak.
Interests	Target users by interests, based on profile information, pages, groups or content they engage with. You can choose from hundreds of categories like sports, movies, music, games, or shopping.
Behaviors	Target users based on what Facebook knows about user behavior, such as the way they shop, the phone they use, or if they plan to buy a house or a car.
Connections	Target users who like your page or app and their friends.
Custom	Target existing customers based on data (e.g., emails, phone numbers) you provide. You can also create Lookalike Audiences – people who are similar to your existing customers.

What is the minimum budget to advertise on Instagram?

The minimum daily budget on Instagram is the same as for Facebook ads and depends on what your ad set gets charged for.

The ad set gets charged for	Min. daily budget
Impressions	INR. 80
Clicks, likes, video views, post engagement	INR. 500
Offer claims, app installs and other low-frequency events	INR. 400

If you want to set up a lifetime budget instead, i.e., a total budget for the duration of the campaign, your minimum budget is calculated by multiplying the minimum daily budget by the number of days the campaign lasts.

3.5 YouTube

YouTube is another popular avenue we all know very well. Advertisements are done in a way to suit the target audience. The type of language used in the commercials and the ideas used to promote the product reflect the audience's style and taste. Also, the ads on this platform are usually in sync with the content of the video requested; this is another advantage YouTube brings for advertisers. Certain ads are presented with certain videos since the content is relevant. Promotional opportunities such as sponsoring a video is also possible on YouTube, "for example, a user who searches for a YouTube video on dog training may be presented with a sponsored video from a dog toy company in results along with other videos. YouTube also enable publishers to earn money through its YouTube Partner Program. Companies can pay YouTube for a special "channel" which promotes the companies products or services.

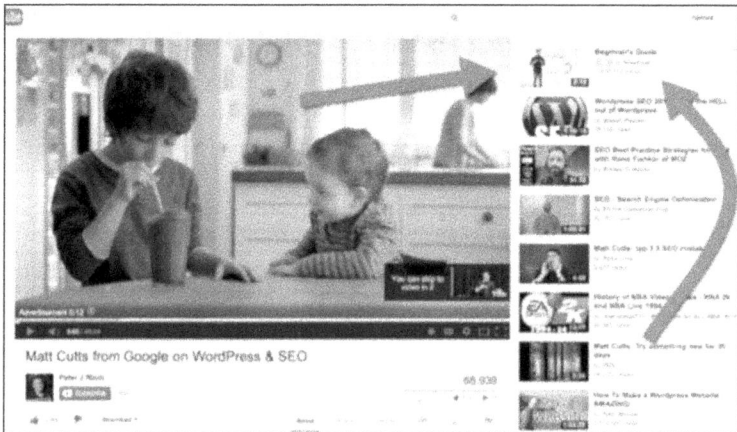

3.6 Blogs

Platforms like LinkedIn create an environment for companies and clients to connect online, Companies that recognize the need for information, originality/ and accessibility employ blogs to make their products popular and unique/ and ultimately reach out to consumers who are privy to social media. Studies from 2009 show that consumers view coverage in the media or from bloggers as being more neutral and credible than print advertisements' which are not thought of as free or independent. Blogs allow a product or company to provide longer descriptions of products or services can include testimonials and can link to and from other social network and blog pages. Blogs can be updated frequently and are promotional techniques for keeping customers and also for acquiring followers and subscribers who can then be directed to social network pages. Online communities can enable a business to reach the clients of other businesses using the platform. To allow firms to measure their standing in the corporate world, sites enable employees to place evaluations of their companies. Some businesses opt out of integrating social media platforms into their traditional marketing regimen. There are also specific corporate standards that apply when interacting online. To maintain an advantage in a business-consumer relationship, businesses have to be aware of four key assets that consumers maintain: information, involvement, community, and control.

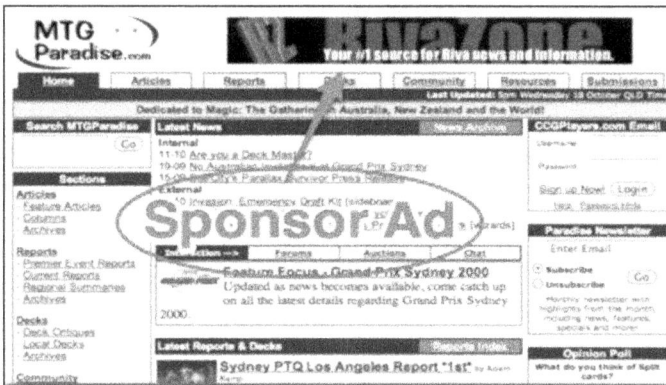

Online Identity Management (OIM), also known as online image management, online personal branding or Personal Reputation Management (PRM), is a set of methods for generating a distinguished Web presence of a person on the Internet. Online identity management also refers to identity exposure and identity disclosure, and has particularly developed in the management on online identity in social network services or online dating services

One aspect of the online identity management process has to do with improving the quantity and quality of traffic to sites that have content related to a person. In that aspect, OIM is a part of another discipline called search engine optimization with the difference that the only keyword is the person's name, and the optimization object is not necessary a single web site; it can consider a set of completely different sites that contain positive online references. The objective in this case is to get high rankings for as many sites as possible when someone searches for a person's name. If the search engine used is Google, this action is called "to google someone".

Another aspect has to do with impression management, i.e. "the process through which people try to control the impressions other people form of them". One of the objectives is in particular to increase the online reputation of the person.

Pseudonyms are sometimes used to protect the true online identity of individuals from harm. This can be the case when presenting unpopular views or dissenting opinion online in a way that will not affect the true identity of the author. Facebook estimates that up to 11.2% of accounts are fake. Many of these profiles are used as logins to protect the true identity of online authors.

The entity)s presence could be reflected in any kind of content that refers to the person, including news, participation in blogs and forums, personal web sites, social media presence, pictures, video, etc. Because of that, online identity management often involves participation in social media sites like Facebook, Google+, LinkedIn, Flickr, YouTube, Twitter, Myspace, Quora and other online communities and community websites, and is related to blogging, blog social networks like My Blog and blog search engines like Technorati.

OIM can also consist in more questionable practices such as the case of buying "likes", "friends", or "subscribers".

The reason why someone would be interested in doing online identity management is closely related to the increasing number of constituencies that use the internet as a tool to find information about people. A survey by CareerBuilder.com found that one in four hiring managers used search engines to screen candidates. One in 10 also checked candidates' profiles on social networking sites such as Myspace or Facebook. According to a December 2007 survey by the Ponemon Institute, a privacy research organization, roughly half of U.S. hiring officials uses the Internet in vetting job applications.

The concept of manipulating search results to show positive results is intriguing for both individuals and businesses. Individuals that want to hide from their past can use OIM to repair their online image and suppress content that damages their credibility, employability and reputation. By changing what people see when searching for an individual, they are able create a completely new and positive identity in its place. In 2014, the EU ruled that people have "The right to be forgotten", and that in some circumstances content can be removed from Google's search index.

3.7 Know your Customer using Digital Marketing Tools

- **Search analytics** is the use of search data to investigate particular interactions among Web searchers, the search engine, or the content during searching episodes. The resulting analysis and aggregation of search engine statistics can be used in search engine marketing (SEM) and search engine optimization (SEO). In other words, search analytics helps website owners understand and improve their performance on search engines, for example identifying highly valuable site visitors, or understanding user intent. Search analytics includes search volume trends and analysis, reverse searching (entering websites to see their keywords), keyword monitoring, search result and advertisement history, advertisement spending statistics, website comparisons, affiliate marketing statistics, multivariate ad testing, et al.

- **Data collection:** Search analytics data can be collected in several ways. Search engines provide access to their own data with services such as Google Trends and Google Insights. Third party services must collect their data from ISP's, phoning home software, or from scraping search engines. Getting traffic statistics from ISP's and phone homes provides for broader reporting of web traffic in addition to search analytics. Services that perform keyword monitoring only scrape a limited set of search results depending on their clients' needs. Services providing reverse search however, must scrape a large set of keywords from the search engines, usually in the millions, to find the keywords that everyone is using.

  Since search results, especially advertisements, differ depending on where you are searching from, data collection methods have to account for geographic location. Keyword monitors do this more easily since they typically know what location their client is targeting. However, to get an exhaustive reverse search, several locations need to be scraped for the same keyword.

- **Accuracy:** Search analytics accuracy depends on service being used, data collection method, and data freshness. Google releases its own data, but only in an aggregated way and often without assigning absolute values such as number of visitors to its graphs.[8] ISP logs and phone home methods are accurate for the population they sample, so sample size and demographics must be adequate to accurately represent the larger population. Scraping results can be highly accurate, especially when looking at the non-paid, organic search results. Paid results, from Google AdWords for example, are often different for the same search depending on the time, geographic location, and history of searches from a particular computer. This means that scraping advertisers can be hit or miss.

- **Market Conditions:** Taking a look at Google Insights to gauge the popularity of these services shows that compared to searches for the term AdWords (Google's popular search ad system), use of search analytics services is still very low, around 1-25% as of Oct. 2009.[9] This could point to a large opportunity for the users and makers of search analytics given that services have existed since 2004 with several new services being started since.

- **Keyword research** is a practice search engine optimization (SEO) professionals use to find and research alternative search terms that people enter into search engines while looking for a similar subject. Search engine optimization professionals research additional keywords, which they use to achieve better rankings in search engines. Once they find a niche keyword, they expanded on it to find similar keywords. Keyword suggestion tools usually aid the process, like the Google AdWords Keyword Planner, which offers a thesaurus and alternative keyword suggestions or by looking into Google Suggest.

Usually, the various search engines provide their own keyword suggestion tools, which also include the number of searches for each of those keywords. The keyword researcher uses this information to select the correct keyword, depending on the SEO goals of the website. Around 20–25% of searches are very specific long tail keywords entered into Google every single day. Ibs easy to rank said keywords when there is the right amount of content and backlinks to match. Keyword research is a valuable and high return activity in the search marketing field.

- **Web analytics** is the measurement, collection, analysis and reporting of web data for purposes of understanding and optimizing web usage.[1] However, Web analytics is not just a process for measuring web traffic but can be used as a tool for business and market research, and to assess and improve the effectiveness of a website. Web analytics applications can also help companies measure the results of traditional print or broadcast advertising campaigns. It helps one to estimate how changes traffic to a website after the launch of a new advertising campaign. Web analytics provides information about the number of visitors to a website and the number of page views. It helps gauge traffic and popularity trends which is useful for market research.

Most web analytics processes down to four essential stages or steps, which are:

- **Collection of Data:** This stage is the collection of the basic, elementary data. Usually, this data is counts of things. The objective of this stage is to gather the data.

- **Processing of Data into Information:** This stage usually takes counts and makes them ratios, although there still may be some counts. The objective of this stage is to take the data and conform it into information, specifically metrics.

- **Developing KPI:** This stage focuses on using the ratios (and counts) and infusing them with business strategies, referred to as Key Performance Indicators (KPI). Many times, KPIs deal with conversion aspects, but not always. It depends on the organization.

- **Formulating Online Strategy:** This stage is concerned with the online goals, objectives, and standards for the organization or business. These strategies are usually related to making money, saving money, or increasing market share.

Another essential function developed by the analysts for the optimization of the websites are the experiments

- **Experiments and testing:** A/B testing is a controlled experiment with two variants, in online settings, such as web developer the goal of A/B testing is to identify changes to web pages that increase or maximize a statistically tested result of interest

Each stage impacts or can impact (i.e., drives) the stage preceding or following it. So, sometimes the data that is available for collection impacts the online strategy. Other times, the online strategy affects the data collected.

3.8 What are Some of the Best Ways to Integrate Email Marketing with Social Media Participation?

Email Marketing is regarded as more effective when compared to social media marketing as the latter one could be messy and daunting to be measured. However, a marketing strategy that has taken the advertising industry by storm is the integration of social media marketing and email marketing. This means that you are taking advantage of two strategies that work in tandem to fetch more customers to your business. While social media sites have influencing click through rates, newsletters swing traffic with the promised content which is available in the form designed by the customers. In order to successfully promote your brand, it has become important for business professionals to rely on these two channels. However, before implementing this strategy to your marketing campaign, you need to understand the importance of integrating social and email marketing.

Here are some easy ways to integrate social and email marketing:

- **Include Social Media Buttons to Emails:** By adding social media buttons to the emails, you can let your readers to know your presence on various social media sites. Moreover, your fanatics can also click those social buttons included within your emails to view the social profiles of your organization. Having a stunning Social Media Page Design is also important to entice the customers. In order to add buttons, you must be in the edit mode of the block. You need to click on social tab on the tools located on screen's left side. You can also choose the kind of button that you want to add just by clicking on any of the networks. Then, you should add the exact link of your page in the link box so that the users will be directly taken to your appropriate page. Following this, you need to click on insert Button to add button to the block. The job is done!

- **Send A Link To Your Email With Simple Share Option:** Not most individuals are aware of the fact that they can send an email whilst promoting it on social media channels using simple share tool. All you need is to go to Schedule Step of the Email and then click on Simple Share Button located at the bottom of the screen. Then, you should choose the social networks that you want the message to be posted to. When you send an email, Simple Share will be posting the messages that you have created to your chosen social sites and thereby providing you with the opportunity of increasing the reach of your message.

- **Add A Share Bar:** The Share Bar is the row of social media buttons which can be added to the top of the email. By doing so, you can enable your readers to share your message with their family and friends through social media. In order to include the share bar, you must go to Header Options and click Pencil Icon. Then click at the check box and OK. Once you have done this, the Share Bar will be appearing at the top of email and just below will be the front name, subject and reply mail. When any of the social buttons are clicked by your readers, they can easily post a link to your email on their social profile page. So, their followers or friends who view those posts can click the link and read your mesas age.

● **Use Social Photos In Emails:** Most people might have heard about the changes to My Library Plus and My Library accounts. These changes allow you to integrate images from your Instagram and Facebook accounts to emails. Once you have obtained the new My Library Tools, click on Social Network Tab and get connected to Instagram and Facebook. Then you can choose your preferred photo to upload and then insert it into your email newsletters. Of course, it is extremely important to inform your audience about the social networks from where you have taken the photos. You must also entertain social media engagement so that your audience could follow you.

Benefits of Social Media And Email Marketing Integration

1. Increasing your viral reach by sharing your emails on all social media sites.

2. Growing your mailing list

3. Getting more subscribers when you want to make your emails to go social, you must always entice your customers so that they can interact with your business and get part in your marketing campaign either directly or indirectly.

Few more tips to create impact further:

● Drip emails after signup

● Use your newsletter to launch social media campaigns

● Always include newsletter in social campaign planning

● Promoting your newsletter in social media

● Newsletter signup page in Facebook

● Sharing links to great content in social channels

● Post links to current newsletter to social media

● Newsletter only offers

3.9 Web Analytics Technologies

There are at least two categories of web analytics, off-site and on-site web analytics.

Off-site web analytics refers to web measurement and analysis regardless of whether you own or maintain a website. It includes the measurement of a website›s potential audience (opportunity), share of voice (visibility), and buzz (comments) that is happening on the Internet as a whole.

On-site web analytics, the most common, measure a visitor›s behaviour once on your website. This includes its drivers and conversions; for example, the degree to which different landing pages is associated with online purchases. On-site web analytics measures the performance of your website in a commercial context. This data is typically compared against key performance indicators for performance, and used to improve a website or marketing campaign's audience response. Google Analytics and Adobe Analytics are the most widely used on-site web analytics service; although new tools are emerging that provide additional layers of information, including heat maps and session replay.

Historically, web analytics has been used to refer to on-site visitor measurement. However, this meaning has become blurred, mainly because vendors are producing tools that span both categories. Many different vendors provide on-site web analytics software and services. There are two main technical ways of collecting the data. The first and traditional method, server log file analysis, reads the log files in which the web server records file requests by browsers. The second method, page tagging, uses JavaScript embedded in the webpage to make image requests to a third-party analytics-dedicated server, whenever a webpage is rendered by a web browser or, if desired, when a mouse click occurs. Both collect data that can be processed to produce web traffic reports.

Visual marketing is the discipline studying the relationship between an object, the context it is placed in and its relevant image. Representing a disciplinary link between economy, visual perception laws and cognitive psychology, the subject mainly applies to businesses such as fashion and design.

As a key component of modern marketing, visual marketing focuses on studying and analyzing how images can be used to make objects the center of visual communication. The intent is that the product and its visual communication therefore become strategically linked and inseparable and their fusion is what reaches out to people, engages them and defines their choices (a marketing mechanism is known as persuasion). Not to be confused with visual merchandising, that is one of its facets and more about retail spaces; here, Marketing gets customers in the door. Once inside, merchandising takes over—affecting placement of products, signage, display materials, ambiance and employee staffing.

Harnessing the power of images and visuals can make a marketing plan more powerful and more memorable. Images — when done deftly – can turn concepts and intangible things into something more concrete influencing the perception of the intended viewer. That helps people envision a brand and its message in their mind's eye — and remember it when it comes time to buy.

Visual marketing can be a part of every aspect of the Communication Mix. Marketing persuades consumer's buying behavior and Visual Marketing enhances that by factors of recall, memory and identity.

Growing trends in the usage of picture based websites and social networking platforms like Pinterest, Instagram, Tumblr, Timeline feature of Facebook justifies the fact that people want to believe what they see, and therefore, need for Visual Marketing.

Visual marketing includes all visual cues like logo, signage, sales tools, vehicles, uniforms, and right to your Advertisements, Brochures, Informational DVDs, and Websites, everything that meets the Public Eye.

Some Important Business Calculations

- **Sessions with Search** = The number of sessions that used your site's search function at least once.

- **Percentage of sessions that used internal search** = Sessions with Search / Total Sessions.

- **Total Unique Searches** = The total number of times your site search was used. This excludes multiple searches on the same keyword during the same session.

- **Results Page views / Search** = Page views of search result pages / Total Unique Searches.

- **Search Exits** = The number of searches made immediately before leaving the site.

- **Percentage of Search Exits** = Search Exits / Total Unique Searches

- **Search Refinements** = The number of times a user searched again immediately after performing a search.

- **Percentage Search Refinements** = The percentage of searches that resulted in a search refinement. calculated as Search Refinements / Page views of search result pages.

- **Time after Search** = The amount of time users spend on your site after performing a search. This is calculated as Sum of all search duration across all searches / (search transitions + 1)

- **Search Depth** = The number of pages viewed after performing a search. This is calculated as Sum of all search depth across all searches / (search transitions + 1)

3.10 Marketing Techniques

Social media marketing involves the use of social networks, consumer's online brand-related activities (COBRA) and electronic word of mouth (eWOM) to successfully advertise online. Social networks such as Facebook and Twitter provide advertisers with information about the likes and dislikes of their consumers. This technique is crucial, as it provides the businesses with a "target audience". With social networks, information relevant to the user's likes is available to businesses; who then advertise accordingly. Activities such as uploading a picture of your "new Converse sneakers to Facebook is an example of a COBRA. Electronic recommendations and appraisals are a convenient manner to have a product promoted via «consumer-to-consumer interactions. An example of eWOM would be an online hotel review; the hotel company can have two possible outcomes based on their service. A good service would result in a positive review which gets the hotel free advertising via social media. However, a poor service will result in a negative consumer review which can potentially harm the company›s reputation.

Social networking sites such as Facebook, Instagram, Twitter, Myspace etc. have all influenced the buzz of word of mouth marketing. In 1999, Misner said that word-of mouth marketing is, «the world›s most effective, yet least understood marketing strategy» (Trusov, Bucklin, & Pawel's, 2009, p. 3). Through the influence of opinion leaders, the increased online «buzz» of «word-of-mouth» marketing that a product, service or companies are experiencing is due to the rise in use of social media and smartphones. Businesses and marketers have noticed that, «a person's behaviour is influenced by many small groups» (Kotler, Burton, Deans, Brown, & Armstrong, 2013, p. 189). These small groups rotate around social networking accounts that are run by influential people (opinion leaders or «thought leaders») who have followers of groups. The types of groups (followers) are called: reference groups (people who know each other either face-to-face or have an indirect influence on a person's attitude or behaviour); membership groups (a person has a direct influence on a person›s attitude or behaviour); and aspirational groups (groups which an individual wishes to belong to).

Marketers target influential people on social media who are recognised as being opinion leaders and opinion-formers to send messages to their target audiences and amplify the impact of their message. A social media post by an opinion leader can have a much greater impact (via the forwarding of the post or "liking" of the post) than a social media post by a regular user. Marketers have come to the understanding that "consumers are more prone to believe in other individuals" who they trust (Sepp, Liljander, & Gummerus, 2011). OL's and OF's can also send their own messages about products and services they choose (Fill, Hughes, & De Francesco, 2013, p. 216). The reason the opinion leader or formers have such a strong following base is because their opinion is valued or trusted (Clement, Proppe, & Rott, 2007). They can review products and services for their followings, which can be positive or negative towards the brand. OL's and OF's are people who have a social status and because of their personality, beliefs, values etc. have the potential to influence other people (Kotler, Burton, Deans, Brown, & Armstrong, 2013, p. 189). They usually have a large amount of followers otherwise known as their reference, membership or aspirational group (Kotler, Burton, Deans, Brown, & Armstrong, 2013, p. 189. By having an OL or OF support a brands product by posting a photo, video or written recommendation on a blog, the following may be influenced and because they trust the OL/OF a high chance of the brand selling more products or creating a following base. Having an OL/OF helps spread word of mouth talk amongst reference groups and/or memberships groups e.g. family, friends, work-friends etc. (Kotler, Burton, Deans, Brown, & Armstrong, 2013, p. 189). The adjusted communication model shows the use of using opinion leaders and opinion formers. The sender/source gives the message to many, many OL's/OF's who pass the message on along with their personal opinion, the receiver (followers/groups) form their own opinion and send their personal message to their group (friends, family etc.)

The platform of social media is another channel or site that businesses and brands must seek to influence the content of. In contrast with pre-Internet marketing, such as TV ads and newspaper ads, in which the marketer controlled all aspects of the ad, with social media, users are free to post comments right below an online ad or an online post by a company about its product. Companies are increasing using their social media strategy as part of their traditional marketing effort using magazines, newspapers, radio advertisements, television advertisements. Since in the 2010s, media consumers are often using multiple platforms at the same time (e.g., surfing the Internet on a tablet while watching a streaming TV show), marketing content needs to be consistent across all platforms, whether traditional or new media. Heath (2006) wrote about the extent of attention businesses should give to their social media sites. It is about finding a balance between frequently posting but not over posting. There is a lot more attention to be paid towards social media sites because people need updates to gain brand recognition. Therefore, a lot more content is need and this can often be unplanned content.

Planned content begins with the creative/marketing team generating their ideas, once they have completed their ideas they send them off for approval. There is two general ways of doing so. The first is where each sector approves the plan one after another, editor, brand, and followed by the legal team (Brito, 2013). Sectors may differ depending on the size and philosophy of the business. The second is where each sector is given 24 hours (or such designated time) to sign off or disapprove. If no action is given within the 24-hour period the original plan is implemented. Planned content is often noticeable to customers and is un-original or lacks excitement but is also a safer option to avoid unnecessary backlash from the public.[93] Both routes for planned content are time consuming as in the above; the first way to approval takes 72 hours to be approved. Although the second route can be significantly shorter it also holds more risk particularly in the legal department.

Unplanned content is an ‹in the moment› idea, «a spontaneous, tactical reaction.» (Cramer, 2014, p. 6). The content could be trending and not have the time to take the planned content route. The unplanned content is posted sporadically and is not calendar/date/time arranged (Deshpande, 2014).Issues with unplanned content revolves around legal issues and whether the message being sent out represents the business/brand accordingly. If a company sends out a Tweet or Facebook message too hurriedly, the company may unintentionally use insensitive language or messaging that could alienate some consumers. For example, celebrity chef Paula Deen was criticized after she made a social media post commenting about HIV-AIDS and South Africa; her message was deemed to be offensive by many observers. The main difference between planned and unplanned is the time to approve the content. Unplanned content must still be approved by marketing managers, but in a much more rapid manner e.g. 1–2 hours or less. Sectors may miss errors because of being hurried. When using unplanned content Brito (2013) says, «be prepared to be reactive and respond to issues when they arise. Brito (2013) writes about having a, «crisis escalation plan», because, «It will happen». The plan involves breaking down the issue into topics and classifying the issue into groups. Colour coding the potential risk «identify and flag potential risks» also helps to organise an issue. The problem can then be handled by the correct team and dissolved more effectively rather than any person at hand trying to solve the situation.

3.11 Purposes and Tactics

One of the main purposes of employing social media in marketing is as a communications tool that makes the companies accessible to those interested in their product and makes them visible to those who have no knowledge of their products. These companies use social media to create buzz, and learn from and target customers. It's the only form of marketing that can finger consumers at each and every stage of the consumer decision journey. Marketing through social media has other benefits as well. Of the top 10 factors that correlate with a strong Google organic search, seven are social media dependent. This means that if brands are less or non-active on social media, they tend to show up less on Google searches. While platforms such as Twitter, Facebook, and Google+ have a larger amount of monthly users, the visual media sharing based mobile platforms, however, garner a higher interaction rate in comparison and have registered the fastest growth and have changed the ways in which consumers engage with brand content. Instagram has an interaction rate of 1.46% with an average of 130 million users monthly as opposed to Twitter which has a .03% interaction rate with an average of 210 million monthly users. Unlike traditional media that are often cost-prohibitive to many companies, a social media strategy does not require astronomical budgeting.

To this end, companies make use of platforms such as Facebook, Twitter, YouTube, and Instagram to reach audiences much wider than through the use of traditional print/TV/radio advertisements alone at a fraction of the cost, as most social networking sites can be used at little or no cost (however, some websites charge companies for premium services). This has changed the ways that companies approach to interact with customers, as a substantial percentage of consumer interactions are now being carried out over online platforms with much higher visibility. Customers can now post reviews of products and services, rate customer service, and ask questions or voice concerns directly to companies through social media platforms. Thus social media marketing is also used by businesses in order to build relationships of trust with consumers. To this aim, companies may also hire personnel to specifically handle these social media interactions, who usually report under the title of online community managers. Handling these interactions in a satisfactory manner can result in an increase of consumer trust. To both this aim and to fix the publics perception of a company, 3 steps are taken in order to address consumer concerns, identifying the extent of the social chatter, engaging the influencers to help, and developing a proportional response.

3.12 Design of an Effective Marketing Strategy-Business Case

Planning

Digital marketing planning is a term used in marketing management. It describes the first stage of forming a digital marketing strategy for the wider digital marketing system. The difference between digital and traditional marketing planning is that it uses digitally based communication tools and technology such as Social, Web, Mobile, Scannable Surface. Nevertheless, both are aligned with the vision, the mission of the company and the overarching business strategy.

Stages of Planning

Using Dr Dave Chaffey's approach, the Digital Marketing Planning (DMP) has three main stages; Opportunity, Strategy and Action. He suggests that any business looking to implement a successful digital marketing strategy must structure their plan by looking at opportunity, strategy and action. This generic strategic approach often has phases of situation review, goal setting, strategy formulation, resource allocation and monitoring.

1. **Opportunity:** To create an effective DMP a business first needs to review the marketplace and set 'SMART' (Specific, Measurable, Actionable, Relevant and Time-Bound) objectives. They can set SMART objectives by reviewing the current benchmarks and Key Performance Indicators (KPIs) of the company and competitors. It is pertinent that the analytics used for the KPIs be customised to the type, objectives, mission and vision of the company.

   Companies can scan for marketing and sales opportunities by reviewing their own outreach as well as influencer outreach. This means they have competitive advantage because they are able to analyse their co-marketers influence and brand associations.

   To cease opportunity, the firm should summarize their current customers' personas and purchase journey from this they are able to deduce their digital marketing capability. This means they need to form a clear picture of where they are currently and how many resources they can allocate for their digital marketing strategy i.e. labour, time etc. By summarizing the purchase journey, they can also recognise gaps and growth for future marketing opportunities that will either meet objectives or propose new objectives and increase profit.

2. **Strategy:** To create a planned digital strategy, the company must review their digital proposition (what you are offering to consumers) and communicate it using digital customer targeting techniques. So, they must define online value proposition (OVP), this means the company must express clearly what they are offering customers online e.g. brand positioning.

   The company should also (re)select target market segments and personas and define digital targeting approaches.

   After doing this effectively, it is important to review the marketing mix for online options. The marketing mix comprises the 4Ps - Product, Price, Promotion and Place. Some academics have added three additional elements to the traditional 4Ps of marketing Process, Place and Physical appearance making it 7Ps of marketing.

3. **Action:** The third and final stage requires the firm to set a budget and management systems; these must be measurable touchpoints such as audience reach across all digital platforms. Furthermore, marketers must ensure the budget and management systems are integrating the paid, owned and earned media of the company. The Action and final stage of planning also requires the company to set in place measurable content creation e.g. oral, visual or written online media.

After confirming the digital marketing plan, a scheduled format of digital communications e.g. Gantt chart should be encoded throughout the internal operations of the company. This ensures that all platforms used fall in line and complement each other for the succeeding stages of digital marketing strategy.

As digital marketing is dependent on technology which is ever-evolving and fast-changing, the same features should be expected from digital marketing developments and strategies. This portion is an attempt to qualify or segregate the notable highlights existing and being used as of press time.

(i) *Segmentation:* more focus has been placed on segmentation within digital marketing, in order to target specific markets in both business-to-business and business-to-consumer sectors.

(ii) *Influencer marketing:* Important nodes are identified within related communities, known as influencers. This is becoming an important concept in digital targeting. It is possible to reach influencers via paid advertising, such as Facebook Advertising or Google AdWords campaigns, or through sophisticated SCRM (social customer relationship management) software, such as SAP C4C, Microsoft Dynamics, Sage CRM and Salesforce CRM. Many universities now focus, at Masters Level, on engagement strategies for influencers.

To summarize, Pull digital marketing is characterized by consumers actively seeking marketing content while Push digital marketing occurs when marketers send messages without that content being actively sought by the recipients.

3. **Online Behavioral Advertising** is the practice of collecting information about a user›s online activity over time, «on a particular device and across different, unrelated websites, in order to deliver advertisements tailored to that user›s interests and preferences.

4. **Collaborative Environment:** A collaborative environment can be set up between the organization, the technology service provider, and the digital agencies to optimize effort, resource sharing, reusability and communications. Additionally, organizations are inviting their customers to help them better understand how to service them. This source of data is called User Generated Content. Much of this is acquired via company websites where the organization invites people to share ideas that are then evaluated by other users of the site. The most popular ideas are evaluated and implemented in some form. Using this method of acquiring data and developing new products can foster the organizations relationship with their customer as well as spawn ideas that would otherwise be overlooked. UGC is

low-cost advertising as it is directly from the consumers and can save advertising costs for the organisation.

5. **Data-driven Advertising:** Users generate a lot of data in every step they take on the path of customer journey and Brands can now use that data to activate their known audience with data-driven programmatic media buying. Without exposing customers› privacy, users› Data can be collected from digital channels (e.g.: when customer visits a website, reads an e-mail, or launches and interact with brand›s mobile app), brands can also collect data from real world customer interactions, such as brick and mortar stores visits and from CRM and Sales engines datasets. Also known as People-based marketing or addressable media, Data-driven advertising is empowering brands to find their loyal customers in their audience and deliver in real time a much more personal communication, highly relevant to each customer's moment and actions.

6. **Remarketing:** Remarketing plays a major role in digital marketing. This tactic allows marketers to publish targeted ads in front of an interest category or a defined audience, generally called searchers in web speaks, they have either searched for particular products or services or visited a website for some purpose.

3.13 Advantages

The whole idea of digital marketing can be a very important aspect in the overall communication between the consumer and the organisation. This is due to digital marketing being able to reach vast numbers of potential consumers at one time.

Another advantage of digital marketing is that consumers are exposed to the brand and the product that is being advertised directly. To clarify the advertisement is easy to access as well it can be accessed any time any place.

However, with digital marketing there are some setbacks to this type of strategy. One major setback that is identified is that Digital marketing is highly dependent on the internet. This can be considered as a setback because the internet may not be accessible in certain areas or consumers may have poor internet connection.

As well as digital marketing being highly dependent on the Internet is that it is subject to a lot of clutter, so it marketers may find it hard to make their advertisements stand out, as well as get consumers to start conversations about an organisations brand image or products.

As digital marketing continues to grow and develop, brands take great advantage of using technology and the Internet as a successful way to communicate with its clients and allows them to increase the reach of who they can interact with and how they go about doing so, There are however disadvantages that are not commonly looked into due to how much a business relies on it. It is important for marketers to take into consideration both advantages and disadvantages of digital marketing when considering their marketing strategy and business goals.

An advantage of digital marketing is that the reach is so large that there are no limitations on the geographical reach it can have. This allows companies to become international and expand their customer reach to other countries other than the country it is based or originates from.

As mentioned earlier, technology and the internet allows for 24 hours a day, 7 days a week service for customers as well as enabling them to shop online at any hour of that day or night, not just when the shops are over and across the whole world. This is a huge advantage for retailers to utilise it and direct customers from the store to its online store. It has also opened up an opportunity for companies to only be online based rather than having an outlet or store due to the popularity and capabilities of digital marketing.

Another advantage is that digital marketing is easy to be measured allowing businesses to know the reach that their marketing is making, whether the digital marketing is working or not and the amount of activity and conversation that is involved.

With brands using the Internet space to reach their target customers; digital marketing has become a beneficial career option as well. At present, companies are more into hiring individuals familiar in implementing digital marketing strategies and this has led the stream to become a preferred choice amongst individuals inspiring institutes to come up and offer professional courses in Digital Marketing.

3.14 Limitations

A disadvantage of digital advertising is the large amount of competing goods and services that are also using the same digital marketing strategies. For example, when someone searches for a specific product from a specific company online, if a similar company uses targeted advertising online then they can appear on the customer's home page, allowing the customer to look at alternative options for a cheaper price or better quality of the same product or a quicker way of finding what they want online.

Some companies can be portrayed by customers negatively as some consumers lack trust online due to the amount of advertising that appears on websites and social media that can be considered frauds. This can affect their image and reputation and make them out to look like a dishonest brand.

Another disadvantage is that even an individual or small group of people can harm image of an established brand. For instance Doppelganger is a term that is used to disapprove an image about a certain brand that is spread by anti-brand activists, bloggers, and opinion leaders. The word Doppelganger is a combination of two German words Doppel (double) and Ganger (walker), thus it means double walker or as in English it is said alter ego. Generally brand creates images for itself to emotionally appeal to their customers. However some would disagree with this image and make alterations to this image and present in funny or cynical way, hence distorting the brand image, hence creating a Doppelganger image, blog or content.

Two other practical limitations can be seen in the case of digital marketing. One, digital marketing is useful for specific categories of products, meaning only consumer goods can be propagated through digital channels. Industrial goods and pharmaceutical products cannot be marketed through digital channels. Secondly, digital marketing disseminates only the information to the prospects most of whom do not have the purchasing authority/power. And hence the reflection of digital marketing into real sales volume is sceptical.

3.15 Lead Generating Techniques for your Business through Digital Marketing

Google AdWords

In the world where everyone begins their online purchase journey by first searching on Google, it's important to make a brand's product/service visible to their potential customers. Google AdWords act as an agent that brings the prospective customers closer to any business by showing up their ad when the customers are searching for a product/service the Brand offers.

Why should a Brand spend on AdWords?

A Brand only pays to Google when the customer clicks on their ad. After clicking on the ad, the visitor comes to a Brand's website and most of the times make a purchase. It's that easy to reach the customers who are looking for your products/services online and to convert them into leads with the help of Google AdWords.

For example:

There is an Interior Designing Company and the company wants to acquire leads online. Say, if someone searches for the keyword Interior Designing, the company's Ad shows up with informative yet crisp and powerful messaging, making the customer click and visit the website- converting into a potential Business Client.

Here are some of the Targeting Parameters that you can use when you run an AdWords Campaign

Location from which user is searching Best suitable time of the day to run the Ad Language Specific Targeting Device Targeting Search Query (keyword) - Most searched keywords on Google Decide what is the objective of running Ads on google is it to bring more traffic on your client's website or on your business website, To get phone calls or to collect email ids. Just choose how much you want to pay per click and get started.

❖ **Retargeting**

What happens to the visitors who come to your a website but go without making any purchase? Study shows that almost 90% of the first time customers leave the website without buying. Reconnect with the customers who have already shown interest and have engaged with a business (Could be yours or your clients) by visiting the website by re-targeting them on the websites the customers visit later.

Running an Ad campaign that re-targets them can be proven highly impactful for the Brand, as it has a recall association, resulting in to the Customer going back to the website by clicking on the Ad and finally making a purchase.

❖ **Facebook Advertisement**

In the times when almost everybody has a Facebook account, It's important for any business to have a presence on Facebook as it increases the brand awareness, gets the brand more reach and adds up to the brand recall. To market a product/service on Facebook, you can create a social media page and

Constantly update it with product and services. The other way to market is by running Facebook Ads.

Facebook ads are not all about clicking that "boost post" button. You have to go behind the curtain to run them in the most effective way. Boosting a post doesn't even present the power Facebook Ads have.

Facebook Ads Manager gives you an access to advanced information and insights about the customers you want to target based on their **location, demographics and interests,** making it easier for you to reach them. It also lets gives you a Pandora of powerful reports that can help you optimize your ads to get more results.

For example:

Nest away, a company that provides apartment, rooms, flats etc... On rent has targeted unmarried women in the age of 17-25 who are either studying or working in this below paid ad.

Targeting through Facebook Ads Manager

1. Show Ads to those who have particular interest like Pets/ Beauty/ Cars / Interior Designing etc...Whatever is relevant to the product/services _

2. Target them based on Occupation, Company, and Colleges etc....

3. Relevant Age Group

4. Those who have liked certain pages (can be your competitor's page as well)

❖ Social Media

Social media is a very fast growing Marketing Technique. It is highly advisable for all the brands to have a presence on social media by creating their profiles on different platforms like Facebook, Twitter and Instagram- whichever platform is most relevant to your business! Not only does Social Media acts as an agent to reach and acquire more fans, it also helps Businesses in Generating Leads via the content that is shared on the Brand pages and profiles. Social media is no more a Brand Building tool. Rather, it's an effective marketing technique that every brand users to get Leads. Understand the platform you are using wisely and build your content that result into Lead Generation. It need not be said that Facebook is one of the famous networking site. About 80% of people spend their time on Facebook to socialise than face to face.

How you can leverage from this Social Media networking site is via Contests, Custom Tabs and by treating your Business FB page as a Website. In the sense that the content you post, the ads you create and the CTA's become the impacting forces for Lead Generation.

❖ Twitter

Use Twitter to generate leads by providing people with an exclusive and compelling offer using Twitter Lead Generation Card. Once you get people to sign up, make sure to follow up with them.

You can also Generate Leads by listening to the Brand Mentions. Monitor the kind of conversations people are having about your business and jump in.

❖ Instagram

Instagram is a compelling visual platform that is fast growing and is being explored by the marketers. Always pay attention on using Instagram, It's important to pay attention to the comments that you are getting on your posts and make sure to respond to each one of them. Make your business likeable and people would want to buy from you.

Use interesting videos to market your products and services and make sure to share the link from where they can buy. Create unique hashtag that are not directly associated with your brand but interested people to use them. When people start using it more often, they spread like wildfire and other people get to know about you.

❖ Video Ads

2016 has seen a drastic growth in the consumption of video content online. According to 2016 Reuters Institute Digital Leaders Survey, over 79% digital leaders have revealed that they are planning to invest in video content much more than they did in the previous year.

Advertising Video Content on Facebook Facebook lets the publishers to reach more people with the help of Facebook Video Adverts. Facebook received over 1 Billion video views per day by the end of 2014 and over 8 Billion views per day by the end of 2015. The growth of the Social Network is predicted to be on the upswing in terms of number of views per day by the end of 2016 Facebook Adverts helps you target and reach people who matter to your business based on their interests, behaviour, age, gender and location. It also gives you the opportunity to target your customers across devices.

❖ Advertising Video Content on YouTube

YouTube is the No. 2 Search Engine in the world and its user base is increasing as you read this.

Advertising on YouTube lets a Brand achieve a lot of goals like Branding, driving traffic to the website or on the Brand's YouTube Channel. If you want to generate more sales through YouTube ads, it is relatively a cost-effective price affair, more than Facebook Advertising and Google Search AdWords, giving you all the more reason to kick start advertising to attract consumers on YouTube right now. Not only this, YouTube has some great built-in metrics available to measure the success of the Ad campaigns.

❖ SEO

A user's purchase journey starts when he/she searches on Search Engines by typing in a lot of Keywords relevant to a Business Category products/ services. It's important to make the Brand visible to people who are searching for it. There are two ways to do so- one is by bringing customers to the Brand website through AdWords which is paid advertising or making the Brand visible on the result pages, organically.

What do we mean by making a Business visible to people searching for it organically on search engines? It means that Building Search Engine Optimization Strategy and implementing simple & effective techniques that will rank the business higher on Google Search Pages without paying anything.

For example:

Real Estate Company wants its website to come on 1st page of Google and be visible to people who are looking to rent an apartment in Noida. Good SEO Practices will help the website rank high on the Google Search pages making the business visible to those looking for it, organically.

Simple techniques for effective Search Engine optimization include:

1. Ensuring that the technical setup of the website is search engine friendly
2. Finding out the Keywords that are most relevant to the business
3. Adding those 2-3 Keywords in the text description of the website's homepage
4. Posting links of the website on Social Media Sites
5. Improving the website's loading time as it is Google ranking factors

❖ Email Marketing

Email marketing is most affordable and effective type of marketing that lets a Brand communicate with the customers about its products and services from time to time. To acquire an Email Database of customers who have shown interest in the business or have had a history of shopping with the brand, acts like the most important asset that the brand can use from time to time. Emailing to the database regularly lets a brand to build a recall amongst its existing customers and attracts the prospective customers by giving out offers and promotional discounts.

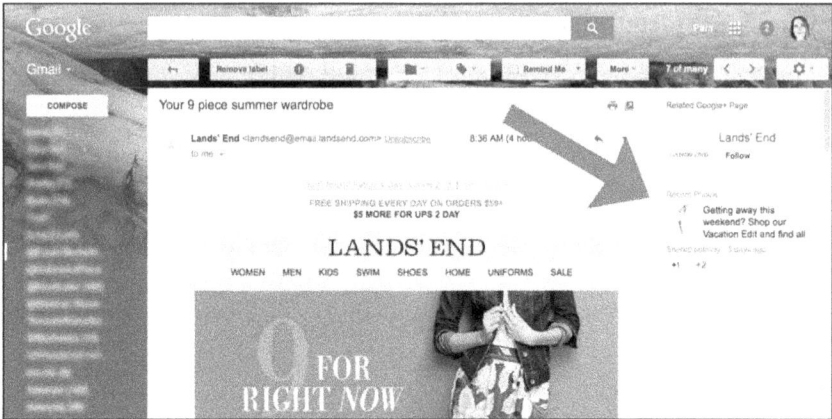

❖ Google Map

If you are a local business or your client is, make sure to register the business on Google Maps. It's amongst the first things that local customers do which is to search for the product/service around the area to extract information. When the customers search, you're Google Maps Location which pops up first. Add the Business address, phone number, hours of operations for customer's disposal. Make sure to add pictures, videos, offers and coupons etc. to convert them. Once converted, make sure you take their reviews on your Google Business page to build credibility amongst the prospect customers and also to boost Map Ranking.

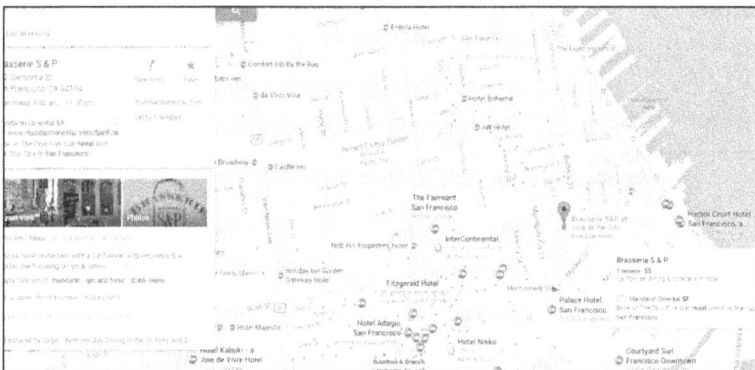

❖ SMS Marketing

Easy, quick & most economical way to reach the consumers and to generate leads is via SMS Marketing. Be it an offer, a promotion or a new service update, SMS marketing is a convenient and faster way to reach out for lead generating activities.

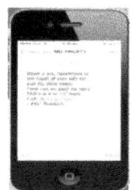

❖ **More on Google AdWords**

Here are some key points for an effective campaign to bring you more leads-

1. Build a Powerful Landing Page Landing pages can be multiple in accordance with the number of services you are offering. For each service, build a landing page to create different ads. This will

    Improve your ad rank & lower down your cost per click.

2. Identify the Right keywords Keep the keywords as relevant to a brand's product/ service. Instead of 'inverters', write 'affordable inverters installation'

3. Use Search Network When you put your money in Display Network, you leave it to chance that your

Customers may see your ad and click on it. Instead use Search Network as people usually begin their purchase journey by first searching you on Google.

Want to run a Google AdWords campaign for your business or for your client's? Here's what you should be doing! First and foremost, **build a funnel comprising of various stages.** Second and most important, **spend some time to identify your customers** before setting out on running any ad campaign. It's important to know their online behaviour to target them at the right places and their needs to devise the right messaging. Once you narrow down your prospective customers- **craft an effective ad copy- (check what your competitors are doing) and target them on various parameters like location, device, best day and time etc.**

❖ **Leverage from Extensions**

Improve the ad's visibility and click through rate (CTR) using Extensions. There is no added cost to add the Extensions in your ad so make the most by providing extra information about your business.

❖ **Deliver an Offer**

Giving an offer along with a Brand's service or product instantly attracts your customer and once the customer avails the offer, it becomes the reason for you to reconnect with your customer to build a lasting relationship.

❖ **Make use of Google Analytics**

Google Analytics provides you with Pandora of insights indicating how the traffic is reacting to your campaign. Take cues from it and take corrective measures to make your campaign effective. Change the messaging of your ad copy, improve your offer, change the targeting, look in through your Keywords strategy etc...

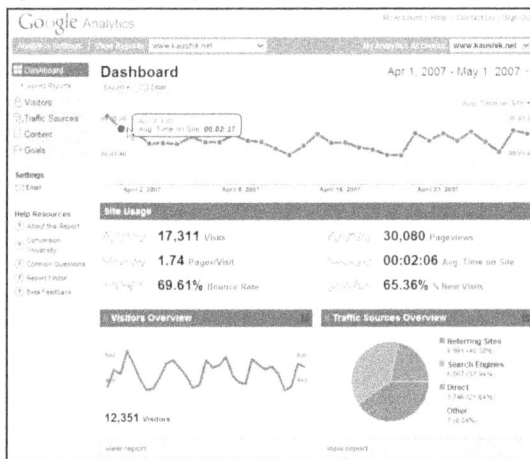

3.16 Performance Review and Efficacy Assessment Techniques of your Digital Marketing Campaign

Digital Marketing and Measurement Model

There is one difference between winners and losers when it comes to web analytics. Winners, well before think about data or tool, have a well-structured Digital Marketing & Measurement Model. Losers don't have that in place.

This chapter shall guide you in understanding the value of the Digital Marketing & Measurement Model (notice the repeated emphasis on Marketing, not just Measurement), and how to create one for yourself. At the end you'll also find some additional examples to inspire you.

The prime reason of failure in most digital marketing campaigns is not the lack of creativity in the banner ad or TV spot or the sexiness of the website. It is not even (often) the people involved. It is quite simply the lack of structured thinking about what the real purpose of the campaign is and a lack of an objective set of measures with which to identify success or failure.

I've developed the Digital Marketing & Measurement Model as a simple, structured, five step process to infuse this much needed thinking. Here is what each step in the process helps accomplish:

Step one is to force us to identify the business objectives upfront and set the broadest parameters for the work we are doing. Sr. Executives play a key role in this step.

Step two is to identify crisp goals for each business objective. Executives lead the discussion, you'll play a contributing role.

Step three is to write down the key performance indicators. You'll lead the work in this step, in partnership with a "data person" if you have one.

Step four is to set the parameters for success upfront by identifying targets for each KPI. Organization leaders play a key role here, with input from Marketing and Finance.

Step five, finally, is to identify the segments of people / behaviour / outcomes that we'll analyse to understand why we succeed or failed.

Simple, right? It is harder than you might think, "soft" work always is. Before we go into each step in detail I want to share something extremely critical. The scope/breadth the model has to cover.

A complete, and competent, Digital Marketing & Measurement Model will focus on three key areas of your marketing, and in each answer the cluster of questions provided:

1. **Acquisition:** How are you anticipating acquiring traffic for your website / YT video / whatever else you are creating? Did you cover all three components of successful acquisition: Earned, Owned, Paid media? How would you prioritize each? Where are you spending most of your efforts?

2. **Behaviour:** What is the behavior you are expecting when people arrive? What pages should they see? What videos should they watch? Should they visit repeatedly? Are there certain actions they should take? What is unique about your effort that ties to an optimal experience for a customer?

3. **Outcomes:** What outcomes signify value delivered to the business bottom-line? It depends honestly on your organizational vision

   ❖ Downloads?

   ❖ Phone calls to your call center?

   ❖ Qualified online lead?

   ❖ Signing up for email promotions?

   ❖ People buying your product / services?

   ❖ 95% task completion rate?

   ❖ 10 point lift in brand perception?

Simply put: Why are we undertaking this digital initiative?

My sincerest hope is that these questions will seed your discussions as you go through the five steps below. If your Digital Marketing & Measurement Model does not cover all three areas of your digital effort, then it is not complete. Please consider revisiting it. Don't accept a mediocre model.

With that macro thought out of the way, let's get going and look at a real example of the five step process to solidify this concept.

The business we are doing this for is a real estate company. I've picked a tough one because the main outcome is offline success. If they can create a good model then your job is much easier!

Step 1: Identify the Business Objectives.

Ask this question: *Why does your website/campaign exist?* (Think of acquisition, behaviour and outcomes.)

This is a difficult question to answer because it requires more thinking that you might anticipate. If you do it right at the end of step one you'll have something that looks like this:

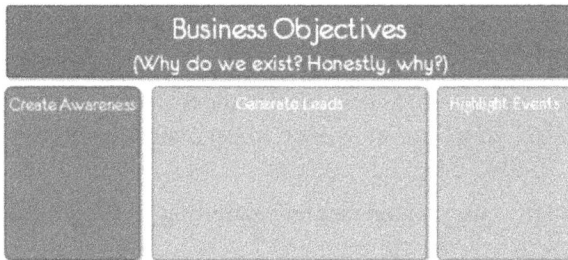

Identifying the business objectives mandates a discussion, multiple discussions, with the senior-most leaders in your company and working with them / sweet-talking their egos and hearts with gentle encouragement, to identify why the site / campaign / digital marketing initiative exists.

Based on those discussions, in our case, we've identified three objectives: *Create awareness, generate leads for the builders and highlight community events.*

Here's a great test. Your objectives should be DUMB:

- **D**oable
- **U**nderstandable
- **M**anageable
- **B**eneficial

If they are too out there, you'll never get anywhere. If they are too vague, nothing will get done. If they are too lame, they'll inspire no one. Go for real world, clear, executable and those that deliver value to the company (short term and long).

Don't you have defined objectives?

Professional Tip: One way to ensure success is to forget that you are creating a set of videos or that you are building a site to host downloads of pdfs or that you are trying to mimic a campaign from Europe. Really, really, really think hard about why you are doing what you are doing. Get the answer from your executive/client.

Step 2: Identify Goals for each Objective.

Drilling down to identify website/campaign Goals requires critical thinking from both the Management, Marketers, and the Analysts – with Management in the leadership role.

My definition: *Goals are specific strategies you'll leverage to accomplish the business objectives.*

After going through some of the acquisition, behaviour questions with stakeholders, here's our model:

Clean. Has a clear direct line between Goal and each objective, provides immense clarity.

To deliver on "Create Awareness," in this case, the site needs to support all the offline efforts along with having a relevant online traffic acquisition strategy.

"Generating Leads" comprises the twin goals of providing all kinds of information that will help potential home buyers to make their decision and to collect e-newsletter registrations as well as e-requests for an onsite tour of the model home by the builder.

Finally, "Highlight Events" is for prospective home buyers (visitors to our site). By making them happy with delightful events, at the construction site hopefully in model homes for sale, they can be converted into Net Promoters (to others) and Buyers (themselves).

These goals provide clarity, but they also contain large chunks of specific marching orders for what the Marketers and Analysts need to get done.

Professional Tip: This is super key, Macro + Micro Conversions! If the goals identified don't cover all the jobs the site/campaign is doing then you might need to revisit your work.

Step 3: Identify the Key Performance Indicators

Finally we get to deal with data!! I know you've been dying to get here. You'll be the ideas leader here.

My definition: *A key performance indicator (KPI) is a metric that helps you understand how you are doing against your objectives.* For each goal, sweat, and find the most hyper relevant KPI. This is what it will look like:

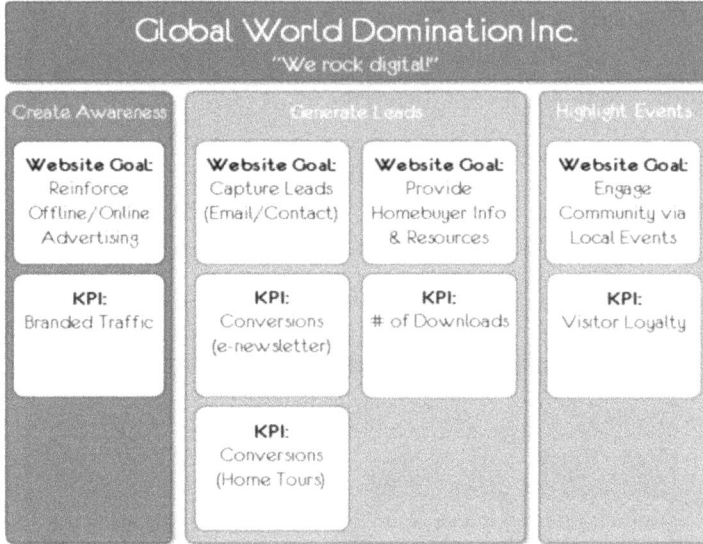

So amazing right?

I am sure your head is buzzing with all the possibilities for custom reports and things to report on, and how much clearer it is what you are supposed to do! Awesome, but hold your horses. We have two more steps to complete.

Professional Tip: Try to look for smart KPIs? Here's specific guidance to help you...

Pick super awesome key performance indicators that truly reveal success or failure.

Step 4: Identify the Targets

It is heart-breaking how few people complete this step. It is absolutely critical, in so many ways.

My definition: Targets are numerical values you've pre-determined as indicators of success or failure.

Why do you need targets? Consider this: You had an amazing campaign on

YouTube. You got 1.2 million views. Is that great or awful? How do you decide? That is why you need targets!

Ok, so you also need them to plan your site / campaign / marketing initiative better. If you were responsible for getting 5 million visits in a month would you execute your campaign differently than if that number was 500k Or if you were supposed to reach 1,000 CMO's would you remember not to use Social Media as your primary acquisition strategy? That's also why you need targets.

Targets can come from historical performance (how you did last time you / someone did something similar). They can come from other efforts (if my one hour long boring video can get 30k views in a week, should your two min peppy video get 1.2 million views?).

Seek people who are accountable (client, management, Finance), they will help you identify targets for each KPI.

Your Digital Marketing & Measurement Model will now look like this

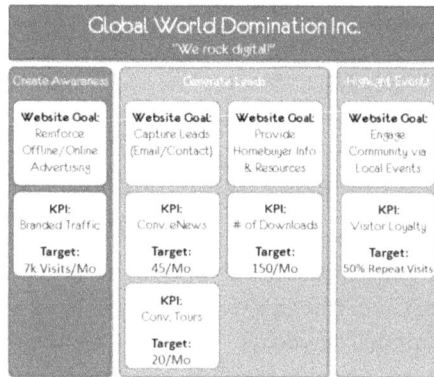

Now everyone knows what the company is shooting for. When you crack open Google Analytics, or other tools you're using, you'll immediately jump with joy or weep when you see the KPI. You'll instantly know what is good and what is bad.

Pro Tip: If you have no targets then make something up. Use a number that if reached won't embarrass you / your management / me. That is a good start; you can revise the number next month after you get the first blush of data. What's important is that you **never** measure without having some sense of what good or bad performance looks like. The more experience you have, the better you'll get at setting targets. Good targets.

Step 5: Identify valuable Segments for analysis

This last part is one that is particularly meaningful to me because of its incredible value.

My definition: A group of people, their sources, onsite behaviour, and outcomes.

When you log into Google Analytics or any other data source you are deluged by data and you could go in a million different directions.

Remember: We not only wanted focus, we wanted hyper-focus.

Take 10 more minutes from the key executives. Have a discussion with them about what the most important segments to focus on are for each goal.

Identify the sources of traffic, types of people desirable, their attributes, their behaviour, business outcomes that they care about the most. And what customers to the site might want to accomplish. Balance for the company and the customers.

You'll provide leadership here and if you did a great job then your DMMM will look something like this:

Global World Domination Inc.			
"We rock digital!"			
Create Awareness	Generate Leads		Manage Events
Website Goal: Reinforce Offline/Online Advertising	**Website Goal:** Capture Leads (Email/Contact)	**Website Goal:** Provide Homebuyer Info & Resources	**Website Goal:** Engage Community via Local Events
KPI: Branded Traffic	**KPI:** Conv. eNews	**KPI:** # of Downloads	**KPI:** Visitor Loyalty
Target: 7k Visits/Mo	**Target:** 45/Mo	**Target:** 150/Mo	**Target:** 50% Repeat Visits
Segments: Traffic Sources Converted Visits	**Segments:** Traffic Sources Site Tools Used	**Segments:** Document Type Geography	**Segments:** 1, 2, 3+ Visits Buckets

What groups of visitors were important? What visitor behaviour is desirable? What a traffic source was Marketing focused on? Who are we trying to attract? What on our site is important – at least according to us? And more such questions are important to answer to get to the optimal segments.

Pro Tip: How to Identify Analytics Segments. Read. Act. Enough said.

This was a lot of work, but I assure you that at this point you will thank God and your Cat that you worked this hard. You now have a structure that will guide your measurement efforts. The insights you derive will be of value because they are grounded in what's important to the business and the leadership. And when you make recommendations based on data… guess what… action will be taken. Worth it, right?

Here's the sexiness: You now know what's important and where to start and what to focus on. Your boss/client knows what success or failure looks like and how to connect her/his business objectives to your data. Prioritized business focus for relevant data analysis!

You have the basis of a solid contract. Get the DMMM signed (preferably in blood!) so that all parties are clear on what everyone is supposed to be solving for.

Punch-line: Always, always, always work with the above "Marketing & Measurement contract" in hand.

Some of you might have noticed that I'd eliminated the Tour Conversions KPI in step five. That was simply to make the image in step five looks prettier. But worry not; with that KPI included our Digital Marketing & Measurement Model will have this beautiful final form…

Can we run the most fantastically actionable web analytics program in any company now? Yes we can!

When you create your own Digital Marketing & Measurement Model you don't have to use the format I've used above, you can add to it as you see fit.

I wanted to share with you a different format, and example. Below is the model for a retail e-commerce website with an online and offline presence:

I hope that the two examples in this blog post will help inspire you to use the Digital Marketing & Measurement Model as the foundation of your web analytics efforts.

3.17 Impact of Social Media on Business & Society

Information and communication technology has changed rapidly over the past 20 years with a key development being the emergence of social media.

The pace of change is accelerating. For example, the development of mobile technology has played an important role in shaping the impact of social media. Across the globe, mobile devices dominate in terms of total minutes spent online. This puts the means to connect anywhere, at any time on any device in everyone's hands.

Why people share information

A fascinating study by New York Times Consumer Insight Group revealed the motivations that participants cited for sharing information on social media. These include a desire to reveal valuable and entertaining content to others; to define themselves; to grow and nourish relationships and to get the word out about brands and causes they like or support.

These factors have caused social networks to evolve from being a handy means for keeping in touch with friends and family to being used in ways that have a real impact on society.

Social media is being used in ways that shape politics, business, world culture, education, careers, innovation, and more.

Here are seven ways the impact of social media is felt by individuals and social groups

The Effect of Social Media on Politics

A new study from Pew Research claims that 62 percent of people get their news from social media, with 18 percent doing so very often.

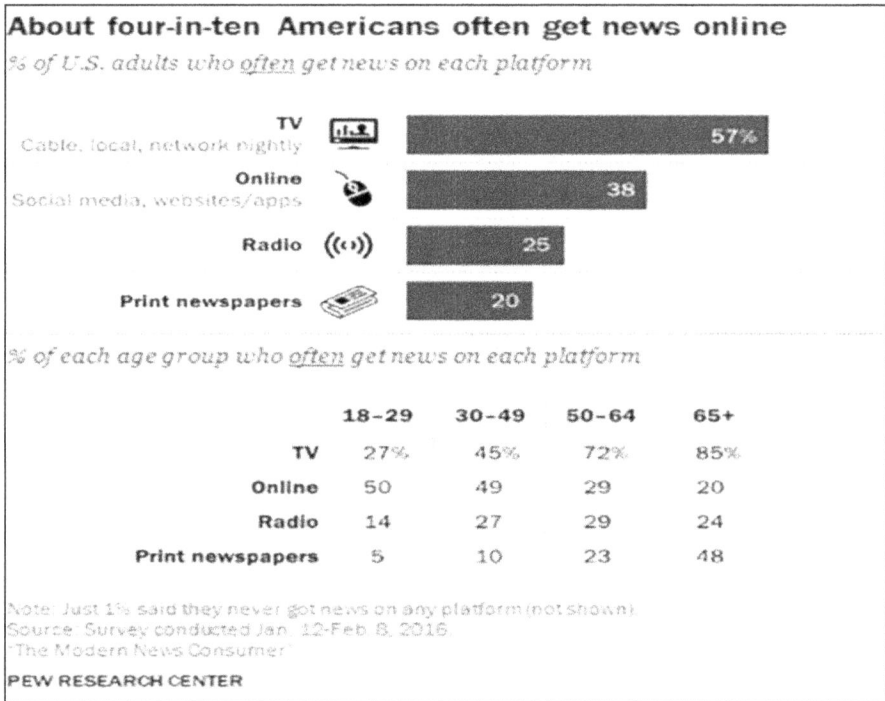

About four-in-ten Americans often get news online

% of U.S. adults who often get news on each platform

Platform	%
TV — Cable, local, network nightly	57%
Online — Social media, websites/apps	38
Radio	25
Print newspapers	20

% of each age group who often get news on each platform

	18–29	30–49	50–64	65+
TV	27%	45%	72%	85%
Online	50	49	29	20
Radio	14	27	29	24
Print newspapers	5	10	23	48

Note: Just 1% said they never got news on any platform (not shown).
Source: Survey conducted Jan. 12-Feb 8, 2016.
"The Modern News Consumer"

PEW RESEARCH CENTER

In comparison to other media, social media's influence in political campaigns has increased tremendously. Social networks play an increasingly important role in electoral politics — first in the ultimately unsuccessful candidacy of Howard Dean in 2003, and then in the election of the first African-American president in 2008.

The New York Times reports that "The election of Donald J. Trump is perhaps the starkest illustration yet that across the planet, social networks are helping to fundamentally rewire human society." Because social media allows people to communicate with one another more freely, they are helping to create surprisingly influential social organizations among once-marginalized groups.

3.18 The Impact of Social Media on Society

Almost a quarter of the world's population is now on Facebook. In the USA nearly 80% of all internet users are on this platform. Because social networks feed off interactions among people, they become more powerful as they grow.

Thanks to the internet, each person with marginal views can see that he's not alone. And when these people find one another via social media, they can do things — create memes, publications and entire online worlds that bolster their worldview, and then break into the mainstream.

Without social media, social, ethical, environmental and political ills would have minimal visibility. Increased visibility of issues has shifted the balance of power from the hands of a few to the masses.

The flipside: Social media is slowly killing real activism and replacing it with 'slacktivism'

While social media activism brings an increased awareness about societal issues, questions remain as to whether this awareness is translating into real change.

Some argue that social sharing has encouraged people to use computers and mobile phones to express their concerns on social issues without actually having to engage actively with campaigns in real life. Their support is limited to pressing the 'Like' button or sharing content.

This is a very human reaction when people are given options that absolve them from responsibility to act. A 2013 study by the University of British Columbia's Sauder School of Business found that when people are presented with the option of 'liking' a social cause, they use this to opt out of actually committing time and money to a charitable cause. On the other hand, when people are allowed to show support in private, they are more likely to show meaningful support in terms of making a financial contribution.

The researchers found that a public endorsement is an action meant to satisfy others' opinions, whereas people who give in private do so because the cause is aligned to their values.

3.19 The Impact of Social Media on Commerce

The rise of social media means it's unusual to find an organization that does not reach its customers and prospects through one social media platform or another. Companies see the importance of using social media to connect with customers and build revenue.

Businesses have realized they can use social media to generate insights, stimulate demand, and create targeted product offerings. This is important in traditional brick-and-motor businesses, and, obviously, in the world of e-commerce.

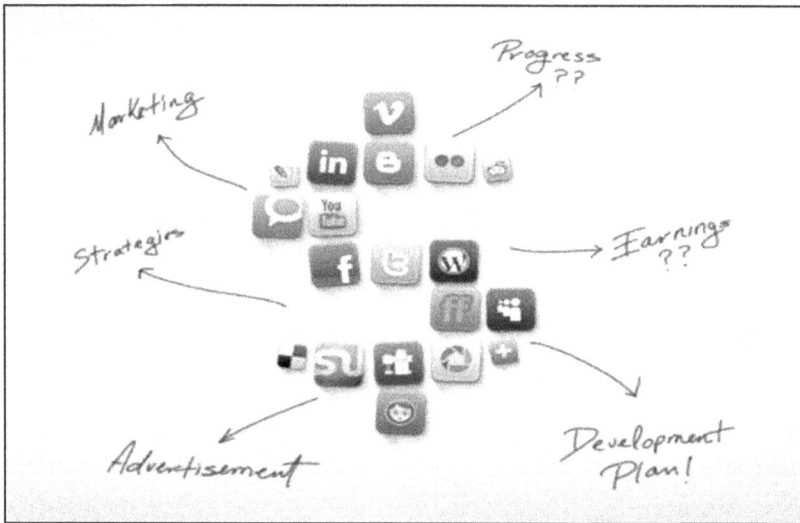

Many studies suggest implementing social networks within the workplace can strengthen knowledge sharing. The result is to improve project management activities and enable the spread of specialized knowledge. Fully implementing social technologies in the workplace removes boundaries, eliminates silos, and can raise interaction and help create more highly skilled and knowledgeable workers.

The Flip Side: Low number of social 'shares' can lead to negative social proof and destroy business credibility

Interestingly, although the use of social sharing has become the norm rather than the exception in business, some companies, after experiencing first-hand some negative effects of social media, have decided to go against the grain and remove the social sharing buttons from their websites.

A case study of Taloon.com, an e-commerce retailer from Finland, found that conversions rose by 11.9% when they removed share buttons from their product pages.

These results highlight the double-edged nature of the impact of social media. When products attract a lot of shares, it can reinforce sales. But when the reverse is true, customers begin to distrust the product and the company. This is what Dr Paul Marsden, psychologist and author of 'The Social Commerce Handbook', referred to as 'social proof'.

3.20 The Effects of Social Media on the World of Work

Social media has had a profound effect on recruitment and hiring. 19 percent of hiring managers make their hiring decisions based on information found on social media. According to CareerBuilder's 2016 social media recruitment survey, 60 percent of employers use social networking sites to research job candidates.

Professional social networks such as LinkedIn are important social media platforms for anyone looking to stand out in their profession. They allow people to create and market a personal brand.

3.21 The Impact of Social Media on Training and Development

Job candidates who develop skills on the latest and most advanced social media techniques are far more employable.

A 2013 survey by Pearson Learning Solutions reported a significant increase in the use of social media in learning. Over half the educators who were interviewed agreed that social sharing encourages interaction, providing an environment that fosters learning.

Blogs, wikis, LinkedIn, Twitter, Facebook, and podcasts are now common tools for learning in many educational institutions. Social media has contributed to the increase in long-distance online learning.

Despite issues of lack of privacy and some instances of cheating among long-distance learners, this has not deterred social platforms from being used in education.

3.22 The Moral Challenges of Social Media

Social media has been blamed for promoting social ills such as:

1. **Cyberbullying:** Teenagers have a need to fit in, to be popular and to outdo others. This process was challenging long before the advent of social media. Add Facebook, Twitter, Snapchat and Instagram into the mix and you suddenly have teenagers being subjected feeling pressure to grow up too fast in an online world.

   Michael Hamm, a researcher from the University of Alberta conducted a study that showed the effects of social media on bullying. 23% of teens report being targeted and 15 percent said they'd bullied someone on social media. Teenagers can misuse social media platforms to spread rumours, share videos aimed at destroying reputations and to blackmail others.

2. **Lack of privacy:** Stalking, identity theft, personal attacks, and misuse of information are some of the threats faced by the users of social media. Most of the time, the users themselves are to blame as they end up sharing content that should not be in the public eye. The confusion arises from a lack of understanding of how the private and public elements of an online profile actually work.

   The Joy of Tech · by Nitrozac & Snaggy
   Unemployable due to stupid personal stuff I put on my facebook page.
   Me too!
   FOR ME, IT WAS AN EMBARRASSING YOUTUBE VIDEO.
   Signs of the social networking times.

   Unfortunately, by the time private content is deleted, it's usually too late and can cause problems in people's personal and professional lives.

3.23 The Impact of Social Media on Personal Relationships

One of the effects of social media is encouraging people to form and cherish artificial bonds over actual friendships. The term 'friend' as used on social media lacks the intimacy identified with conventional friendships, where people actually know each other, want to talk to each other, have an intimate bond and frequently interact face to face.

The Bottom Line

It's been said that information is power. Without a means of distributing information, people cannot harness the power. One positive impact of social media is in the distribution of information in today's world. Platforms such as Facebook, LinkedIn, Twitter and others have made it possible to access information at the click of a button.

Research conducted by parse.ly shows that the life expectancy of a story posted on the web is 2.6 days, compared to 3.2 days when a story is shared on social media. That's a difference of 23%, which is significant when you consider that billions of people use the internet daily.

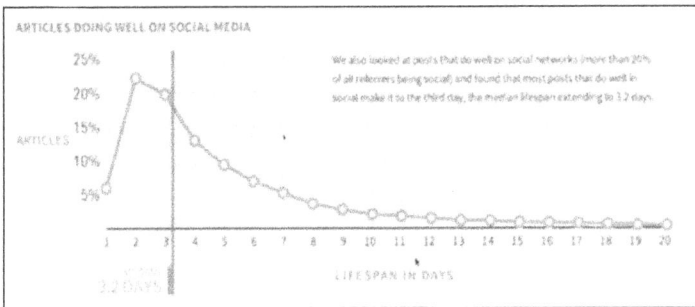

This means that the longer the information is in circulation, the more discussion it generates and the greater the impact of social media.

While the world would be a much slower place without social media, it's caused harm as well as good. However, the positive impact of social media is astronomical and far surpasses the ills associated with sharing.

At the end of the day, sharing is about getting people to see and respond to content. As long as the content is still relevant and the need for information still exists, it's always worthwhile for any organization using social media to keep publishing.

❑❑

Chapter 4: Web Analytics

4.1 Introduction

I personally love their form analytics the most – it shows which fields the users have filled, and which ones they leave out. This becomes highly significant when it comes to analysing exit rates.

SeoChat reviewed Clicktale, and this is what they had to say about the tool.

You can check out detailed reviews of these tools before you invest in one. However, to make your life easier, here's a checklist that provides a comparison of all the above mentioned Web Analytics tools (there are 10 of them) for your easy reference.

Never ignore web analytics – it's often what makes the difference between an ordinary marketer and a powerful, savvy digital marketer!

Google Analytics

Google Analytics is a freemium web analytics service offered by Google that tracks and reports website traffic. Google launched the service in November 2005. Google Analytics is now the most widely used web analytics service on the Internet. Google Analytics is offered also in two additional versions: the subscription-based Google Analytics 360, previously Google Analytics Premium, targeted at enterprise users, and Google Analytics for Mobile Apps, an SDK that allows gathering usage data from iOS and Android Apps.

Integrated with AdWords, users can now review online campaigns by tracking landing page quality and conversions (goals). Goals might include sales, lead generation, viewing a specific page, or downloading a particular file. Google Analytics' approach is to show high-level, dashboard-type data for the casual user and more in-depth data further into the report set. Google Analytics analysis can identify poorly performing pages with techniques such as funnel visualization, where visitors came from (referrers), how long they stayed on the website and their geographical position.

It also provides more advanced features, including custom visitor segmentation. Google Analytics e-commerce reporting can track sales activity and performance. The e-commerce reports show a site's transactions, revenue, and many other commerce-related metrics.

Google Analytics includes Google Website Optimizer, rebranded as Google Analytics Content Experiments. Google Analytics' Cohort analysis feature helps understand the behavior of component groups of users apart from your user population. It is beneficial to marketers and analysts for successful implementation of a marketing strategy.

As a business owner or marketer, you understand the importance of having information that allows you to make informed decisions on how to grow your business. Whether you're running a small boutique in town, or working at a large brand, the odds are your business has a presence on the web. You might be selling products online, running a blog, or just using your site to provide information about your services. But no matter the purpose of your website, you're to going to want to fully understand the customer journey as they interact with your content. And Google Analytics does just that.

It's a free service, with some premium options that helps you analyze visitor traffic, and paints a complete picture of who your audience is, and what their needs are. It's a platform that connects to every page on your website. And through various dashboards and reports, you'll have the opportunity to unlock tremendous data. Google can provide you the routes people take to reach your site, the content they viewed, and even the devices they used to get there. Their software can also measure sales and goal conversions, say, getting someone to sign up for your newsletter.

And with advanced tools such as funnels and attribution, you can see exactly how all the pages on your site are working with or against you. At its core, Google Analytics helps you understand what's working and what isn't. It gives you the insights you need to make changes so you can meet your performance goals. You'll be able to uncover the why behind the data. If you see a strong uptick in traffic, you might uncover the source as a blog you haven't heard of. If you're seeing a strong decline, you might identify a problem with your site or a competitor that's poaching traffic with better SEO or paid ads.

Let's think about Google Analytics alongside your business objectives. In the online world, it can seem like there's endless ideas. But, I think we can boil online objectives into five common categories: ecommerce, lead generation, content publishing, online information, and branding. For ecommerce, your objective is to sell products or services. You'll use Google Analytics to find ways to increase those sales and track your performance over time.

For lead generation, your aim is to collect user information and you'll test strategies and the landing pages to find a working combination. For content publishers, the goal is to encourage repeat visits and engagement. So, you'll be tracking what keeps people clicking and interacting with the site. For online information, it's important that users find what they're looking for when they need it. So, you'll be interested in what content they're finding or not finding. And for branding, the key objective is awareness and loyalty.

Is your site being shared, linked to, and engaged with on the greater web? It's more than just looking at how many people visit your site. That information is just a fraction of what you'll need to make informed decisions. Every site will have actions. And Google Analytics tracks all of those actions, and then it boils it down into easy to understand reports. This equips you with the right data to understand what you need to do to improve the outcome of your site.

4.2 How Google Analytics Work?

Before we dive into the Google Analytics platform, I want to talk first about what's going on under the hood. By understanding how Google Analytics works, you'll be better equipped to identify problems with your setup or understand why certain data anomalies might occur. There are four components to how the Google Analytics system works: Data Collection, Configuration, Data Processing, and Reporting. To track a website, Google Analytics uses a small snippet of JavaScript code. You'll place this code on every page of your website and when a user arrives, the code comes alive and starts to collect data on how the user engages with your site.

Some of the data comes from the website itself, like the URL of the pages that the user is viewing. Other data is collected from the user's browser, like the language the browser is set to, the browser name, and the device and operating system used to access the site. And this is how you can see, say, if most of your users are Mac or PC, or iPhone or Android. The JavaScript can also collect information on what content is viewed, for how long, and even the referring source that brought the user to the site in the first place, say, a blog that linked to your site, or a Facebook post.

All of this information is then pushed to Google Analytics servers to await processing. Google looks at each piece of data as an interaction or a hit. And every time your user visits a new page on your site, the code collects and sends new or updated information about the user's activity.

And now that Google has all of this information, they'll start processing it. And this can take anywhere from four to 24 hours. You can think of processing as the step that takes all of this raw information and turns it into something useful.

From there, Google will organize the information. It's going to categorize users by whether they're new or returning. It'll determine their length of the stay on the site, and it'll even link together all the pages they've viewed in the order they viewed them in. It's also at this stage that Google applies any configuration settings you've pre-set for that raw data. And we're going to talk more on those later, but an example of this would be if you want to exclude, say, yourself or your office from appearing in your reports. Once your data is then processed, it's going to be stored in a database.

From here, the last element is reporting. And this is what we'll be spending the majority of this course looking at. You're going to be accessing reporting through the Google Analytics web interface, and it's there that you can interact with all of your data. Now, it is possible to grab the data using Google's API but we're not going to be covering that in this course. Now, there's a lot more that does go on under the hood to make Google Analytics possible. If you're really curious, you can explore Google's documentation in the Google Developer Guidelines.

It's dense reading but it does give you an even closer look at how all of these elements work together.

4.3 Performance Measurement of a Content Assessment using Google Analytics

Effective Content Marketing has always been based on a well-organised content strategy, clearly defined targets, and constant analysis of the results.

How can you determine the success of your digital content? How do you figure out what kind of content attracts your audience and allows you to achieve your marketing goals? You start by measuring and analysing your content performance by looking at the right metrics.

In this article, you will find 23 essential content metrics and learn how you can interpret, analyse, and measure them.

User Behavior Metrics

Page views

Shows the total number of times a particular page on your website was visited.

Page views can give you a basic understanding of how good your content has performed in comparison with other posts published in the same period. This metric can show what kind of topics attract the most attention from your audience.

How to measure

Google Analytics - Behaviour > Site content > All Pages tab, You can sort it by Unique Pageviews. When the data displays you can see which posts perform best, as well as check traffic for specific URLs.

Unique Visitors

Indicates the total number of visitors who viewed a particular page on your website

This metric is similar to Page views, but it can provide you with more accurate insights on how many new visitors your content attracts. Evaluating the number of unique visitors helps you to determine the scope of your audience.

How to Measure

Google Analytics - Audience > Overview > Top row, second from left, choose the date period in the upper right corner.

New and Returning Users

Shows the ratio between new and returning visitors

The number of new visitors indicates the number of potential leads, while the number of returning visitors shows if the visitors like your content. It is better to have a healthy mix of both: that means, your content can attract new users and retain the old ones.

How to measure

Google Analytics - Audience > Behaviour > New vs. Returning

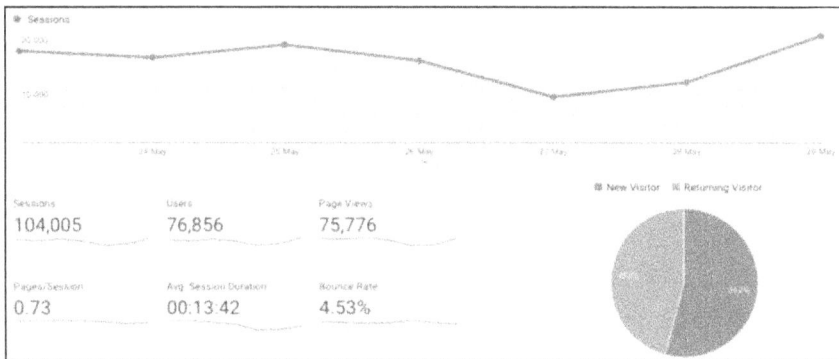

Page Depth

Demonstrates the average number of pages your users visit per session beyond the landing page.

This metric indicates how engaging your overall content is. If this number is too low, this might be a sign of poor content interlinking, or low-quality website design and navigation. You can check the most highly-visited pages on your website and optimize them to get better conversions.

How to measure:

Google Analytics - Audience > Behaviour > Engagement > in the Distribution tab select Page Depth.

Average Time on Page

Indicates if the visitors are attentively reading your content or just skimming it, If the «time on page» on some content pieces is significantly lower than on others, it can show you which types of content are liked more and less. Analyse the best-performing articles and compare them to the least-performing articles. Try to determine why some are doing better than others. Do they differ by length, by form or by topic? Do they include infographics, images or video? Replicate what works.

How to measure

Google Analytics - Behaviour > Site Content > All Pages

Bounce Rate

Indicates the percentage of users that left the particular page without visiting any other website pages

A high bounce rate can indicate that something isn't quite right with the page. If you have an e-commerce site, a high bounce rate can be a worrying signal, because it means that most customers leave your website without making a purchase.

Check your page load speed and your CTAs. Maybe your SEO needs some tweaking or people are not finding what they were looking for on this particular page.

Analysis and interpretation of a bounce rate should depend on the type of website or web page, so don't panic. For example, a high bounce rate on a blog may be normal if you have a number returning visitors who read new articles, find relevant information, and leave your website after that.

How to Measure

Google Analytics - Behaviour > Site Content > All Pages

Pages per Session

Indicates the average number of pages viewed during a session on your website.

This metric shows if your content is engaging and organized well enough to motivate a visitor to discover another web page. If your blog or website has proper and helpful interlinking (links to posts with more detailed information on the subject), users will be more likely to visit more than one page.

How to Measure:

Google Analytics - Audience > Overview > Pages/Session

Traffic Sources

Shows which sources bring traffic to your website.

This can help you discover the best and the worst marketing channels for you and help you determine what is, and what is not, working for you. Does the majority of your audience come from search engines, or is your social media strategy stronger than your SEO? Or maybe your brand is already well-known, and you mostly get direct traffic?

Analysing traffic sources allows you to identify which marketing channels and strategies are working best for your content distribution. You can also identify the channels with good potential and perhaps a larger investment in resources or a tweaking of strategy would make a massive difference.

How to Measure:

Google Analytics - Acquisition > All Traffic > Channels.

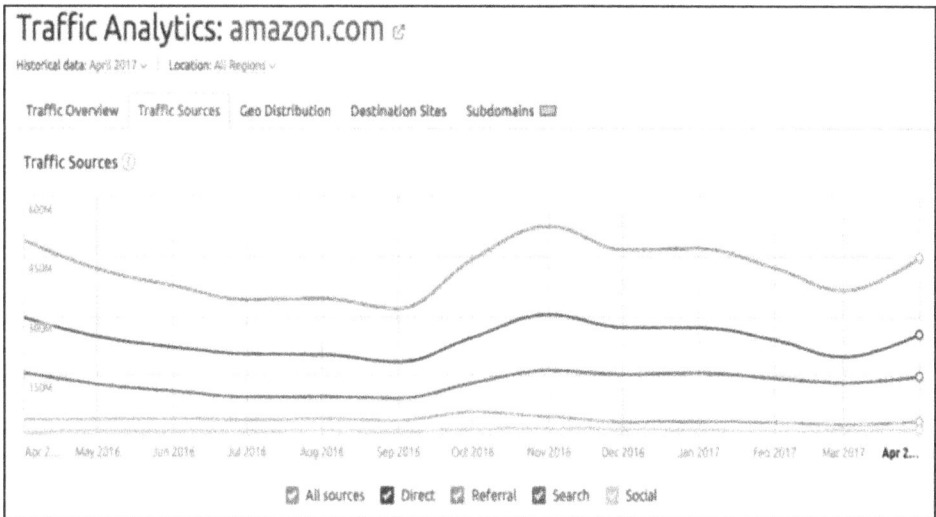

4.4 Engagement Metrics

Likes and Shares

These are indicators of your content engagement and popularity among your audience. However, a share is more significant than a like because it not only shows that someone found your content interesting but also expanded its reach.

How to measure:

1. **(website name) Content Analyser:** Projects > Set up a project > Post Tracking tab > Add a URL or a group of URLs. You can see the total number of shares as well as the number of shares for each piece of content (including your external publications).

2. **(website name) Social Media Tracker:** Projects > Set up a project > Overview > Engagement. You can see the total engagement of your content on social media.

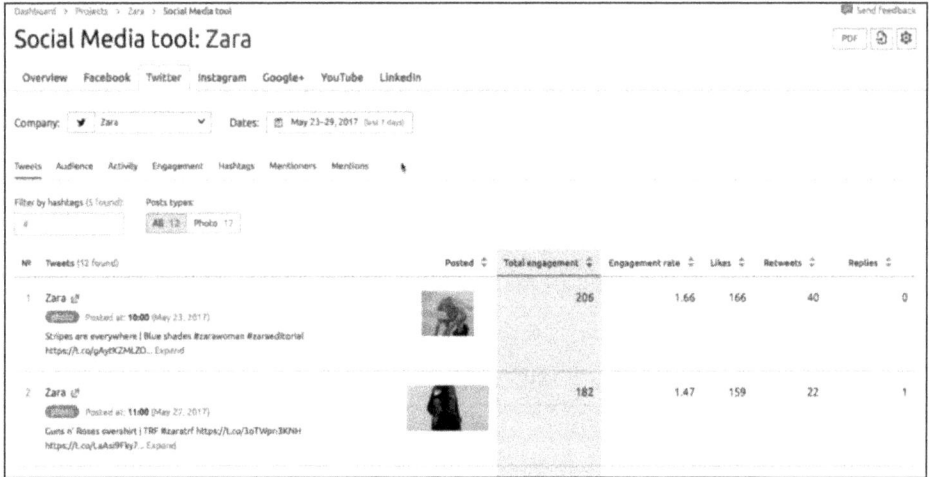

Comments

The number of comments under the post demonstrates the level of content engagement even better than social likes and shares do. It takes more time to write a comment than to like or share a post (of course, we are talking about valuable comments). So, if a reader was motivated enough to express his opinion in a comment section, it is often a good sign.

How to measure:

1. **Social Media Tracker:** Projects > Set up a project > Overview > Choose a social media you are interested in. You can see the number of comments and replies to your posts on social media.

2. To manage your blog comments, use Commentful (tracking of your comments and online conversations).

Mentions

Mentions measure performance and engagement from your content. Track mentions of your content both in social media and other media channels; pay special attention to their sentiment, context, and authors.

How to Measure:

1. **Brand Monitoring Tool:** Projects > Set up a project > Mentions. You can track your mentions by source, period, presence or absence of backlink.

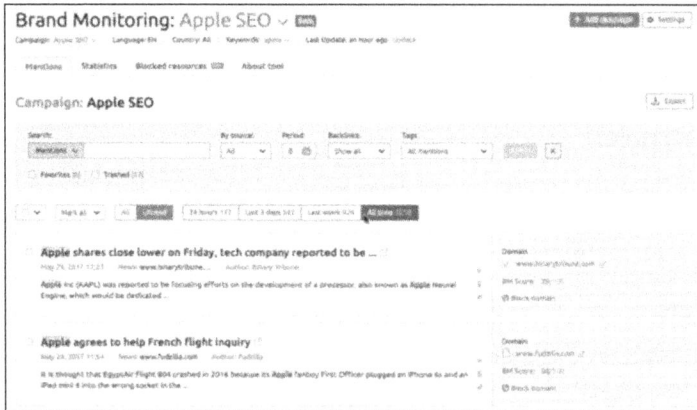

2. **Buzzsumo -Monitoring.** You can filter your mentions by brands, competitors, backlinks, keywords or authors.

Re-publications

If another article partly quotes your content or refers to it as a source, this can be considered as a mention. And if the full text of your article, your infographic, video or another piece of content is published on a third-party website, this counts as a republication.

When you find a republication of your content, make sure the author included the link to the original post. It will help you to attract a more targeted audience to your website.

How to Measure:

You cannot measure the exact traffic coming to your article, but checking the average traffic of this website with Similar Web or SEMrush Traffic Analytics you will understand the potential reach you gain with this republication.

You can also ask the author to include an utm link. In this case, you can track referral traffic to your website via Google Analytics - Acquisition > Campaigns > All campaigns.

Incoming Requests

A high number of incoming requests is a straight indicator of your content quality, whether it is an invitation to write new material, to give an interview, to share your knowledge base, or to cooperate in any other way.

4.5 SEO Outcome Metrics

Organic Traffic

Shows the number of people who found your website through a search engine

Low figures may indicate that an article or page was not optimized properly. So to increase organic traffic, you need to pay attention to proper search engine optimization.

How to Measure:

Google Analytics - Acquisition > All Traffic > Channels > Check the Organic search group. By clicking on it, you will get information on keywords that people have used to find your website.

Dwell Time

Dwell Time indicates the average length of time a visitor spends on the page before returning to the SERPs.

This metric is very important for your SEO: if a user comes to your webpage and returns right away to the search results, this is a negative signal to search engines and it affects your ranking.

How to Measure:

Analyse your bounce rate, session duration, and time on page. If you have a low bounce rate and high time on page, it means users stay on your web page or website, so you have a high dwell time.

Backlinks

Backlinks are one of the most important Google ranking factors, and therefore one of the key content and PR metrics. Pay special attention to the number of links (do not forget to exclude spams), the number of unique domains, and the quality of the referring domains.

How to Measure:

1. **SEMrush:** Domain Analytics > Backlinks. You can find the total number of backlinks, your referring domains and IPs, new and lost backlinks, top anchors and much more.

2. **Brand Monitoring Tool:** Projects > Set up a project > Mentions > Apply filters > Backlinks > Show mentions with backlinks. You can see all mentions of your brand or product that include links to your website.

3. **Content Analyser:** Projects > Set up a project > Post Tracking tab > Add a URL or a group of URLs. You can see the total number of backlinks and discover websites pointing to a particular publication.

Keywords

Check the performance of your post for your targeted keywords. How many keywords is your content ranking for in the Google top 3? How is this page performing compared to your competitors?

How to Measure:

1. **SEMrush Content Analyser:** Projects > Set up a project > Post Tracking tab > Add a URL or a group of URLs. You can see for which keywords your webpage is ranking in SERPs.

2. **SEMrush Position Tracking:** Projects > Set up a project > Add keywords you are interested in. Track your positions for your target keywords.

4.6 Company Revenue

Number of Leads

The number of potential clients, who have shared their personal details throughout the content produced by you. You can get them through contact forms, sign-ups for updates and newsletters, downloads of materials and so on.

How to Measure:

To track leads generated by your content you need to set up corresponding goals in Google Analytics.

Existing Leads Touched

It is not enough to just get a new lead. To achieve your marketing and business goals, it is very important to accompany your prospects in their purchasing processes. By analysing the number of existing leads that interacted with your content you can evaluate and develop better lead nurturing.

How to Measure:

Track the number of returning users in Google Analytics.

Conversion Rate

The percentage of visitors who took a desired action (click, registration, download, etc.) after interaction with your content

How to Measure:

Track the number of conversions and divide it by the number of total clicks on your link, banner or CTA during the same time period.

```
Conversion Rate = Conversions/Total clicks
```

Revenue Influenced / ROI

Return on investment (ROI) is the percentage of revenue we take from different actions. In this case, it will be the revenue related to the content created by you or your team.

How to Measure:

Take the profit of your investment, subtract the cost of the investment, and divide the total by the cost of the investment:

```
ROI = (Return - Investment)/Investment
```

4.7 Choosing Relevant Content Metrics

To start, think about your marketing and business goals. What is "success" for you? What ROI are you looking for? If your brand has good visibility, then metrics such as likes, shares or web traffic may not be the key metrics in your content marketing strategy. In this case, you could focus on the number of new visitors you attract and/ or new leads generated by your content.

Don't forget the metrics that will help you track success in regards to reaching your target audience and the effectiveness of your distribution channels. If your content does not bring you desired results, try to assess your distribution channels. Maybe, the channels you are using are not relevant to your audience, and you should invest your efforts in other marketing channels.

And last but not least, don't analyse your data using just one metric. Always try to take into consideration different data based on various metrics. By examining all available data as a whole, you will gain a clear and complete picture of your content results.

Measure and analyse your digital content to improve your strategy and stay on top with various intelligent measurements!

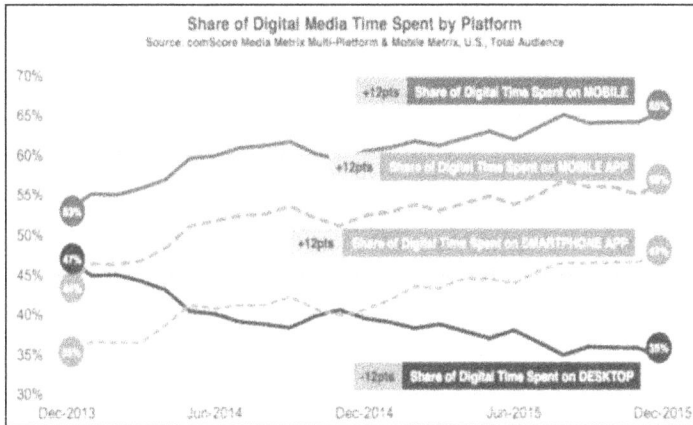

Share of Digital Media Time Spent by Platform
Source: comScore Media Metrix Multi-Platform & Mobile Metrix, U.S., Total Audience

4.8 Summary

Web analytics is often considered as monitoring and evaluation tool for any digital marketing exercise an organization conduct to promote its brand and maximize revenue. Web Analytics plays a critical role in any Digital Marketing campaign not only to show how effective their strategy and implementation was but also clearly reflect their loop holes to rectify it way forward.

Web Analytics as an effective tool helps an organization to identify consumer behaviour as a whole including their decision making parameters behind buying a product from any producers across the globe. Therefore, it tells you who all being your competitors have an edge over you in terms of products quality and features, which you may develop further with some innovative ideas.

It tells you why, when and how much people consume the product on a particular period, it even tells you what is the time cycles you should approach them more often and on a regular interval till when.

Since it tells you about consumer behaviour and about their buying patter up to a large extent, you as a business can always improvise that leverage that opportunity to customize your existing product, plan for launching new products and services with additional features in the market keeping in mind the current demand scenario.

For example in early in 90s all of us know that Nokia has a market share of more than 98% in India, but the boom came to an end in 2010, when blackberry came with their business phones with additional features to compete Nokia in the market, such an innovative business initiative brought down Nokia's market share to 70% in India and then we all know how drastically Samsung tapped the market with their new innovation called "Smartphones" with a different look and experience.

During this process of transformation Samsung captured the entire mobile market in India and Nokia was nowhere in the market, even blackberry for the matter of fact almost withdrew their offerings from Indian marketing seeing a strong challenge from Samsung.

Why did I use this case is to make you understand that even if you're market leader in your space today doesn't guarantee that you won't be bankrupt 10 years down the line. Many a times Nokia top management has asked in various public forum that they didn't do anything wrong with their product quality or customer service, it's true in all sense but the only area they couldn't focus was the changing consumer behaviour and buying pattern.

The only mistake Nokia committed was not to survey what consumer is looking for; they didn't bring any innovations to please their customers being the market leader in their respective sector. As a result your competitor came with certain better offerings and dragged away all your assets from you so easily, this case teaches us how to stay ahead of your competitors, how to continuously develop your product range and introduce new variants to pleasantly surprise your customer to stay healthy in terms of market share in your sector.

Now, web Analytics is a kind of tool which can help you to monitor not only your performance but track your competitor's activities very closely too. It will give you an edge over 1000 other players in your sector and ensure you're updated on what's going on in the market.

I would like to talk about another similar business case in the field of Consumer Durables; we all recognise who is Redmi today without thinking twice which is a sister concern of Xiaomi China. Now look at how they have gained significant market share in India by launching one after one innovative mobile model within a reasonable price range. Since they are into a highly competitive business environment, challenged by old veterans in the market like "Samsung" "Motorola" "LG" "Sony" to name few Redmi has realised that they can't play in premium price segment and doesn't have luxury to spend big on advertisement too being a start-up.

Therefore they have utilized Digital Marketing up to an optimum level of utility and have used strong analytics to assess their efficacy in the market. The result was evident in front of all of us; Redmi launched around 15 smartphone models within 2 years of their inception and all of them performed well in their portfolio. They never continued a model beyond six months and brought a new variant with additional features always in their offerings. They were focused on their strength and therefore tried to convince buyers that innovation comes cheap today and they should always take the opportunity to experience it at a low investment risk.

You might be surprised to know that Redmi has grabbed 26.5% of the Indian smartphone market share within two years of their inception just similar to what

Samsung did with Nokia a decade back. If you analyse Samsung is committing the same mistake what Nokia did years back is stop innovations, Design inadequacy and riding on the brand equity and existing market share blindly which is slipping fast out of their kitty.

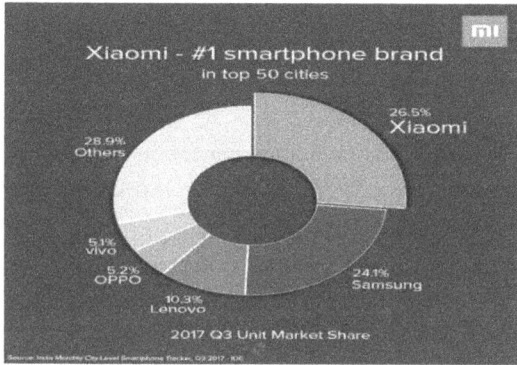

The case of Redmi is relevant and applicable here because they realized the strength of Digital Marketing and utilized all kind of analytics like Data Analytics, Web Analytics, Ecommerce Affiliated Efficacy test, Social Media Analytics widely and wisely up to the possible optimum extent.

Similarly if your business can realize the potential of Digital marketing and Web Analytics you can do wonder provided the applications are implemented usefully into your business. You should never forget the fact that good strategy combined with innovations at your business shall always fetch you the desired result you may want to achieve.

4.9 A case where Analytics says about Buying Decision made by the Target Audience of a Business

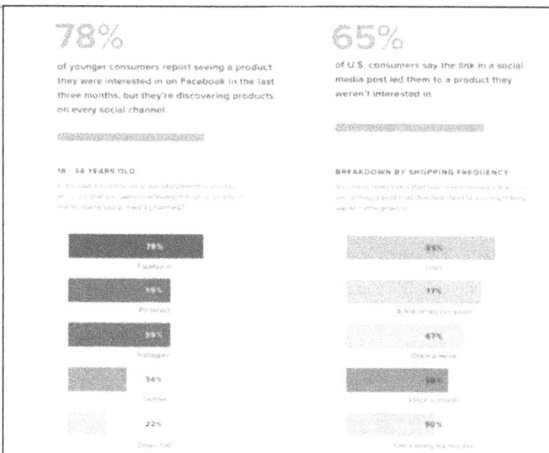

4.10 The Future Evolution of Digital Marketing and Role of WordPress in it

The future evolution of marketing is termed as **'Digi Marketing'** where-in there is a shift from mass broadcast to digital, participatory, two-way and primarily viral. The Digital Darwinism will force marketers to engage the customers continuously by adopting new media and digital channels thereby re-crafting the way we approach marketing.

- **From Viewers to participants:** Consumers are no longer just docile viewers but are likely to be participating and watching by expressing their opinions through blogs, podcasts and web.

- **From Impressions to Involvement:** Involvement is necessary today and hence SOV (Share of Voice) becomes key driving force for marketers. Creating ongoing engagement is needed which is not just by logging many times on the channel but by continuously interacting and responding and connecting emotionally to the discussions.

- **From Broadcast to Addressable:** Shift from thinking about mass audience to individuality and interactivity where by even if there are millions of people with the same type of device, you can still connect with them as individuals displaying their buying habits and preferences.

- **From Schedule-Driven and Location-Bound content to Time-shifted and Borderless:** Freedom from scheduling, freedom geographic boundaries, freedom to scale and freedom from formats.

- **From Mass messaging to opt-in messaging:** Messaging to consumers should be on opted – in basis which directs towards individual needs and preferences.

- **From Traditional media planning to New media planning:** The traditional media plan included signage, billboards by including a telephone number. But by making the billboards digital we mean that we can display a video and not a standard image which would make the billboards more interactive.

- **From managed PR to Digital Influence:** It is more to do with image management. It is necessary that marketers map real-time conversations of consumers by monitoring blogs, disseminating new information digitally and responding to blogs rather than only concerned of image control.

- **From integrated marketing to unified marketing:** Unification of individual customers experience by using individual customer data to support continuous participant dialogue.

4.11 Growth of Internet Sites and Smartphone

According to the eMarketer research firm, around 10 billion people across the world are going to use a mobile phone in 2018 and the Smartphone users would total 1.75 billion in 2014 by surpassing the global Smartphone audience of 3 billion by 2020. The trajectory of Smartphone is going to grow faster through 2017 and the penetration among mobile phone users globally would near to 50% as per the eMarketers forecast period. This has made it possible because the Smartphone is getting affordable with the adoption of 3G and 4G networks. It is also expected that more than 5.23 billion people globally or 68.9% of the mobile phone users would go online via mobile at least monthly in 2018. It is also estimated that total number of mobile phone internet users will increase to 76.5% in 2018.

These forecasts are made based on the worldwide and local trends in the economy including technology changes and population changes and changes in the companies including demographic trends and trends in consumer behaviour. The top countries which are fuelling the internet growth in the order of importance include China followed by India although a small percentage i.e. 11% of the total population of India being online.

4.12 How do you use Web Analytics effectively to Make most out of it for your Business?

Web Analytics – Keeping a track of it all can be one tedious, overwhelming process.

But thanks to Web Analytics tools, number-crunching and making sense of data has become quite simple!

What used to be the exclusive sidekick of Data Scientists has now become a friend of every digital marketer. Web Analytics is about figuring out what works and what does not. It helps figure out actionable tactics and aids in making informed decisions while planning the next move.

Before I tell you anything about these tools, you need to know a few basics that might help you along the way.

Assumptions don't work.

As a digital marketer, your decisions should involve qualitative and quantitative (yes, both!) analysis of your website's data.

You already know that? Good. Then let's get started and look at what you should be doing from 1 to 3.

Step 1 – Set a goal

Don't look for hits. I mean, don't look ONLY for hits. Focus on the overall business goal.

Website visits should translate into conversions, so shift your focus from hits to conversions.

As a digital marketer, you need to constantly ask yourself questions like: What is the conversion rate? How many views are dripping through the funnel? Are there any bottlenecks?

Decide your goals based on what action you want your visitors to take:

- Should they be downloading your content?
- Do you want them to register for a course? *wink-wink*
- Or are you tempting them to purchase your product?

Set your goals based on the actions YOU want the visitor to take. And once that goal is set, it's time for step 2.

Step 2 – Understand where the Problem Lies

"Why did you leave me?" Your Ex might not give you a proper answer to this question, but Web Analytics tools certainly will.

Look for pages with high exit rates. This will give you an insight into user behaviour and help you optimize content.

Once you understand why people leave, you will know what puts them off – and you can figure out how to retain them.

It's as simple as that. Now if only you could apply this to your personal life, wouldn't things be easy?

Step 3 – Optimizing user experience

If your website isn't user-friendly, congratulations! You've successfully pushed away millions of users already.

Terrified? No worries! Just avoid these 5 bad UX elements in your design and you'll be well on your way to major improvement:

1. Slow load time (the cardinal sin)
2. Error 404 (Miss Links, Miss Users)
3. Bad colour combinations (the quickest way to turn someone off)
4. No social sharing buttons (the biggest blunder in this digital age)
5. Contact details not found (what's the point of your website, then?)

Make a note of what you need to sort out, fix those problems, and then look at how it impacts your website data. You'll be surprised!

4.13 What details you can get from Web Analytics Tools?

Depending on how you plan to use the tools, you can get a lot of details from the data gathered by various Web Analytics tools. However, I've listed a few important details that you should have your eyes on.

1. **What do users search for?**

   You can find out the keywords that people search for, which lead them to your website via search results.

This helps you to:

❖ Draw parallels between keyword sets

❖ Understand what clicks (literally) and what doesn't

❖ Create content that interests users

In fact, the blog post you're reading right now was written by drawing insights from keyword variations that marketers searched for, i.e., "Web Analytics Tools".

2. **Best and Worst Performing Content:** Analyse and redesign your strategy based on your content performance report.

You can, for instance:

❖ Update the content of your articles

❖ **Repurpose Content** by adding elements such as Infographics, Slide shares, and Case Studies

❖ Try different promotional methods

❖ Use paid promotions to get an extra boost

Maybe, a new and refined approach designed with the help of insights from Web Analytics tools will make your content work!

And even when it doesn't, you'll definitely know about it from analytics tools.

3. **The Reason why people abandon your website:** When, where, and why does the user stop his/her journey on your website?

Knowing this is the best thing for an internet marketer. Instead of dismissing your entire strategy, just get rid of the element that isn't working. Is it the price? An annoying payment procedure or a compulsory action that the user doesn't want to take Identify that, redesign the experience thereon, and see the difference!

4. **Campaigns that Work:** John Wannamaker, one of the pioneers of Marketing, once said, "Half the money I spend on advertising is wasted; the trouble is, I don't know which half."

Well, you don't have that problem! Measure the success and failure of your online campaigns, understand what works, and experiment with new things.

Set up UTM tags on various URLs to tag which of the articles/campaigns are working. I use this approach whenever I'm doing a guest post. This helps me to know whether that post resulted in driving traffic to my blog or not.

Here is a Step-by-Step guide on UTM tag Builders.

5. **Location-based data:** Websites are universal. But not all businesses are.

If your business is one that caters to just one country or city, your Web Analytics needs to reflect data based on your location.

There's isn't much of a point if the website of a local store in Ohio gets most of its traffic from Ho-Chi Min Lane, Kolkata is there?

Here's why location is so important:

❖ Your customers look for offers and discounts based on your region's festive season or special occasions

❖ The language, tone, or topic dealt with in your content is relevant to the people of your place

❖ The sensibilities of your target audience differ from those of others

6. **The device that is used to view content on your website:** I know you've heard this before, and I'm sure you've read it everywhere, but I'll say it again Mobile is the present and the future. Do not ignore it.

In fact, I wouldn't be surprised if some of you are reading this on your phone or tablet. There are millions of people using mobile to access the internet and complete tasks on a regular basis (almost 53% of mobile-users worldwide). In fact, in the next couple of years, there will be a 10% increase in the number of people accessing the internet on their mobile phones!

Now can you imagine the damage you've done to your business if your website is not tailored to meet this requirement?

Check what devices and browsers your audience is most on, and optimize accordingly.

And now that you've understood what Web Analytics Tools can do for you, let's take a look at some of the best ones.

Google Analytics wins!

And here's why: will discuss more in this chapter following

● It helps you track your ROI

● The internal split testing feature is really cool

● It's got an awesome conversion tracking software

● Data integration with AdSense is a unique characteristic

● Report generation is simple and relevant

Besides this, I've listed 10 Web Analytics tools in two sections: Free and Paid.

4.14 5 Best Free Web Analytics Tools and their Features

1. **Clicky:** The best thing about Clicky is its simplified dashboard which makes it very convenient to check statistics and take quick actions. Plus, it offers:

❖ Real time data

❖ Twitter Search tracking

❖ **Cost:** Free. Pro version for $9.99/Month onwards

I particularly love their "Spy" feature, similar to the online feature on Google

Analytics. It's easy on the eye and offers a detailed view of what users are doing on your site, from where they were referred, the country they are in, and the browser and platform they are using to access your content. All of it, in real time

Ramsay Taplin gives a solid review of Clicky and goes to the extent of saying that it's better than Google Analytics! Blasphemy is what it is!

2. **Open Web Analytics (OWA)**

   Few features:

   ❖ Open source

   ❖ Self-Hosted

   ❖ Heat maps and mouse tracking

   ❖ Funnel Analytics

   ❖ **Cost:** Free

   And what makes it absolutely irresistible is that it's fast. You can see that special care has been taken to make information visually appealing and easier to read.

3. **Piwik:** Here's what Piwik's features are:

   ❖ Self-hosted (PHP, MySQL)

   ❖ Privacy and data ownership

   ❖ Customized dashboard, with adjustable widgets for displaying stats

   ❖ Faster interface and quicker insights

   ❖ Community support in 53 different languages

   ❖ **Cost:** Free; the Piwik pro starts at $65 per month

   Piwik, apart from giving you complete control over data, is really helpful if you intend to create your own plugins. This is basically because it's a plugin-based tool.

   Here, WebAppstorm has a detailed review of Piwik Analytics.

4. **Woopra:** These features of Woopra make it worth trying:

   ❖ Ability to have a live chat with visitors

   ❖ Its "Appconnect" feature

   ❖ Customized dashboard for each user

   ❖ **Cost:** Free (till 30000 visitors), Pay $80-$1200+ per month to get more.

   What I found the most interesting was its "Appconnect" feature. With it, you can utilize the services and features of 3rd party applications through Woopra. This can also include analysing user behaviour and triggering third party applications. For example, triggering a live chat based on certain user behaviour.

   Trey Ratcliff reviews Woopra in a quick video which you can check for a detailed review.

5. **Heap Analytics:** Here's what impressed me about Heap Analytics:

   ❖ User-friendly, with point-and-click interfaces

   ❖ Define custom events to use the Event Visualizer

   ❖ **Cost:** Free; Pro version starts $59-$399

This is a tool that efficiently tracks everything – video play, file downloads, form submissions, and literally anything you can place a tracking code on to! Heap records all bits of data and this helps you answer any question you have later.

Now we will move on to paid tools – the ones that bring out every marketer's deepest apprehensions. But trust me; the ones I'll be listing out will be worth every buck.

4.15 5 Best Paid Web Analytics Tools and their Features

1. **Mint:** So why should you pay for Mint?

   ❖ Self-hosted and downloadable analytics program

   ❖ Real-time stats

   ❖ Customizable, with a special feature called "Peppermill"

   ❖ Separate view for traffic generated from images

   ❖ **Cost:** One time cost of $30!

   Mint enables you to have more control over your site's analytics and the ease of its extremely user-friendly dashboard is a huge plus. It's quite refreshing! (No wonder they call it "Mint"!) It also uses native web charts instead of flash.

2. **Kissmetrics:** A few features of Kissmetrics:

   ❖ Analyzes changes in user behavior

   ❖ Timeline view of visitors

   ❖ Easy-to-understand visual format

   ❖ Track URLS by adding parameters

   ❖ **Cost:** $149/month with a 30-day free trial!

One of the most important features is "Path Report," which will help you analyse the pattern of user interaction with your site. Few features, which are essential to Google Analytics, like "Traffic Data" are missing in Kissmetrics.

Leslie Poston tells you How to combine Kissmetrics with Google Analytics.

3. **Mouseflow:** Here' are a few features from Mouse Flow:

   ❖ Mouse-tracking, Click, Movement, and Scroll heat maps

   ❖ Form and Funnel Analytics

   ❖ Performance and usability testing

❖ **Cost:** $19 per month

The scroll heat-map feature is the best, because it tells you how far your users scroll down through your content, with the complete mouse trail of a user. Besides, there are attention, geo, movement, and click heat maps as well.

4. **Crazy Egg:** Why Crazy Egg?

❖ Its "Scrollmap" tells you where visitors abandon the page and where you need to add elements to keep them interested

❖ Feature called "Confetti": Distinguish clicks based on categories like referral sources and search terms

❖ SEO update tracking

❖ Chart intelligence – Google analytics overlay listing published Google updates.

❖ **Cost:** $9-$99 per month (based on unique pages)

You can read the in-depth review of Crazy Egg by Seriously Simple Marketing.

5. **Clicktale:** Features which make Clicktale click

❖ Visual guide to user interactions, just like Crazy Egg

❖ Mouse move and click heatmaps

❖ JS errors tool and bounce report

❖ Form analytics

❖ **Cost:** Between $99-$790

❏❏

Chapter 5: WordPress Blogging

Advent of Blogging as a Social Media and Birth of CMS (Content Management System) The term 'blog' was coined in the year 1997 and the word's creation is attributed to the process of 'logging the web' as one browsed. The early 2000s was seen by a period of rampant spurge for blogs and by 2001 'meta-blogs' (blogs about blogging) made a substantial portion of the popularity of blogs.

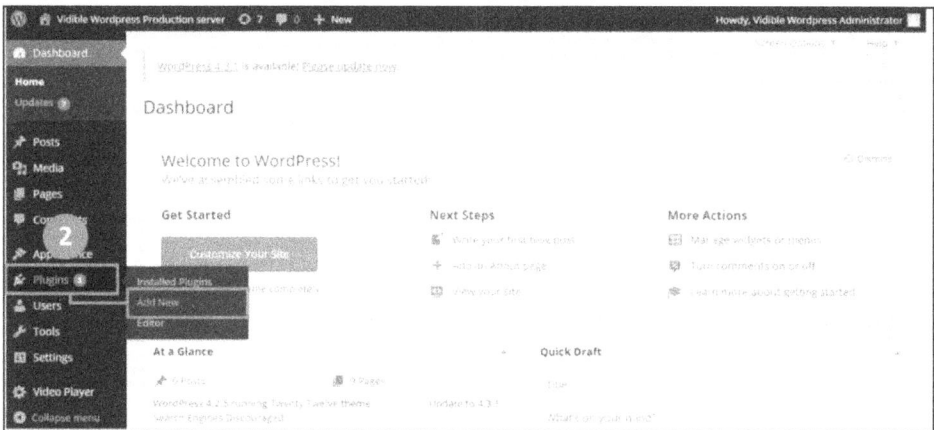

It was in 2003 that blogging platforms like Word Press got started which brought blogging to the mainstream by 2015 as 132 million Americans were seen reading blogs. Around this time the process of blogging increased even more with greater than 192 million blogs being online and active by the end of 2018. Thus the future of blogging in growing rapidly as it has become an integral part of one's online culture with the advent of social media and social networking which is seen in the last 5 years. Blogs are definitely going to have a bright future to the extent that the content available through blogs bring in growth and innovation which will need a system create content, manage content, publish content and present it finally. This gave birth to the process of CMS which facilitates the process of creation, management, distribution, publishing and discovery of corporate information. The most common use where-in CMS is put for is to manage web content and hence in some instances these systems are called web management systems.

5.1 WordPress Blogging – Leading to CMS

WordPress started in the year 2003 having a single bit code to facilitate the typography and writing skills with fewer users. Today it has grown tremendously to be the largest self-hosted blogging tool in the entire world adopted on millions of sites and used by tens of millions of users. WordPress is an open source project which is being worked on by hundreds of people and is free to use either for homepage or website without paying anybody licensing fee. The keystone element in the Marketing domain has been the word "Content". Significant changes have been brought about by technology for numerous processes in terms of supporting the collection and publication of information on varied forms and mediums. All these set of processes collectively are known as content management. Thus the term Content Management System has been evolved through the sheer necessity of managing and maintaining the enormous data available on blogs, Webpages and websites. The 3 most popular CMSes online are Drupal, Joomla and WordPress. All the three are open source and built on PHP + MySQL and differ significantly with respect to features, capability, flexibility and ease of use.

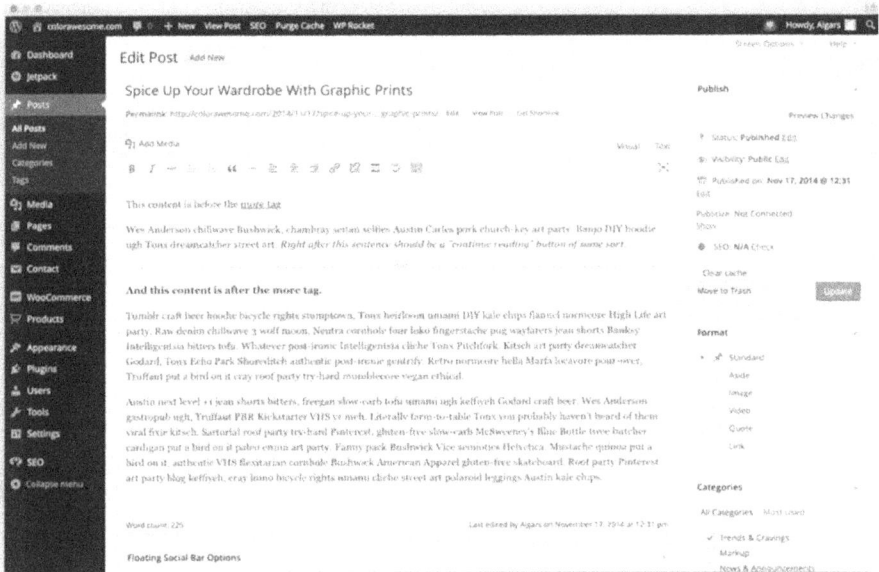

- **Advantages of WordPress** as a CMS Even traditionally less innovative organizational bodies like government owned businesses and funds (e.g. pension fund) could benefit from the developments in big data. Lev Manovich opined that humanists should use data analysis and visualization software in their daily work, so that they can combine quantitative and qualitative approaches in all their work.

- **Importance of Plugins While Using WordPress:** WordPress Plugins allows easy modification, customization, and enhancement to a WordPress blog. Instead of changing the core programming of WordPress, you can add functionality with WordPress Plugins. Plugins can extend WordPress to do almost anything you can imagine and primarily supports in enhancing WordPress as a CMS.

- **Importance of Widgets While Using WordPress:** Widgets were originally designed to provide a simple and easy-to-use way of giving design and structure control of the WordPress Theme to the user, which is now available on properly "widgetized" WordPress Themes to include the header, footer, and elsewhere in the WordPress design and structure5. Widgets primarily support in enhancing the look and feel of the webpages.

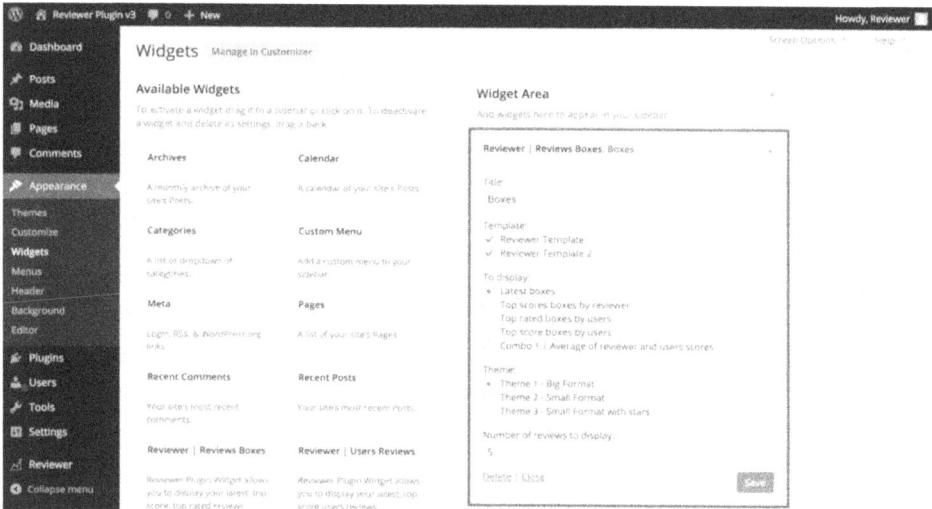

- **Ease of Use While Using WordPress:** It is an easy-to-use authoring environment setting especially designed to work like Word. It primarily supports creating new pages and updating content without using the technical platform of HTML. Plugins are tools which extend the functionality of WordPress. The core of WordPress is designed to be lean, to maximize flexibility and minimize code bloat. Plugins offer custom functions and features so that each user can tailor their site to their specific needs. Look & Feel - The web site can be kept fresh by easily changing the site layout and appearance by swapping themes. One can plan layouts for holidays or special events etc. – all by clicking on one button.

- **Ease of Use While Using WordPress:** WordPress themes are responsive themes that automatically adjust the layout to fit into mobile screens. This eliminates the need to create a separate website to meet mobile/smart phone requirements.

- **Ultimate in SEO Friendliness:** WordPress code is streamlined without excessive HTML code that Google finds very easy to index. Also, it is relatively simple to customize every page to give you the highest possible probability of getting your pages in high search results positions. In addition, there are plugins that help in refining the process even further which would be discussed in the later section. WordPress can enhance search engine rankings there by supporting in showing on the first pages of search results using Google or Yahoo.

5.2 WordPress & SEO in Digital Marketing

Over 6 million websites with over 8 billion Webpages constitute what is now called the World Wide Web. In order that the desired customer makes his way into our website, it is important that our webpage appears in the Search Engine Results Page (SERP) when the customer searches for a keyword or phrase. All search engines – Google, Bing, Yahoo, have developed algorithms which enable the visitor to zone into those links that are mostly likely to provide him additional information and content based on relevance and authority. This process in general is called SEO. SEO helps improve the websites interaction with the users and the search engine. SEO supports onsite visibility in search engines by appropriate usage of keywords, making the content the most relevant to the users. SEO also provides offsite advantage to the website by building authority to the website via link building i.e. the more other websites offer my website by backlinks, the more the authority my website gains. As mentioned earlier Word Press code is streamlined without excessive HTML code that Google finds very easy to index. However, in order to make it more effective, there are quite a large number of plugins that can further help in improving the position of the page in search results. Built-in Features: WordPress encourages the web designer to make use of the menu and the categories so that each page can address a particular topic or subject.

The use of categories helps in further classifying the pages. This enables the website creator to use keywords precisely in each of the pages and subcategories which help the google spider to index each page accurately and thus enable a better search rank. WordPress also allows the creator to caption and give an alternate text to multimedia that further aids the search engine spider. Creations of tags and slugs are yet another feature that is quite simple to implement.

5.3 Role of WordPress in Digital Marketing

Digital marketing landscape has gained tremendous importance during the last decade and has played a pivotal role in creating 'relationship marketing'. Technology advances have punctuated the evolution of communication of businesses with their customers. What is important to note is that none of these later advances in communication has actually depreciated the ones that came before. In fact they have actually supplemented them. Even today, the earliest forms of communication are still around and thriving. The advent of newer technologies has been exploited by marketers to use Digital marketing as a new tool to woo their customers. Digital marketing has also been bolstered with the proliferation & penetration of mobile phones. Over 250 million Indians are currently using phones to browse the internet. Digital Marketing has been built around the emerging technologies – be it internet expansion or the mobile revolution. The website has become the center of this universe with various technologies deployed to lure the customers to it.

Therefore, the Key Requirements for a Comprehensive Digital Marketing Solution is that it should enable

- Search Engine Optimization
- Search Engine Marketing
- Social Media Marketing

Having attracted the prospect, it then becomes important that the customer is engaged on the website that could result in some pre-determined call to action like download, purchase etc. With "content" being the core creative activity of increasing customer engagement, it is imperative that an easy yet comprehensive solution be available that simultaneously performs the two tasks of creating the required content and enabling users at all levels – experts to novices - in propagating the content to the customers at large. Figure shown below: It is in this context that we have examined the various CMSes. WordPress **"the darling of google"** is fundamentally a CMS package that provides the fundamental benefits to both a novice and an expert in web designing.

Value of Plugins and its Importance While Using WordPress for SEO, SEM & SMM A few Plugins that aid SEO plugins in WordPress are:

WordPress SEO Plugin by Yoast This plugin is written from the ground up by Joost de Valk and his team at Yoast to improve your site's SEO on all needed aspects. While this WordPress SEO plugin goes the extra mile to take care of all the technical optimization, it first and foremost helps you write better content. WordPress SEO forces you to choose a focus keyword when you're writing your articles, and then makes sure you use that focus keyword everywhere. Using the snippet preview you can see a rendering of what your post or page will look like in the search results, whether your title is too long or too short and your Meta description makes sense in the context of a search result. This way the plugin will help you not only increase rankings but also increase the click through for organic search results. In addition to the above plugins which actively help in SEO, there are a lot of plugins that enhance the functionality of WordPress without affecting SEO. We have listed 10 such plugins that make using WordPress a great experience. Some of the plugins also help in search engine marketing and social media marketing.

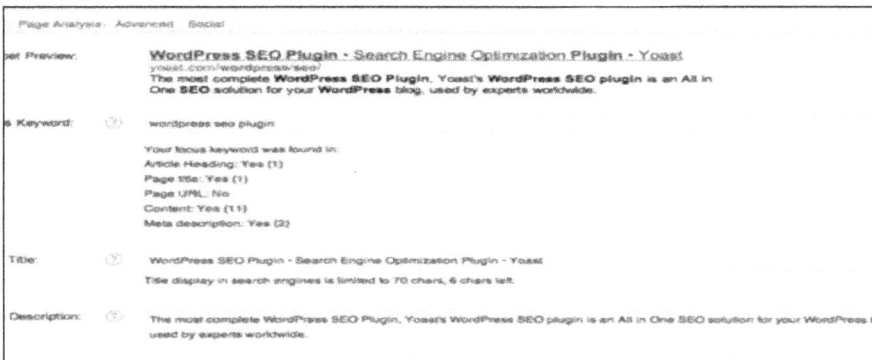

NextGen Gallery and Lightbox plus NextGen are plugins for image gallery management. You can define lots of things such as the image's title and alt tags, which solves any SEO image problems. The two plugins have been combined into one entry because they work hand-in-hand. Lightbox Plus uses Color box – a lightweight Query image gallery script that is the friendliest for performance and doesn't hinder on-page SEO. Lightbox Plus offers a lot more options for the appearance and behavior of Lightbox's execution.

5.4 NextGen Gallery

Lightbox Plus

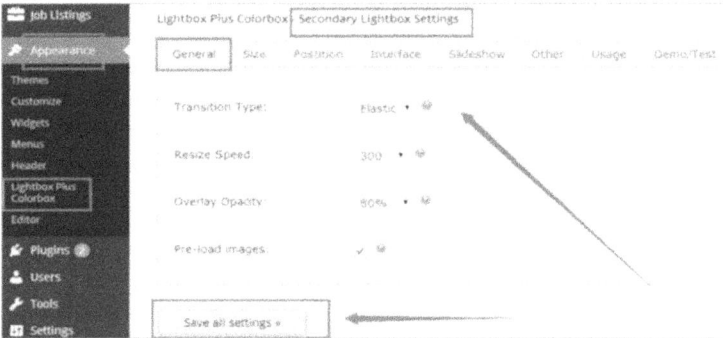

- **Meta Slider:** Meta Slider is the most popular slideshow plugin for WordPress. Creating slideshows with Meta Slider is fast and easy Meta Slider enables creation of SEO optimized responsive slideshows with Nivo Slider, Flex Slider, Coin Slider and Responsive Slides.

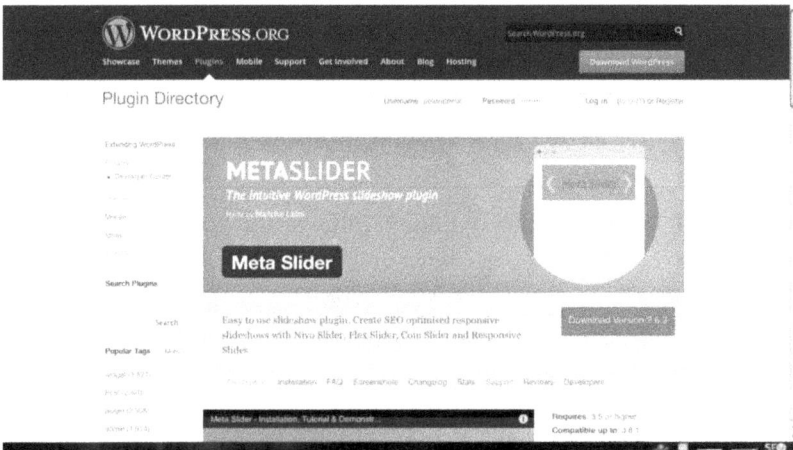

Simple Page Sidebars This plugin gives WordPress users, designers, and developers the ability to assign custom sidebars to individual pages--without making any template changes. Existing sidebars can also be assigned in quick edit and bulk edit modes, saving time. Simple Page Sidebars aims for basic, core-like functionality and integration that is easy to use - it utilizes built-in WordPress caching, so your site won't be bogged down with additional queries. Simple Page Sidebars also ships with a "Widget Area" widget for pulling all the widgets from one sidebar into another.

Contact Form is another plugin which can manage multiple contact forms embedded with a webpage. One can easily customize the form and the mail contents flexibly with simple markup. The form supports Ajax powered submitting, CAPTCHA, for spam filtering and so on. Moreover this plugin has add-ons like Contact 7 Skins plugin which makes it easy for the WP user to customize the look & feel of the contact form. By using Flamingo – another plugin, the user can track the user's details when they comment on a page.

Plugins for SEM in Digital Marketing The process of SEO to be really effective takes considerable time and effort. In the meanwhile, the website publisher has an option of projecting his website by incurring some expenses in promoting his site by advertising on various sites including search results page on a Cost per Mille (CPM) or Cost per Click (CPC) basis. It then necessitates creation of landing page. While WP has the capability, there are several plugins that can make the task easier and 'professional.

WordPress Landing Pages/WordPress Calls to Action/WordPress Leads While Landing pages plugin is a standalone, combined with the other two enhances the capabilities and effectiveness of the landing page and thus conversion.

SMM in Digital Marketing With the explosion of Social media with over 5000 registered social media sites, peer group interaction has started dominating the decision making process of the individual customer. The move from WOM to "Word of Keyboard" is pretty apparent. There are quite a number of social media plugins and also plugins that can display your twitter feed, Facebook like box, google+ reference and social media icons.

WordPress Social Media Feather This plugin is a super lightweight free social media WordPress plugin that allows WP user to quickly add social sharing and following features to all pages. The differentiating feature of this plugin is its focus on simplicity, performance and unobtrusive impact.

Facebook like Box Widget This plugin enables Facebook Page owners to attract and gain Likes & Recommendation Comments from their own website. The Like Box enables users to: see how many users already like this page, and which of their friends like it too, read recent posts from the page and like the page with one click, without needing to visit the page.

Google+ Plugin This plugin allows WordPress user to post directly from G+ to your WordPress website. The Google+ plugin supports post formats so a hash tag system can be used to decide on the post format.

WordPress Responsive themes are made in a way to handle the requirements of all the 3 screens.

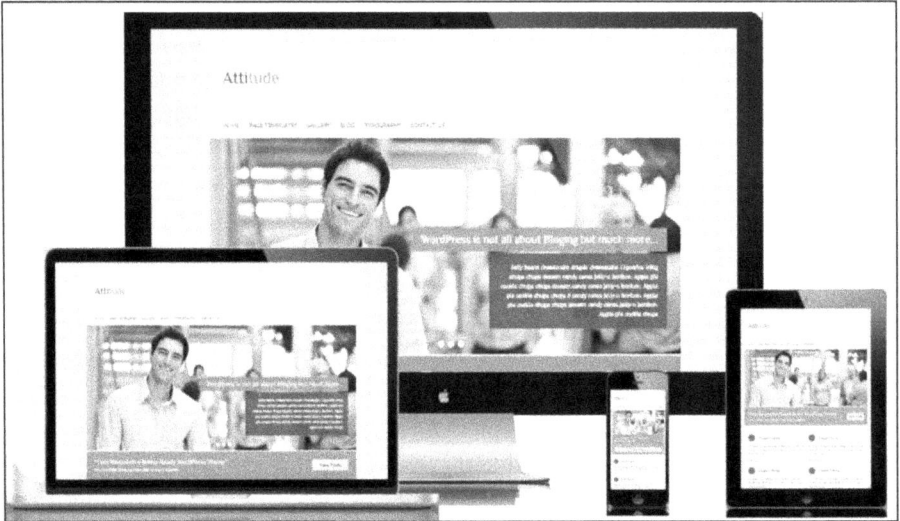

Example: Most smart TVs today have built in browsers which handle websites just like the standard internet browsers. Mobile phones, given the screen size would show distortion in earlier web-designs and hence there was a need for creating sites exclusively for mobile web browsing. However responsive themes from Word Press have surmounted this shortcoming and the webpage automatically arranges itself within the screen. This is true even for different screen resolutions in desktops and PCs.

The WP advent of Responsive themes in website has truly extended the reach to customers irrespective of the devises they use thus enabling uniformity and consistency. Responsive Theme is a flexible foundation with fluid grid system that adapts a website to mobile devices and the desktop or any other viewing environment. Advent being a calendar inbuilt system manages the content on webpage as per the exact requirement of the business.

WordPress is responsible for 24.5 % of the top million websites worldwide representing small, medium and big business because of its cheap development cost and readily available templates on open sources. If you are using WordPress, you are in company alongside. The New York Times, Wall Street Journal's Speakeasy, Ford, New York University Library, CNN, Harvard Law School, Ben & Jerry, People Magazine, NASA .Some of the other leading organizations like Bata, CNN, and Huffington Post also use WordPress to develop their website or blogs. What is even more surprising is that there are quite a few celebrities who use WordPress like Usain Bolt, The Rolling Stones, Snoop Dogg, and Bill Cosby.

This is clearly an indication of the versatility of WordPress that it can cater to such varied segments of users. As of March 2012, WordPress is on 72.4 million sites in the world. WordPress.com hosts about half of them. As of a moment today, WordPress 3.3, the latest version, has been downloaded 12,179,538 times – which is phenomenal by itself if you look at the number of versions released to date.

Our study clearly brings out the simplicity, the versatility and the value of the various plugins that go a long way in enhancing the basic CMS software – a definite advantage with respect to the other CMSes and Digital Marketing as a whole.

With newer versions of WordPress coming out almost every month, the numbers of developers are increasing every day. This would culminate in higher and more sophisticated versions of plugins. We look forward to study this evolution during the coming years.

5.5 Digital Marketing- A great tool for Market Research

Marketing research is "the process or set of processes that links the consumers, customers, and end users to the marketer through information- information used to identify and define marketing opportunities and problems; generate, refine, and evaluate marketing actions; monitor marketing performance; and improve understanding of marketing as a process. Marketing research specifies the information required to address these issues, designs the method for collecting information, manages and implements the data collection process, analyzes the results, and communicates the findings and their implications.

What is Online Market Research?

A set of strategies used by various companies irrespective of their business volume or scale of their business operations to determine how their products are performing on the market and with individual customers. Strategies Product Performance Trends Wider audience More information on target audience like their age bracket, choice of products, Frequency of buying so on and so forth..

Advantages of Internet Surveys

- Convenient
- Less expensive/Inexpensive depending on the scale
- Accurate Automation

Why market research?

You need few insights to decide on your business/product strategies on how, when, what to launch in the market to gain maximum revenue out of this campaign/drive/ product cycle.

Online VS Offline Research

Offline High cost Need interviewer to collecting Less flexibility for respondent High chance of error Time consuming Limited research area Need to find specific criteria Cannot implement Logics Online Low cost Image and video availability Complex questionnaire handling Inconsistence answer elimination Speed delivery Error free No interviewer Implement Logics, therefore online market surveys are often hassle-free provided it has good analytics embedded in it to simplify the complex and large databases.

Why Online Research?

The Era OF Multiple Gadgets Connected 25.2% from Featured Phone, 49.1% Accessing from Desktop PC, 71.3% from their Smartphone, 73% Accessing from Laptop, 26.3% from their Tablet.

5.6 Online Research Flow

Online Survey Process

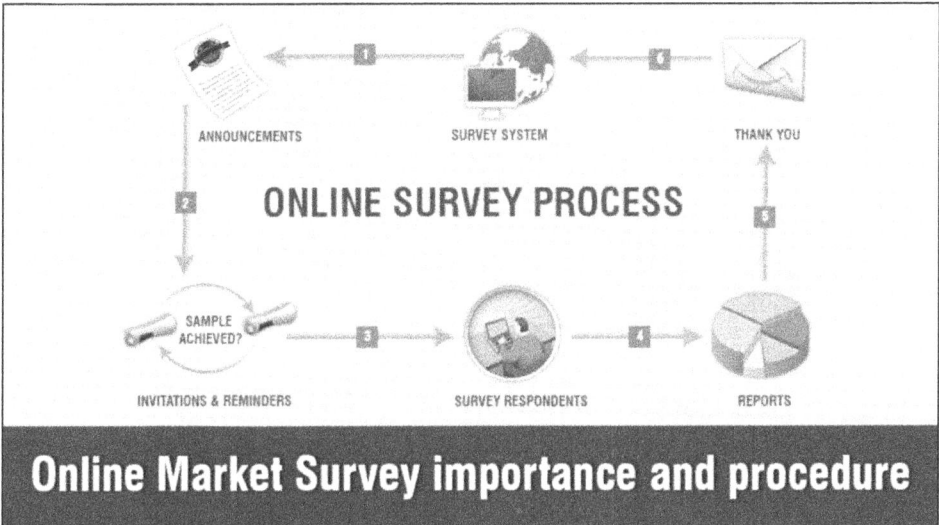

ANNOUNCEMENTS   SURVEY SYSTEM   THANK YOU

ONLINE SURVEY PROCESS

SAMPLE ACHIEVED?

INVITATIONS & REMINDERS   SURVEY RESPONDENTS   REPORTS

Online Market Survey importance and procedure

1. **Clarify Your Research Objectives:** All research begins by defining the goals of the study. What do you want to learn by conducting an online survey? Commit the goals to writing. Doing so will help to keep your survey focused. The number one reason for the failure of surveys is a lack of well-defined objectives. Poorly defined objectives yields excessively long surveys and ambiguous results. Clarify your research objectives to focus on the important information needed for decision making. The online survey itself should be designed to directly address the research goals. In other words, stay away from "fishing expeditions".

2. **Decide on a Sampling Method:** Proper sampling is essential for all research. If you select the wrong people, then the results will not reflect the true attitudes of the population. If you choose the right people, then the results will provide a solid foundation for decision making. The goal in sampling is to select people who represent the population.

   Equally important is to get a high response rate, if the response rates it too low; we question the reliability of the data. Are the responders in some way different from the non-responders? So it's extremely important to choose a sampling method that maximizes response rate.

   Sending e-mail invitations seems to be the only method that produces high (but wildly varying) response rates (15%-80%). Of course, this requires that you have the e-mail addresses of the sample. We strongly advise you not to send "spam". While StatPac can be used to send bulk e-mail to any e-mail list, we suggest that you send e-mail only to people with whom you've had previous contact.

Publishing the URL to a web survey in written form (e.g., newsletters, newspapers, postcards, letters, etc.) will likely elicit a low response rate (<5%). Additionally, pop-up or pop-under windows also get poor response (typically 2%-4%).

One sampling method that appears to work on the Internet is called a snowball sample. In the e-mail invitation, you ask potential respondents to forward the e-mail invitation to other people who might also be interested in the topic. The potential for bias is high with a snowball sample, so we discourage the use of this method. However, it may be appropriate for some surveys, especially when the researcher has a severely limited e-mail list.

There are four things that most affect response rates:

(i) The interest of the respondent in your research topic

(ii) The quality of the invitation

(iii) The use of an incentive

(iv) The number of questions asked

3. **Questionnaire Design:** Internet surveys are more critical than paper and pencil surveys. Our research has shown that an online survey must be shorter than traditional mail questionnaires. Respondents' willingness to participate and complete a questionnaire depends heavily on its length. Thus, when conducting a online survey, it becomes imperative to ask as few questions as necessary to get the information you need.

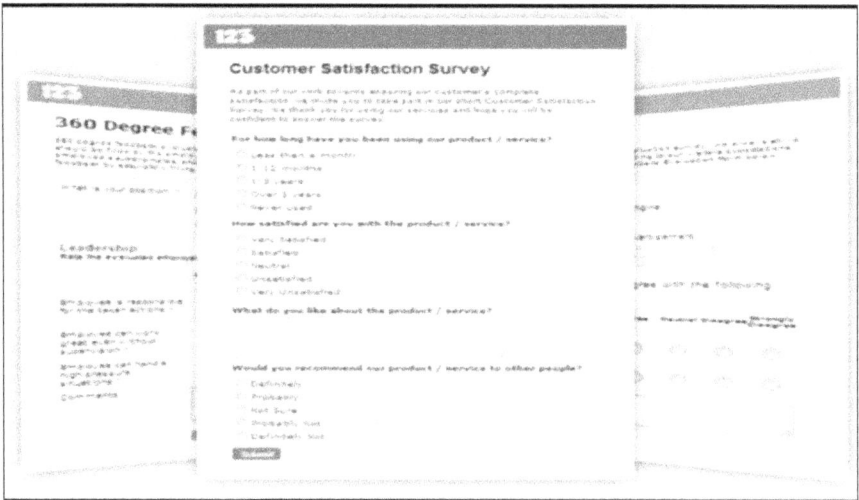

4. **Invite the Sample to Participate:** In a typical online survey, potential respondents are sent an e-mail inviting them to participate by clicking on a link in the e-mail. While you can use any e-mail program to send the invitations, StatPac for Windows can customize each e-mail with a personal greeting or other information you want to be included. More importantly, it can serialize each e-mail with an ID number in order to track who responded and who didn't.

The e-mail invitation you send can be thought of as a "sales pitch". Sell the potential respondent on why they should complete your questionnaire. What benefit will they receive by completing the questionnaire? One way to provide a benefit is to offer an incentive. Potential incentives are drawings for prizes, donations to charities, a small tangible gift, cash, and a copy of the results. Altruistic appeals are usually not effective.

5. **Host Your Surveys on the Internet:** You need access to a server to host your surveys on the Internet. Users of our software can host their surveys on their own Web site or our Web site (for free). StatPac for Windows software has selections to use our free server.

If you are using the free version, the link to your survey will be:

http://take-survey.com/guest/YourSurveyName.htm   or
https://www.take-survey.com/guest/YourSurveyName.htm   (SSL secure)

If you are using the registered version, you can create a private folder on our server so the link will be:

http://take-survey.com/PrivateFolderName/YourSurveyName.htm   or
https://www.take-survey.com/PrivateFolderName/YourSurveyName.htm (SSL secure)

Note 1: Our server is UNIX based so all links are case sensitive.
Note 2: SSL secure surveys must contain the www as part of the link.

All the server management tools are built into StatPac. You'll be able to upload surveys and download responses. Apart from StatPac www.Surveymonkey.com is another widely used and one of the most popular online survey platforms globally with its auto enabled analytics.

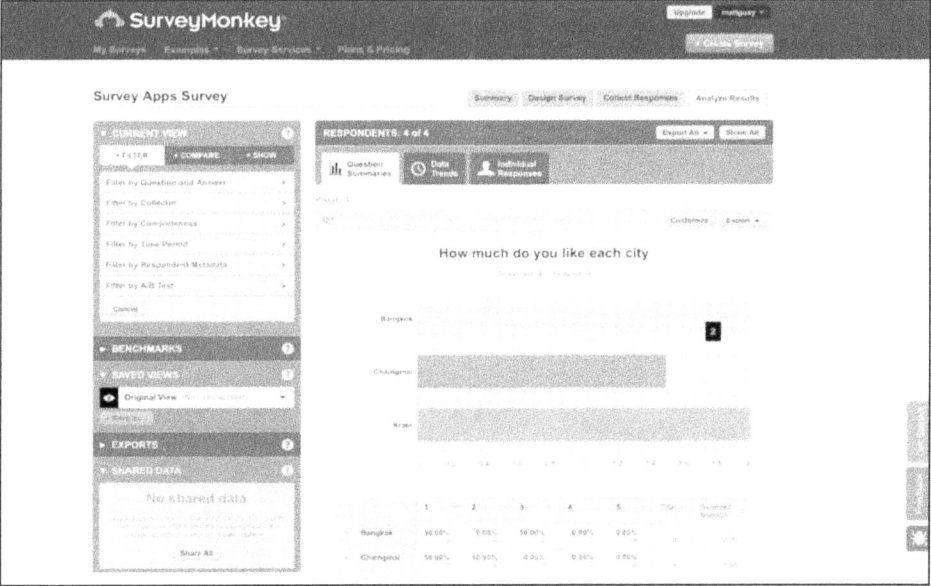

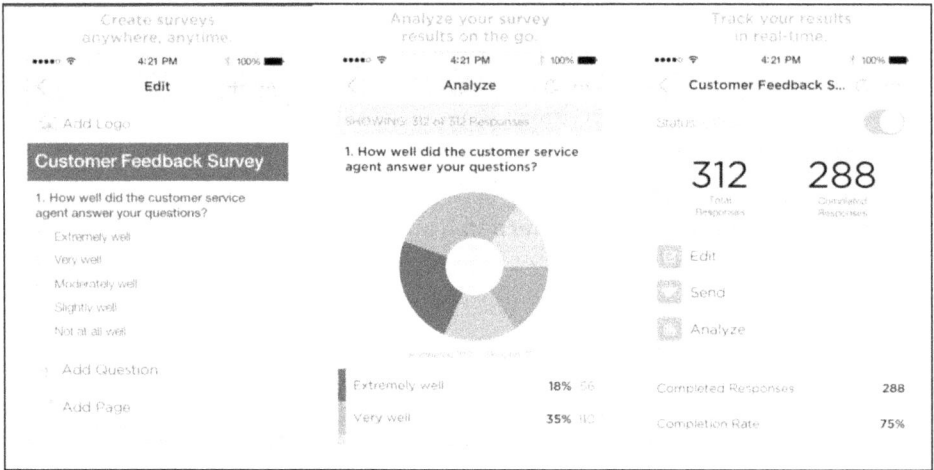

6. **Data Verification and Collection:** Internet surveys are different from paper and pencil questionnaires. Data checking and verification are performed immediately while the respondent is taking the survey. All the data is captured electronically and no manual data entry is involved.

There are two basic methods of capturing the data electronically. The first method is by e-mail. When a respondent completes a survey his or her answers are e-mailed to you and the data is captured from the e-mail. The e-mail is method is not frequently used. The second method is to store responses in a file on the server and then download all of them to your local computer at once. The file method is recommended because all the data is kept on the server and it uses fewer Internet resources. If you have more specific questions about the technical aspects of Internet surveys please see our frequently asked questions.

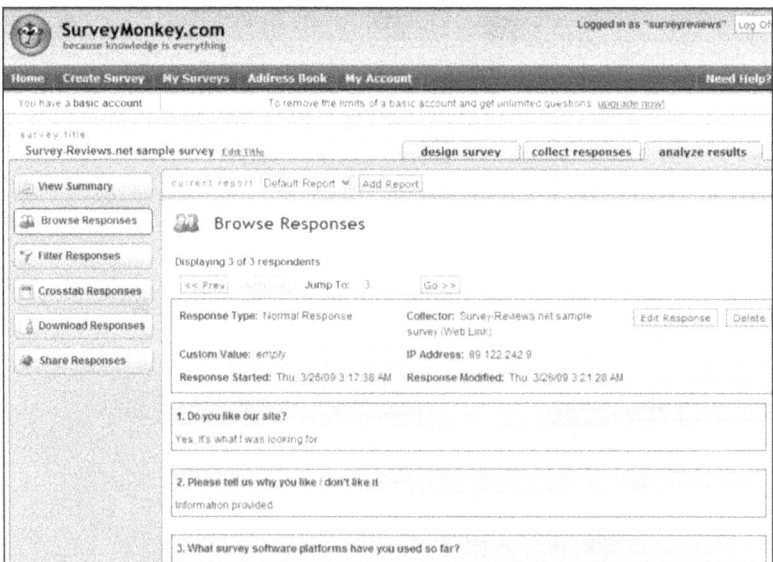

7. **Statistical Analysis Reports:** The whole idea behind doing surveys is to get decision making information... which means clear and comprehensive reports. Look for software that creates reports as MS Word documents so you can easily customize the output.

Typical reports include "top-line" frequencies with graphics, and crosstab and banner tables that show your key variables broken down by the demographics of the sample. Banner tables give the information you need to identify opportunities and to make knowledgeable decisions based on the data.

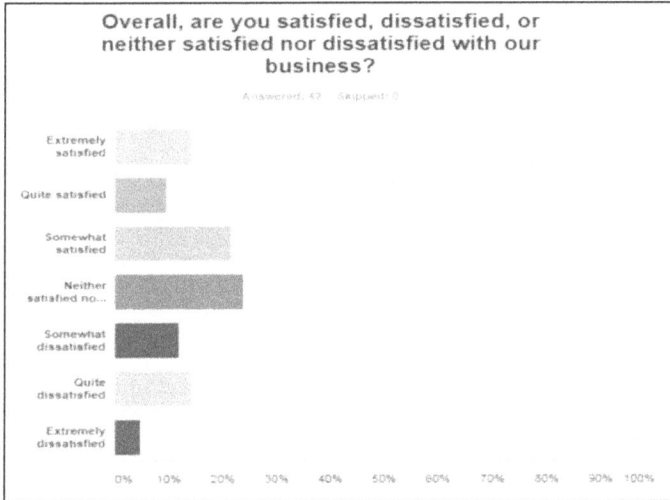

5.7 Copy write- An art or science?

Copywriting is critical for success online in the current digital age. Design, content marketing, SEO, and growth hacking are all parts of a complete digital marketing plan, but copywriting is the glue that ties it all together. Copy gives your design meaning and lays the foundation for your content marketing, SEO, and growth hacking. Writing better copy enables you to convert more readers into customers, and we wanted to provide a guide that would give you an advantage when writing copies both on and offline.

Copywriting is the art and science of writing copy *(words used on web pages, ads, promotional materials, etc.)* that sells your product or service and convinces prospective customers to take action. In many ways, it's like hiring one salesman to reach all of your customers. A sales team contacts customers' one at a time; a copywriter reaches all of them at once through billboards, magazine ads, sales letters, blog posts, and more.

Copywriting is the act of writing text for the purpose of advertising or other forms of marketing. The product, called copy, is written content that aims to increase brand awareness and ultimately persuade a person or group to take a particular action.

Copywritershelpcreate billboards, brochures, catalogs, jingle lyrics, magazine and newspaper advertisements, sales letters and other direct mail, scripts for television or radio commercials, taglines, white papers and other marketing communications.

They are generally known as website content writers if their work appears mostly on the Internet. A content writer helps create online advertisements, web pages, email newsletters, blog posts and social media.

Cross discipline copywriters who look at the wider context of their work are called digital copywriters. The distinction is that these individuals consider the mechanics of the user journey, the external links that are included in the copy for search engine optimization and are highly focused towards creating online sales and dealing with technical issues such as bounce rate.

One of the easiest ways to answer — what does a copywriter do? — is to say, "You know all the stuff you get in your mailbox (mostly advertisement and promotional materials)?"

"Well, a copywriter wrote that. Copywriters also write other marketing materials like websites, emails, brochures, catalogues, and more."

If you're interested in copywriting, it's probably because you heard:

1. It's a great way to make money working at home.

2. You can be up-and-running quickly with very little investment.

3. A formal education is not required.

All of these things are true.

In fact, professional copywriting skills continue to be in high demand and copywriting jobs are some of the highest paid projects for freelance writers.

Many copywriters make six-figures working full-time. Others only work part-time, but enjoy a full-time income. The best part is, there is still plenty of room in this huge and expanding industry.

So what is copywriting?

Copywriting is the process of writing advertising promotional materials. Copywriters are responsible for the text on brochures, billboards, websites, emails, advertisements, catalogues, and more. This text is known as "copy." Copy is everywhere — it's part of a $2.3 trillion industry worldwide.

Unlike news or editorial writing, copywriting is all about getting the reader to take action. That action might be to purchase, opt-in, from a company or engage with a product, service, or company.

That's why a copywriter is often referred to as "a salesman in print."

Copywriting should not be confused with "copyright." Copyright means an individual or company has the exclusive legal right to reproduce, publish, sell, or distribute someone's work (such as books, music, artistic items). The purpose of a copyright is to protect that material and prevent illegal use of it by unauthorized agents. The owner designates the material is copyrighted with the symbol.

5.8 Copyright: A Globally Practiced Method to Prevent Plagiarism and Control Data Duplicity

What is copyright and why it is important?

Copyright is a legal right created by the law of a country that grants the creator of original work exclusive rights for its use and distribution. This is usually only for a limited time. The exclusive rights are not absolute but limited by limitations and exceptions to copyright law, including fair use. Copyright legally protects an author's works — and, therefore, is vitally important to book publishing livelihoods. According to the U.S. government, "Copyright is a form of protection grounded in the U.S. Constitution and granted by law for original works of authorship fixed in a tangible medium of expression."

What is NOT protectable under copyright provisions?

•Ideas • Facts • Titles • Names • Short phrases/Blank forms "Work Made for Hire?" etc.

It's either prepared by an employee within the scope of his or her employment, or a work specially ordered or commissioned by express written agreement.

Exclusive Rights Granted by court of law:

1. Reproduce phone records

2. Prepare derivative works

3. Distribute by sale rental, lease, or lending

4. Publicly perform literary, musical, dramatic, and choreographic works, pantomimes, and motion pictures and other audio-visual works

5. Publicly display literary, musical, dramatic, and choreographic works, pantomimes, and motion pictures and other audio-visual works

6. Publicly perform sound recordings, by digital audio transmission

Why to Register?

1. Necessary for enforcement

2. Claim Statutory damages (no need to prove Actual Damages) ENFORCEMENT

3. INFRINGEMENT (When your stuff is used without your permission)

4. DMCA – Take Down notices

5. PLATFORM-Specific Rules

Copyright in Social Media

1. Photographs

2. Authorship (Who owns the photo?)

3. People in the background (Get waivers?)

4. Trademarks in the background? (Get release?)

5. Text & links

6. Attribution

7. Is it OK to post on Twitter / Facebook / LinkedIn / Instagram?

The purpose and character of the use, including whether such use is of a commercial nature or is for non-profit educational purposes The nature of the copyrighted work; The amount and substantiality of the portion used in relation to the copyrighted work as a whole and The effect of the use upon the potential market for or value of the copyrighted work.

Ownership & Management Tips one thing I have learned: my clients should have consulted me first!

● Identify and document

● Identify Copyright assets early

● Protect through registration and contracts

● Use "Work-made-for-hire" Language for employees, contractors

Why copyright is important for online enterprises

Copyright laws protect certain kinds of original works. Any creation that is fixed in a recording medium -- whether paper, compact disc, film or digital -- is subject to copyright. The industries dealing with copyrighted material such as books, newspapers, recorded music, movies and software in 2002 made up more than 5 percent of the U.S. gross national product and totaled almost $350 billion. This high value results from the protection copyright laws give to the owners of the underlying intellectual property.

Copyright was initially relevant primarily to published and sold works. The Internet has changed the way in which people seek and publish information, making it important to understand the ways in which copyright laws affect Internet use. Internet-based businesses and businesses that use the Internet for promotion and publication of information should be aware not only of how to avoid copyright infringement, but also of the protections copyright laws afford to website operators.

Definitions

A key part of copyright law defines what creators can protect with copyright. Copyright comes into effect automatically when the author permanently fixes an original work on a recording medium. Such works include literature, music, choreography, pictures, sculpture, movies, software and architectural works. The originators or discoverers of facts, ideas, news, methods or processes can't copyright them, and any applicable intellectual property rights are governed by patent law.

Control

Copyright laws let creators control their works. By assigning exclusive rights to copyright holders, the laws ensure that only the originators and those who receive their permission can copy, perform or change the works. Control encourages artists of all disciplines to create original works that enrich public life. American copyright law came about to benefit the public from the original works of authors.

Income

By assigning the exclusive right to copy and distribute original works to creators, copyright laws ensure that the holders of the copyright can earn income from their work. Authors may sell, rent or license their own works or give permission to others to use them and collect royalties. Such income allows creators to continue their activities and produce new works.

Fair Use

In addition to establishing what works may be protected and assigning exclusive rights, copyright laws include fair use as a limitation on copyright. Members of the public may reproduce small sections of a copyrighted work for the purposes of criticism, teaching, commentary or research. Fair use of copyrighted material is generally non-commercial, restricted to a small part of the work and limited to activities that do not substantially affect the commercial value of the work. The "Fair Use Doctrine" provides an exception to copyright laws for scholarly and educational purposes. Fair use permits people to take limited excerpts of works for articles, critiques and other public services. Parodies of copyrighted works are also generally protected. There is no standard excerpt that is permissible under law, and guidelines about fair use are relatively unspecific. If your small business has had copyrighted material copied from your website, courts examine the purpose of the use of copyrighted work, the financial effect the use has on the copyright holder, the degree to which an item was excerpted and the nature of the copyrighted work when determining whether a violation has occurred. For example, a person cannot excerpt a photo, so re-posting a photo from your website might constitute copyright infringement, but excerpting a line from a book you sale might not.

Infringement

Copyright law defines what constitutes infringement and specifies the applicable penalties. While infringement by making physical copies is a clear violation, copyright violations in a digital environment required the extra clarifications provided by the Digital Millennium Copyright Act of 1998. The law provides for a notification procedure for suspected copyright infringement and makes it illegal to circumvent copyright measures taken by copyright holders.

Copyright Law Basics

Copyright protection is automatic for any creative work that is created after 1978 and fixed in some tangible form. You don't have to display a copyright symbol or register rights to your item for it to receive copyright protection. For this reason, you should assume all content on the Web is copyrighted unless it explicitly states otherwise. Copyright laws are federal laws, which mean you generally have to sue in federal court if someone violates your copyrights. If someone from another country steals your items -- an increasingly common phenomenon given the worldwide reach of the Internet -- it can be extremely difficult to enforce your copyright protection.

Digital Millennium Copyright Act

The Digital Millennium Copyright Act removes liability from websites whose users commit copyright infringement so long as the websites take the material down. This means that even if YouTube or Facebook allows you to upload something on your small business page, you could still be committing copyright infringement and the material can be removed. Some Internet users believe that if they state that no copyright infringement was intended they might escape liability. For example, people frequently re-post songs on YouTube with a disclaimer stating they are not violating copyright laws. This does not, however, absolve users from liability, so it is important to check the copyright status of any material you upload to a website.

Illegal Downloads

Illegal downloads have cost musicians, authors and other creative professionals millions of dollars. It is illegal to download or upload copyrighted material, such as books, songs and movies without the explicit permission of the copyright holder. The Recording Industry Association of America has sued many individuals for illegal downloads. If you plan to use music on your business website, ensure that you obtain the music legally and that you have permission to use the music.

Preventing Infringement

The simplest way to avoid infringing on another person or business' copyrights is to seek permission to use anything that is not yours. Even using a photographer's photo on a personal blog could constitute copyright infringement. If you are concerned about your copyrights being infringed upon, insert watermarks and upload material in formats that are difficult to copyright, PDF files. There is no guaranteed method for preventing infringement, but registering your copyrights and prominently displaying a copyright symbol can deter would-be thieves.

The Effects of Copyright Violation

Copyright violations generally occur when one party utilizes another party's creative or scientific work without his permission. The U.S. Copyright Right Act makes copyright violation a federal crime. It also allows injured parties to file civil lawsuits against copyright violators to recover money damages. Many businesses rely on copyrights for their means of revenue. Copyright laws carry stiff penalties to protect creators of unique works, and to safeguard the economic benefits they deliver for society.

Economics

Copyright and intellectual property violations cost U.S. businesses approximately $28 billion yearly and deprive the U.S. economy of approximately 2.1 million jobs. Copyright violations also result in lower quality consumer goods through substandard counterfeit products. The U.S. government suffers tax revenue losses from illegal counterfeit sales and also must spend money on copyright enforcement efforts.

Penalties

Copyright violations can result in significant legal penalties. Copyright violators can be held liable for civil damages, court costs, and attorneys' fees. Separate criminal fines of up to $250,000 per offense, and even jail time, may also apply. Employees can also face employment discipline and discharge for violating copyright laws, and students who violate copyrights can face disciplinary actions by college ethics committees.

How Not to Violate Copyright Laws

Copyright laws protect the rights of people who create or own creative works such as books, articles, movies and photographs. It might seem as though avoiding copyright infringement should be as simple as not taking someone else's work and claiming it as your own, but copyright laws offer broad protections to copyright holders. Business owners unfamiliar with copyright laws may inadvertently violate another person's copyright, and this violation can carry stiff penalties.

Using Others' Works

Any original, creative work is eligible for copyright protection, and copyright holders don't have to place a copyright symbol on the item or register the copyright to claim copyright infringement. Consequently, any time you use any item that is not yours, you may be violating copyright laws. For example, using an image from someone's website or a search engine on your own website could be copyright infringement. Copying a work, even for personal use -- such as making a copy of a book to distribute in a business meeting -- can also be copyright infringement. The sure-fire recipe for avoiding copyright infringement is to never use any work that is not yours without getting permission to do so.

Contacting Copyright Holders

If you find a creative item you want to use, you'll need to contact the copyright holder to get permission. Search for the copyrighted item on the U.S. Copyright Office website to locate the copyright holder. While not all copyrighted items are registered, if it is registered, this resource can help you locate the owner. You can also contact site owners or publishing and distribution companies for creative works such as books and videos. You'll need to get explicit, written permission to use the item, and the copyright holder can charge you a licensing fee for your use.

Fair Use

Fair use is an exception to copyright laws that allows people to use limited excerpts for scholarly, non-profit or educational purposes. For example, you could excerpt a book as part of a book review or show part of a movie for a college class. There is no legally codified list of specific fair uses and no specific limit on the size of excerpts, so determining whether something constitutes fair use can be challenging. If you're not sure, you should contact the copyright holder. Even if your use of an item falls under the fair use exception, you'll still need to credit the original source.

Penalties for Violation

If you violate copyright laws, the copyright owner can sue you for financial damages she incurred as a result. For example, if an author sells fewer copies of a book because you are distributing the book for free online, she could sue you for the cost of each free book. In addition to actual damages, copyright violators can also be sued for each violation. Deliberate, wilful or repeated copyright violations can also carry a prison sentence.

5.9 How to Gain Permission or Acknowledge Copyrighted Material

Violating someone's copyright is an expensive mistake. If your company uses a copyrighted photo in a brochure without permission, a judge can impound all the printed brochures and order you to print future fliers without the image. The copyright holder can sue you for damages, as well as court costs. Getting permission is a safer alternative.

Permission

A simple way to get permission to use an image, an architectural design or a piece of writing is to ask. If you contact the copyright holder and he agrees to grant you permission, you're home free. If you have no idea who holds the rights, contact the U.S. Copyright Office. You can search the agency's post-1978 records online to find the rights owner. Earlier records are in hard copy, so you either look through them at the office in Washington, D.C., or pay to have the agency's staff handle it.

Fair Use

You don't have to get permission if you make "fair use" of the copyrighted material. A short quote from a copyrighted work might be acceptable, for instance, or a photograph that accidentally includes a copyrighted painting in one corner. It's tricky because there's no hard-and-fast rule to what's acceptable. A quote from a long novel might be acceptable, but not if you borrowed the same amount from a short work. Fair use is harder to claim if you make commercial use of material than if it's part of a non-profit or educational effort.

Acknowledgement

Acknowledging the source of the material doesn't give you the right to use it or turn a case of infringement into fair use. If the copyright holder grants you the right to use her work, she'll probably tell you what acknowledgement she wants and how to phrase it. When you make fair use of someone else's material or use material that's out of copyright, it's still courteous and professional to acknowledge who created it.

Considerations

When you take information or statistics from someone else's work but use your own words, you don't need to seek permission. Information isn't copyrightable. If you're not sure if your company's use of copyrighted material is legal, it's better to play it safe and consult an attorney rather than forge ahead and get sued. A lot of material is protected by copyright even if it isn't obvious. With wedding photos, for example, the photographer, not the couple, usually holds the copyright.

5.10 What Is a Statement Giving Permission to Reproduce Copyrighted Material?

A statement giving permission to reproduce copyrighted material is a type of copyright license that gives the licensee the right to reproduce copyrighted material -- usually subject to specific restrictions of time and scope and in return for compensation to the copyright holder. As a small-business owner, you may wish to license the material of a copyright holder for the benefit of your business. Understanding license terms and restrictions is essential to remaining compliant with your desired licensing arrangement, and the same rules apply when someone else wants a license to use your original work.

Rights of Copyright Holders

Copyright holders maintain the exclusive right to distribute and make copies of a work, the right to make derivative works and the right to publicly perform or display a work. Because these rights are exclusive to copyright holders, anyone desiring to exploit these rights must obtain the permission of the copyright holder. For works created after Jan. 1, 1978, copyright protection lasts for 70 years plus the life of the author. Due to the long term of protection granted to copyright holders, the use of a protected work often requires a license.

Copyright License

Although it is possible to give an oral statement granting the use of copyrighted material, it's better for all parties that such statements are formalized in writing as copyright licenses. Copyright licenses contain the essential terms of the licensing agreement between the parties. They may be exclusive or nonexclusive, and generally the copyright holder is compensated in some manner. If you want to license material from a copyright holder, ask if she has a standard copyright licensing agreement that she uses.

Right to Reproduce

A license granting a right to reproduce copyrighted material should state where the material may be reproduced, how many times the material may be reproduced and any potential time restrictions for reproduction. For example, it is common to limit a license to a certain geographic area or for only a particular number of copies. A license should also state how the copyright holder will be compensated, if the copyright holder may also continue to reproduce the work, if the license can be renewed and when the copyright holder has the right to revoke the license. The agreement should address renewal and termination, as most licenses are not infinite. A well-drafted renewal or termination clause will give the author of the copyrighted material a chance to renegotiate in the future if the value of the work has increased.

Creative Commons License

One type of copyright license often used is the creative commons license. Copyright holders can use creative commons licenses if they would like to provide a blanket license for the general public to use or reproduce their work. Creative commons licenses allow copyright holders to specify how the material will be used and what attribution rights must be provided to the creator of the work.

5.11 How a Business can Convert its Visitors into Qualified Business Leads using CRM/AI

What is Lead Generation?

Lead generation is the process of attracting and converting strangers and prospects into someone who has indicated interest is you company's product or service. Some examples of lead generators are job applications, coupons, and online content.

We've all been through it. You know, the moment you're about to dig into the best darn pile of spaghetti and meatballs you've ever seen.

Just as you twist your fork in the pasta, spear a mouth-watering meatball, and go in for the first greeting bite ... the phone rings. "May I speak to Mr. X?" asks the telemarketer on the other end. "This is an important message regarding your oven preferences."

This frustrating interruption is exactly why we're here to discuss inbound lead generation. What is inbound lead generation? It's a solution that can save your business or organization from being that annoying, disruptive cold caller who is ruining spaghetti nights for pasta lovers all over the world.

What Is a Lead?

Let's start with the basics. A lead is a person who has indicated interest in your company's product or service in some way, shapes, or form.

In other words, instead of getting a random cold call from someone who purchased your contact information, you'd hear from a business or organization you've already opened communication with.

For example, maybe you took an online survey to learn more about how to take care of your car. If you got an email from the auto company that hosted the survey on their website about how they could help you take care of your car, it'd be far less intrusive and irrelevant than if they'd just called you out of the blue with no knowledge of whether you even care about car maintenance ... right?

And from a business perspective, the information the auto company collected about you from your survey responses would help them personalize that opening communication to meet the existing needs of the potential client.

What Is Lead Generation?

Lead generation is the process of attracting and converting strangers and prospects into those leads we just talked about.

Whenever someone outside the marketing world asks me what I do, I can't simply say, "I create content for lead generation." It'd be totally lost on them, and I'd get some really confused looks.

So instead, I say, "I work on finding unique ways to attract people to my business. I want to provide them with enough goodies to get them naturally interested in my company so they eventually warm up to the brand enough to want to hear from us!"

That usually resonates better, and that's exactly what lead generation is: It's a way of warming up potential customers to your business and getting them on the path to eventually buying.

Why Do You Need Lead Generation?

By showing an organic interest in your business, it's those strangers and prospects that are initiating the relationship with you -- versus you, the business, initiating the relationship with them. This makes it easier and more natural for them to want to buy from you somewhere down the line.

Within the larger inbound marketing methodology, lead generation falls in the second stage. It occurs after you've attracted an audience and are ready to actually convert those visitors into leads for your sales team. As you can see in the diagram below, generating leads is a fundamental point in an individual's journey to becoming a delighted customer of your business.

ATTRACT	CONVERT	CLOSE	DELIGHT

Strangers — Visitors — Leads — Customers — Promoters

Blog	Forms	CRM	Surveys
Keywords	Calls-to-Action	Email	Smart Content
Social Publishing	Landing Pages	Workflows	Social Monitoring

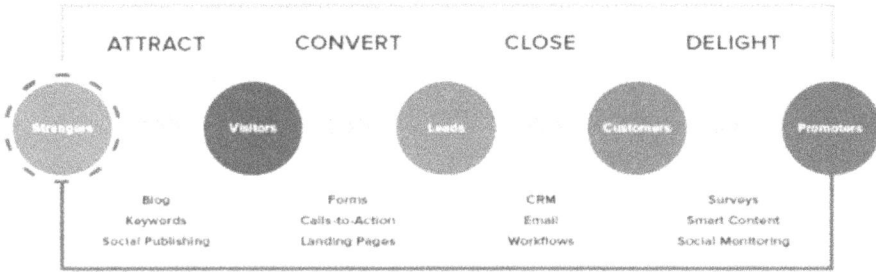

How to Qualify a Lead

As you now know, a lead is a person who has indicated interest in your company's product or service. Now, let's talk about the ways in which someone can actually show that interest.

Essentially, a sale lead is generated through information collection. That information collection could come as the result of a job seeker showing interest in a position by completing an application for the job, a shopper sharing contact information in exchange for a coupon, or a person filling out a form to download an educational piece of content, like an ebook, kit, podcast, tool, trial, or something else.

Below are just a few of the many ways in which you could qualify someone as a lead. Each of these examples also highlights the fact that the amount of information you can collect to qualify someone as a lead, as well as the person's level of interest in your company, can vary. Let's assess each scenario:

Job Application: Any individual filling out an application form is willing to share a lot of personal information because he/she wants to be considered for the position. Filling out that application shows their true interest in the job, therefore qualifying the person as a lead for the company's recruiting team.

Coupon: Unlike the job application, you probably know very little about someone who has stumbled upon one of your online coupons. But if they find the coupon valuable enough, they may be willing to provide their name and email address in exchange for it. Although it's not a lot of information, it's enough for a business to know that someone has interest in their company.

Content: While the download of a coupon shows an individual has a direct interest in your product or service, content (like an educational eBook or webinar) does not. Therefore, in order to truly understand the nature of the person's interest in your business, you'll probably need to collect more information -- you'll need enough information for a sales rep to actually understand whether the person is interested in your product or service, and whether they're a good fit.

These three general examples highlight how lead generation differs from company to company, and from person to person. You'll need to collect enough information in order to gauge whether someone has a true, valid interest in your product or service, but knowing how much information is enough information will vary depending on your business.

Let's look at EPiServer, for example. They use web content reports for lead generation, collecting six pieces of information from prospective leads:

As you can see, EPiServer asks for:

- **Full Name:** Basic information needed for communication with the to-be lead.

- **Email:** The email address will allow your business to communicate with the to-be lead through your email marketing campaigns.

- **Company:** This will give you the ability to research what the business does and how the lead might benefit from your product or service. (Mainly for B2B)

- **Role:** Understanding an individual's role in the business will help you understand how to communicate with them. Every brand stakeholder will have a different take and perspective on your offering. (Mainly for B2B)

- **Country:** Location information needed for qualifying the to-be lead and sending it to the correct sales team, if applicable.

- **State:** Location information needed for qualifying the to-be lead and sending it to the correct sales team, if applicable.

If you'd like to learn more intermediate-level tips on information collection and what you should ask for on your lead gen forms, read our post about it here. But we're getting ahead of ourselves.

5.12 How to Generate Leads: The Mechanics of Lead Generation

Now that we understand how lead generation fits into the whole inbound marketing methodology, let's review the actual components of the lead generation process.

- **Visitor:** A visitor has discovered your business through one of your marketing channels, whether that's your website, blog, or social media page. On any of these channels, you'll need to have a tracking mechanism.

- **Call-to-Action (CTA):** A call-to-action or CTA is an image, button, or message that calls website visitors to take some sort of action. When it comes to lead generation, this action is to navigate.

- **Landing Page:** A landing page is a web page a visitor lands on for a distinct purpose, while a landing page can be used for various reasons, one of its most frequent uses is to capture leads.

- **Forms:** Forms are typically hosted on landing pages, although they can technically be embedded anywhere on your site. They consist of a series of fields (like in our example above) that collect information in exchange.

- **Offer:** An offer is the content or something of value that's being "offered" on the landing page. The offer must have enough value to a visitor to merit providing their personal information in exchange for access to it.

See how everything fits together?

(If you're looking for a free lead generation tool, take a look at HubSpot Marketing Free, which lets you set up contact and lead capture forms on your website and/or scrape contact info from your existing forms. It's really easy to set up.)

Once you put all these elements together, you can use your various promotional channels to link and drive traffic to the landing page so you can start generating leads. Here are some example pathways for lead generation:

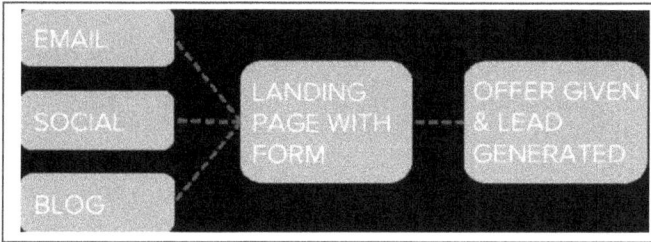

Hold Up ... Why Not Just Buy Leads?

Marketers and salespeople alike want to fill their sales funnel -- and they want to fill it quickly. That's where the temptation to buy leads comes in. Buying sale leads, as opposed to generating them organically, is much easier and takes far less time and effort, despite being more expensive. So why shouldn't you just buy leads?

First and foremost, any leads you've purchased don't actually know you. Typically, they've "opted in" at some other site when signing up for something, and didn't actually opt in to receiving anything from your company. The messages you send them are therefore unwanted messages, and sending unwanted messages is intrusive, not inviting. (Remember that disruptive call I got when I was trying to eat my spaghetti? That's how people feel when they receive emails and other messages from people they didn't ask to hear from.)

If the prospect has never been to your website, indicated an interest in your resources, products, services, or even industry, then you're interrupting them ... plain and simple.

If they never opted in to receive messages from you specifically, then there's a high likelihood they could flag your messages as spam. This is quite dangerous for you. Not only does this train their inbox to show only emails they want to see, but it indicates to their email provider which emails to filter out. Once enough people click flag your messages as spam, you go on a "blacklist," which is then shared with other email providers. Once you get on the blacklist, it's really, really hard to get back off of it. In addition, your email deliverability and IP reputation will likely be harmed.

It's always, always, always better to generate leads organically rather than buy them. Read this blog post to learn how to grow an opt-in email list instead of buying one. (And if you're just starting your business and are looking for more marketing tools and resources, check out our comprehensive guide for how to start a business.)

Lead Generation Trends & Benchmarks

You're getting web traffic and generating leads. But how are you doing compared with other companies in your industry? How many leads should you really be generating?

It's tough to figure out whether your lead generation strategy is working if you aren't looking at industry data. That's why we partnered with Qualtrics to survey more than 900 marketers from all different industries in North America and Europe. Using this data, we created a demand generation report with data on website visitors, leads, opportunities, customers, and revenue.

For example, did you know that 74% of companies that weren't exceeding revenue goals didn't know their visitor, lead, MQL, or sales opportunities numbers? How about that over 70% of companies not achieving their revenue goals generate fewer than 100 leads per month, and only 5% generate more than 2,500 leads per month?

For the in-depth reports, download our Demand Generation Benchmarks Report. Here are some highlights:

Cost per Lead, by Industry

The media and publishing industries report the lowest cost per lead, at $11–25. Software, information technology and services, marketing agencies, and financial services companies all report the highest average cost per lead, at $51-100.

Leads Generated per Month, by Annual Revenue

Unsurprisingly, the more revenue a company has the more leads they generate. The differences are most drastic at the highest and lowest end of the spectrum: 82% of companies with $250,000 or less in annual revenue report generating less than 100 leads per month, whereas only 8% of companies generating $1 billion in annual revenue report less than 100 leads per month.

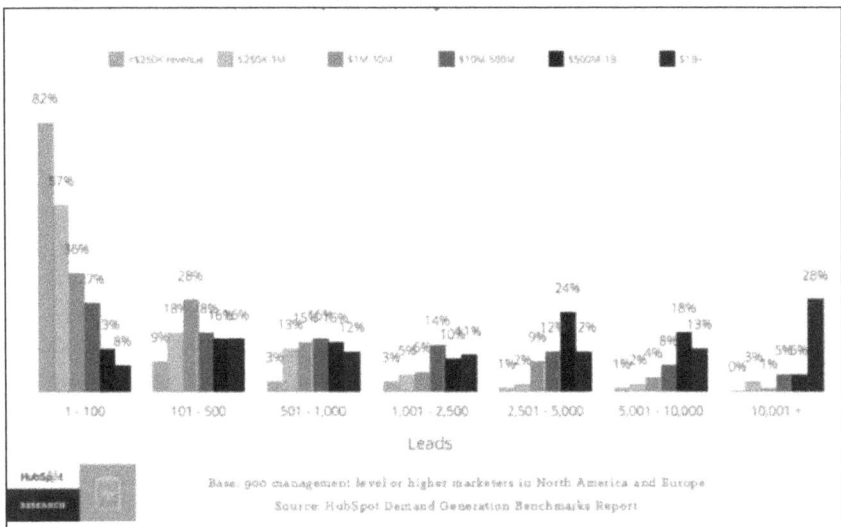

Leads per Month

We found that, in general, 58% of companies generated 500 leads per month or fewer and 71% generate 1,000 or fewer. However, as we saw previously, the companies having the most success are also the ones generating the most leads.

Here's how the data broke down by company size:

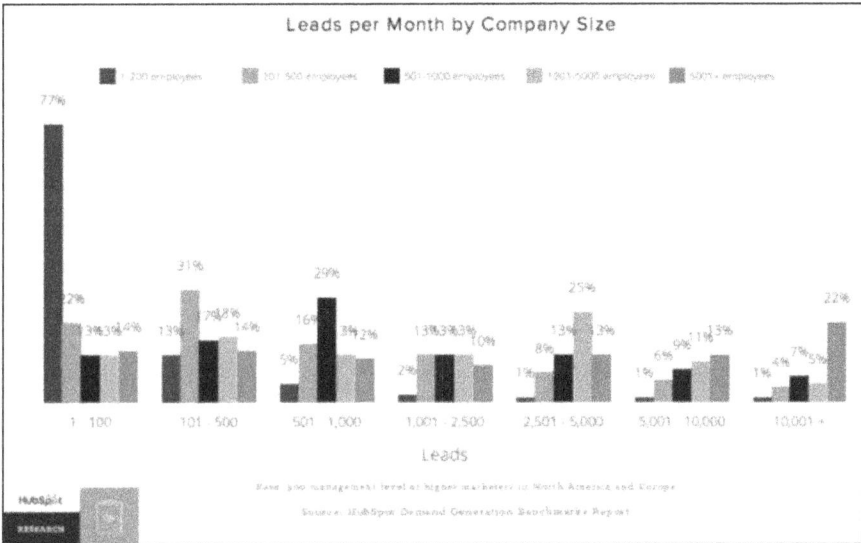

Lead Generation Software (CRM/AI)

We found that the most successful teams use a formal system to organize and store leads: 46% use Google Docs, 41% use marketing automation software, and 37% use CRM software. (HubSpot customers: Google Drive integrates both with HubSpot Marketing and with HubSpot CRM.)

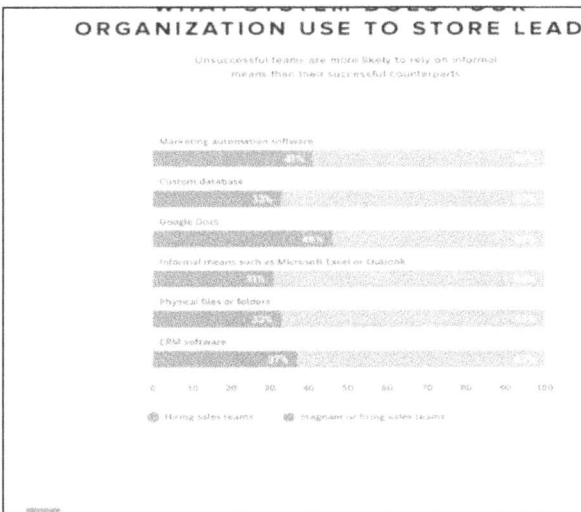

Tips for Lead Generation Campaigns

In a given lead generation campaign, there can be a lot of moving parts. It can be difficult to tell which parts of your campaign are working and which need some fine-tuning. What exactly goes into a best-in-class lead generation engine?

Use the Right Lead Generation Tools

As you saw in our data, the most successful marketing teams use a formal system to organize and store their leads. That's where lead generation tools and lead generation software comes in.

How much do you know about the people visiting your website? Do you know their names or their email addresses? How about which pages they visit, how they're navigating around, and what they do before and after filling out a lead conversion form?

If you don't know the answers to these questions, then chances are, you're having a hard time connecting with the people who are visiting your site. But these are questions you should answer -- and you can, too, with the right lead generation tools.

There are a few different tools and templates out there that'll help you create different lead gen assets you can put on your site:

CTA Templates

50+ free, customizable call-to-action (CTA) templates in PowerPoint that you can use to create clickable CTA buttons you can put on your blog, landing pages, and elsewhere on your site.

HubSpot Marketing Free: A free lead generation software tool from HubSpot that includes lead capture and contact insights features, which will scrape any pre-existing forms you have on your website and add those contacts to your existing contact database. It also lets you new pop-ups, hello bars, or slide-ins -- called "lead flows" -- that'll help you turn website visitors into leads immediately.

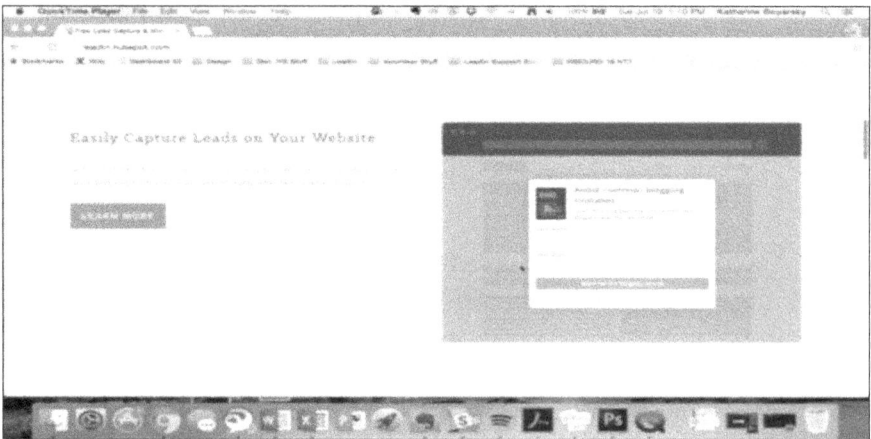

Hotjar: A great tool to help you understand what users want, care about, and do on your site using heatmaps, visitor recordings, analyses of your forms, feedback forms and surveys, and more.

A form scraping tool that collects submissions on your website's existing forms, so you can consolidate all your leads into your contacts database regardless of which form visitors submit on your website. If you're a HubSpot customer, you can create and embed forms using HubSpot. Non-HubSpot customers can use a form creation tool like Contact Form 7, Jetpack, or Google Forms, and then use HubSpot Marketing Free's Collected Forms feature to automatically capture these form submissions and put them in your contacts database.

Create amazing offers for all different stages of the buying Cycle

Not all of your site visitors are ready to talk to your sales team or see a demo of your product. Someone at the beginning of the buyer's journey might be interested in an informational piece like an eBook or a guide, whereas someone who's more familiar with your company and are near the bottom of the cycle might be more interested in a free trial or demo. Make sure you're creating offers for each phase and offering CTAs for these offers throughout your site.

Yes, it takes time to create valuable content that teaches and nurtures your leads down the funnel, but if you don't offer anything for visitors who aren't ready to buy, then they may never come back to your website. From checklists to templates to free tools, here are 23 ideas for lead generation content to get you started.

If you want to take personalization a step further for a higher conversion rate, try using smart CTAs on your webpages and blog posts. Smart CTAs are CTAs that detect where that person is in the buying cycle -- whether they're a new visitor, a lead, or a customer -- and change accordingly. Personalized CTAs convert whopping visitors than basic calls-to-action.

Link your CTA to a dedicated landing page

This may seem obvious to some of you, but you'd be surprised how many marketers don't create dedicated landing pages for their offers. CTAs are meant to send visitors to a dedicated landing page where they receive a specific offer.

Don't use CTAs to drive people to your homepage, for instance. Even if your CTA is about your brand or product (and perhaps not an offer like a download), you should still be sending them to a targeted landing page that's relevant to what they are looking for, whether it's a feature-specific landing page for your product, or something else. If you have the opportunity to use a CTA, send them to a page that will convert them into a lead.

If you want to learn more about how to build and promote high-converting landing pages, then download our eBook on optimizing landing pages for conversions.

Use social media strategically

While marketers typically think of social media as best for top-of-the-funnel marketing, it can still be a helpful and low-cost source for lead generation. The key is using social media strategically for lead gen.

How do you do that? Start by regularly posting links to your Facebook, Twitter, LinkedIn, and other social media posts directly to the landing pages of high-performing offers. Make sure you make it clear to visitors that you're sending them to a landing page, though. That way, you're setting expectations fairly. Here's an example from one of our Facebook posts:

You can also do a lead generation analysis of your blog to figure out which posts generate the most leads, and then make a point of regularly linking posts to them, too.

Another way to generate leads from social media? Run a contest. They're fun and engaging for your followers, and they can also teach you a ton about them. It's a win-win. Read our step-by-step guide for growing your email list using social media contests here, which covers everything from choosing a platform, to picking a winner, all the way to analysing your results.

Finally, take advantage of the lead gen opportunities each social media platform already gives you. For example, Facebook has a feature that lets you put a simple call-to-action button at the top of your Facebook Page, helping you send Facebook followers directly to your website. Here's an example from Canvas's Facebook Page.

Twitter has Twitter Lead Gen Cards, which let you generate leads directly within a tweet -- without having to leave Twitter. A user's name, email address, and Twitter username are automatically pulled into the Card, and all they have to do is click "Submit" to become a lead. (HubSpot users: You can connect Twitter Lead Gen Cards to your HubSpot Forms. Learn how to do that here.)

If you're looking for more lead generation tips for social media, here are lead gen tips for Facebook and here are lead gen tips for Twitter.

There you have it, folks. Now that you know more about how to generate leads for your business, we recommend you try HubSpot's free lead generation tool. Use it to add simple conversion assets to your site (or scrape your existing forms), and then learn more about your site visitors and what content prompts them to convert.

The basics we've gone over in this blog post are just the beginning. Keep creating great offers, CTAs, landing pages, and forms -- and promote them in multi-channel environments. Be in close touch with your sales team to make sure you're handing off high-quality leads on a regular basis. Last but not least, never stop testing. The more you tweak and test every step of your inbound lead generation process, the more you'll improve lead quality and increase revenue.

5.13 How an Entrepreneur Setup an Online Store for their Online Business (Business Case- I with Shopify)

Here's a step-by-step guide on how to build your own online shop with Shopify.

I'll cover all the basics and bit more, so you could get your online store up and running ASAP (We're all busy, I know).

If you're not sure about using Shopify, you can always try WooCommerce. Here's

How to Set up Your Own Online Shop with the Help of Shopify

Signing up with Shopify and starting your store couldn't be any easier and they even offer a 14 day free trial to get you going.

To launch your Shopify store, you must sign up for an account.

1. **Sign Up with Shopify**

   To start, visit Shopify.com. Use the signup form to start creating an account.

   Enter the required details and then click the 'Create your store now' button.

   Your store name needs to be unique or Shopify will ask you to choose something else.

   After this initial screen you'll be asked for a few more details, these include your name, address, country and a contact number.

   You will also be asked if you have products and, if so, what you aim to sell. If you're just trying out Shopify to see if it works for you, you can select 'I'm just playing around' in the 'Do you have products?' dropdown, and 'I'm not sure' in the 'What will you sell?' section.

   Once complete, click 'I'm done'.

2. **Start Setting up Your Online Shop**

   After you've signed up you'll be directed straight to your store admin screen. Now you are ready to start customising your store's look, uploading products and setting up payments and shipping.

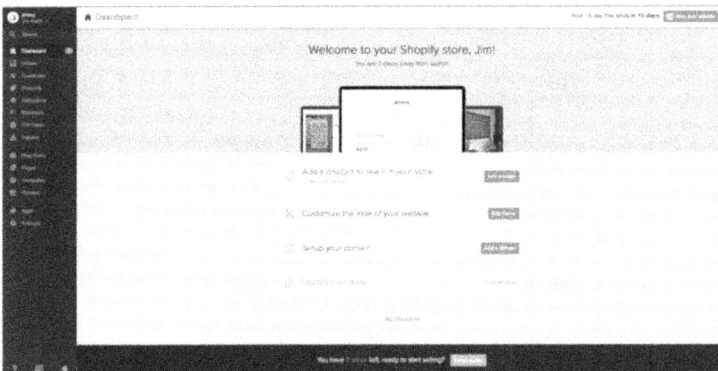

Your home admin screen tells you all you need to know to get you up and running.

3. **Choose a "Theme" or "Layout"**

Shopify has its own official theme store. These themes are all guaranteed to have full support from the designers so you know your store is in good hands.

All themes come with a comprehensive list of modifications you can make without having to touch a line of code. The premium themes come with more modifications, but that's not to say you can't achieve a great looking site with a free one. These changes are outlined in the next section.

If you want to make wholesale changes to a theme, there are very few limitations on what can be achieved by accessing the HTML and CSS. Don't worry if you haven't got any coding experience. Shopify has an international team of design agencies they call 'Shopify Experts' that you can hire to fully customise your site.

To find a theme that suits your needs we recommend the following:

1. **Browse the Theme Store**: Log into Shopify and visit the Shopify Theme Store at themes.shopify.com. Here you'll find over 180 theme variations to choose from, including a good selection of free ones.

You can filter by paid or free, industry and by features. You can also sort themes by price, popularity, and most recent.

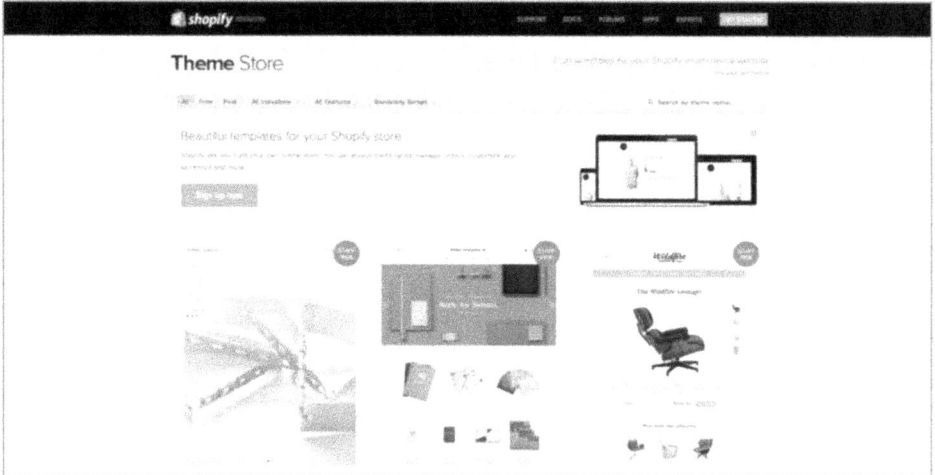

The Shopify Theme Store.

2. **Check the functionality and reviews:** Once you've found a theme you like, click on the theme's sample image. You'll be given more information about the theme, such as whether the theme is responsive/mobile ready among other features.

Scroll down to read some reviews to find out what e-tailers using the theme think of it.

3. **Preview the theme:** To see the theme in action, click View Demo. You'll see this below the green 'Preview Theme in your Store' button.

   If the theme comes in a range of styles, you can also view demos of the different styles by clicking on them.

4. **Get the theme:** Once you've found a theme you like, click the green button.

   Shopify will ask you to confirm that you want to install the theme.

   Click Publish as my Shop's Theme.

   Don't worry if you're not 100% sure it's the right theme for you. You can always change your mind later.

   After the theme has installed, Shopify will let you know, and will give you the option to Go to your Theme Manager. Click this.

   Your theme manager shows published themes (the one you installed or activated most recently) and unpublished themes below (previously installed themes).

4. **Edit Shopify Settings:** The majority of Shopify themes allow you to make simple changes that can massively change the appearance of your store, so you can rest assured knowing you won't end up with a website that looks like a clone of thousands of other stores.

These stores are all built using the same theme.

On your admin screen, select 'Themes' from the left hand navigation menu. On this page you will see your live theme in a box at the top, in the top right hand corner of that box will be two buttons. The first one is of three dots, which gives you some basic settings changes. One of these allows you to make a duplicate of the theme. We highly recommend you do this in case you make some changes you don't like, then you can delete the duplicate and start again. The second button says 'Customize Theme'. If you click that you will be taken to a page that controls all the basic functionality of your store. This is a great time for you to have a thorough play with the settings and test out all the features so you can find out what your site is capable of.

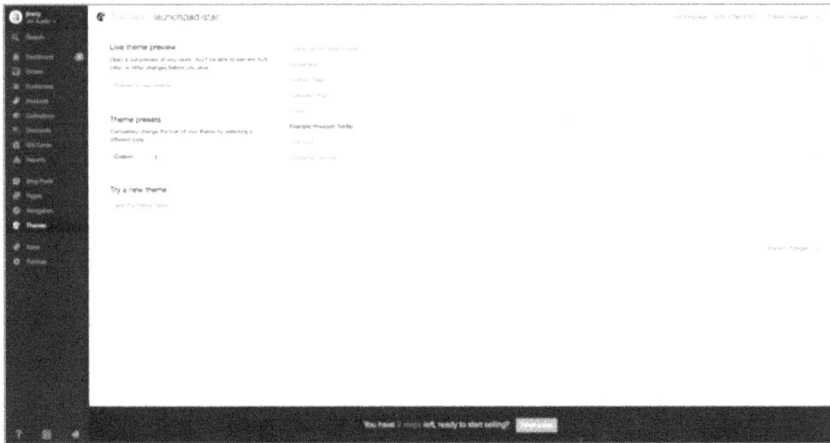

Your themes custom settings

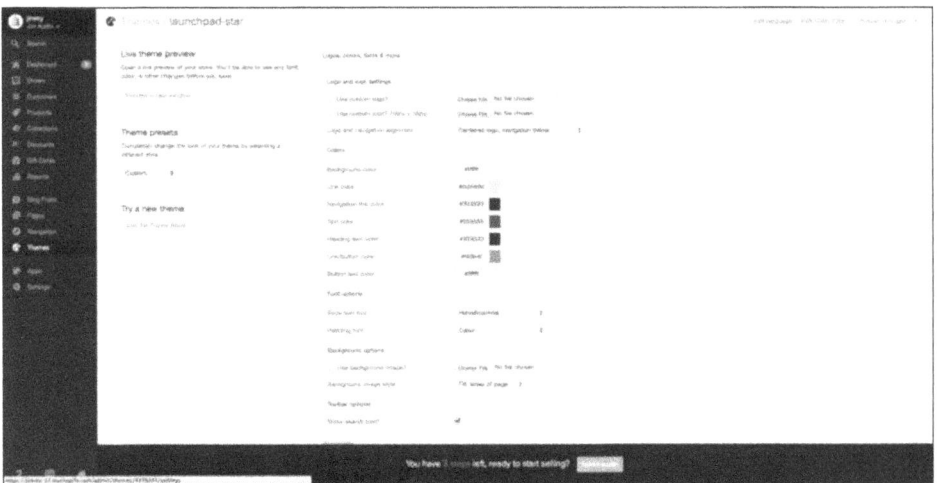

Changing colours in your theme

The most common features will include:

❖ uploading logos

❖ uploading slides to a homepage carousel

❖ adding related item functionality to product pages

❖ choosing how many items appear on each line of the collection pages

❖ colour schemes

❖ font choices

Some themes will also allow you to reposition elements on pages such as showing product images on the left, right or center of the page. You can also choose whether you want to display social like/tweet/pin/+1 buttons.

5. **Add Your Products to the Store:** Again, navigating from the bar on the left select 'Products', You will then see a blue 'Add a product' button in the top right hand corner of the page. Use the following screen to add as much detail as needed about your products. Especially look at those that will help with SEO such as name, description and URL. Also include as much detail about variants as possible to help inform customers about your items.

This is also the screen where you upload product pictures. Once the images are uploaded you can rearrange them so don't worry about uploading them in any particular order.

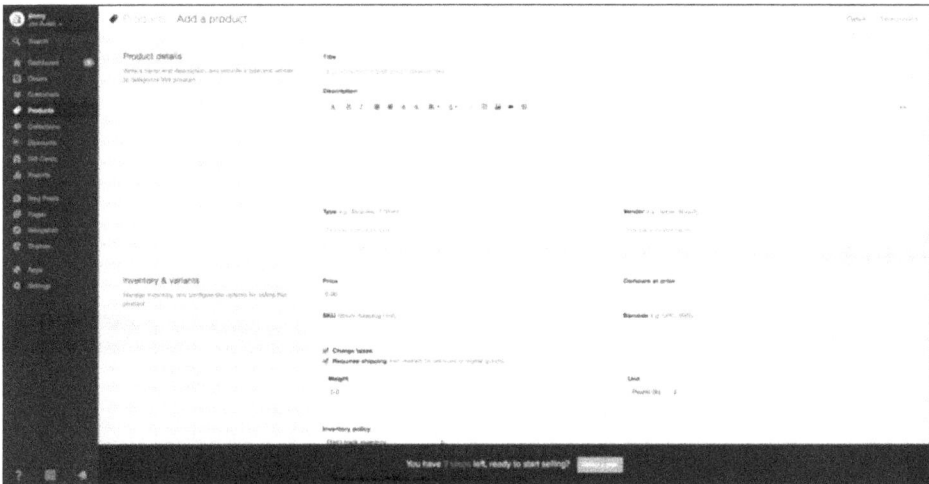

The Product screen (Make sure you fill out as much information as possible)

Product images can make a sale so make sure you show your products off to their best and highlight any special or unique features with close up photos. To keep your store looking tidy we suggest you keep all images the same dimensions. Unless of course you plan to make your collection pages look like a Pinterest board.

Once everything is filled out always remember to click the 'Save product' button in the top and bottom right hand corners.

Set up collections (group of products)

A collection is any group of products that have some feature in common that customers might look for when visiting your store. For example, your customers might be shopping for:

❖   clothes specifically for men, women, or children

❖ items of a certain type, such as lamps, cushions, or rugs

❖ items on sale

❖ items in a certain size or color

❖ Seasonal products such as holiday cards and decorations.

Products can appear in any number of collections. Usually, you would display your collections on your homepage and in the navigation bar. This helps customers find what they're looking for without having to click through your whole catalogue.

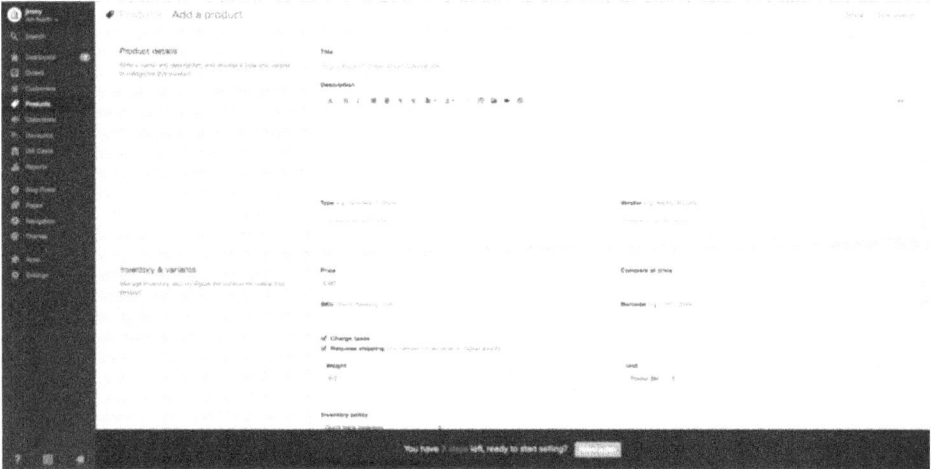

The Collection set up screen works in exactly the same way as the Product screen

Manual and automatic collections

When you add a new collection, you can select how products should be added to it. These are the two options:

❖ **Manually:** You add and remove products in a manual collection individually.

❖ **Automatically:** You can set up selection conditions to automatically include products that meet certain criteria.

Payment gateways

A payment gateway allows you to take payment from your customers via your website. The price and commission rate is important, but it's also important to see what features they offer. Not all payment gateways are created equal.

You need to look at the following when choosing the right payment gateway for you.

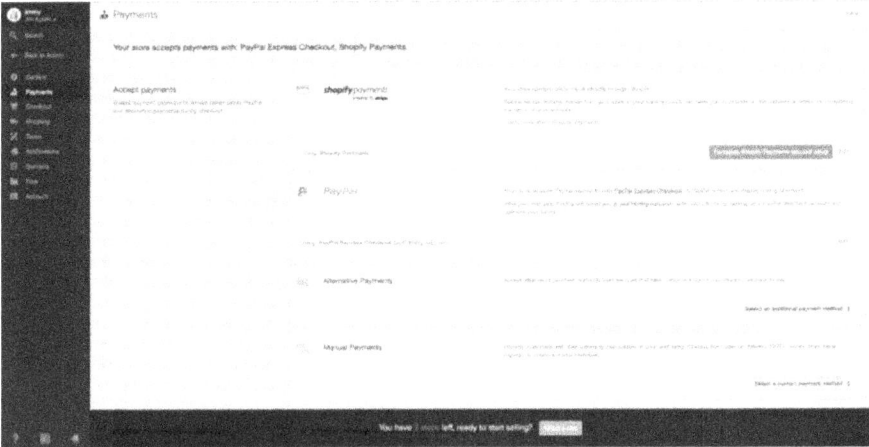

(i) **Transaction Fees:** When you take a payment, some gateways will keep a small percentage or flat fee (or sometimes both) for letting you use their service. Compare these based on what your anticipated sales are.

(ii) **Card Types:** You need to know what types of card are accepted by your chosen Payment Gateway. All accept VISA and MasterCard, while most accept American Express. PayPal is also becoming popular for online payments.

(iii) **Offsite Checkout:** Some gateways will take the payment on their own servers via their own form. This means the customer is taken away from your checkout and they pay on the form provided by your payment gateway. They are then redirected to your confirmation page once the customer successfully pays. This allows you to have a bit more control of the checkout process. Now you can circumvent Shopify's limitations in that they don't let you customise the checkout other than with CSS.

Payment gateway transaction fees are added on top of Shopify's own transaction fees. However as of November stores based in the US and UK can use Shopify Payments. Depending upon your Shopify plan, you can save on these extra costs. Relative to your plan you will receive these highly appealing rates.

❖ Basic 2.4% + 20p

❖ Professional 2.1% + 20p

❖ Unlimited 1.8% + 20p

Depending on how many transactions you make every month it could be worth upgrading to take advantage of these savings.

If you live in the US or UK your store will automatically use Shopify Payments. To complete this, click the 'Complete Shopify Payments account setup' button found in Settings > Payments. If you wish to use a third party gateway you can use the 'enable payment gateways' link on the same page.

6. **Get Your Online Shop "LIVE":** Before your site can go live you need to add a few more details about your company and how you plan to make deliveries and pay tax.

General

Make sure all your business information is filled out on this page. Also make sure to make use of the Google Analytics feature. This can prove to be an invaluable source for tracking your stores visitors.

Taxes

(i) Go to the Products page of your admin

(ii) Click on the name of a given product.

(iii) Scroll down to the section called "Inventory & variants".

(iv) Click on the edit link next to your Product Variant to open a dialog window.

(v) Make sure the checkboxes next to Charge taxes and Requires shipping are checked if you need to include these with your products.

(vi) Some stores won't need to charge taxes or shipping on products like digital goods. On the other hand, a T-shirt store will likely need to charge both.

(vii) If you are planning to ship your product to customers, make sure to enter the product's weight in the appropriate field.

Shipping: If your shipping rates are too narrow, or you don't give enough options, you may lose out on some sales. Shopify will only calculate a shipping rate for your customers based on the rules that you define in the Shipping page of the admin. To make sure you won't lose any sales:

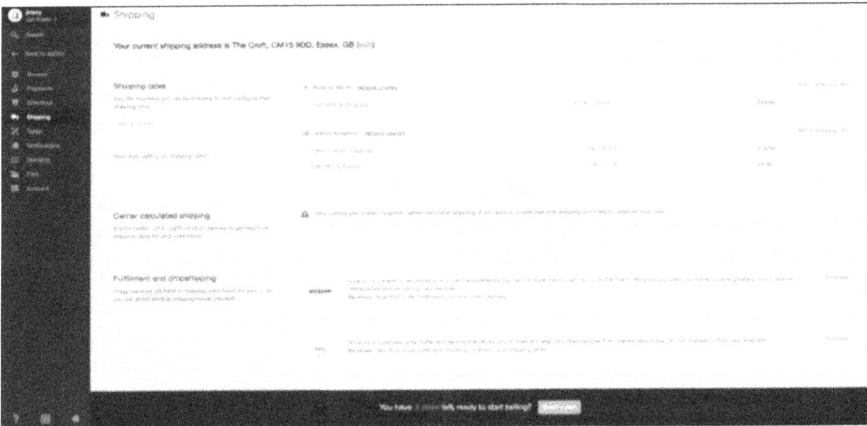

(i) From your store admin, go to the Settings > Shipping page.

(ii) In the "Shipping rates" section, look to see if you have set a weight-based shipping rate and adjust it according to your product's specifications.

Test your order system

To test your system you can simulate a transaction using Shopify's Bogus Gateway.

To use the Bogus Gateway:

(i) From your store Admin, click Settings, then Payments to go to your Payments settings

(ii) If you have a credit card gateway enabled, deactivate it before continuing. (Click Edit, then Deactivate, then confirm your deactivation.)

(iii) In the Accept credit cards section, click Select a Credit Card Gateway to open the drop-down menu.

(iv) Scroll down the list to Other, then click (for testing) Bogus Gateway.

(v) Click Activate (or Reactivate, if you've used the Bogus Gateway before).

(vi) Go to your storefront and place an order as a customer would. At checkout, enter the following credit card details instead of genuine numbers:

Testing a real payment gateway with a genuine transaction:

(i) Make sure you've set up the payment gateway you want to test.

(ii) Make a purchase from your store as a customer would, and complete checkout using genuine credit card details.

(iii) Cancel the order immediately, to refund yourself and avoid paying transaction fees.

(iv) Log in to your payment gateway to make sure the funds went through.

Is this free?

Yes – just be sure to cancel and refund the order soon after you place it.

If your billing cycle hits after you've placed the test order but before you cancel it, the transaction fees will appear on your bill. You can still cancel after paying your bill to Shopify, but you'll receive the refund as a transaction credit on your account. You can use transaction credits to pay future transaction fees.

7. **Consider Buying a Domain Name:** To get your site live you'll need a domain name. You have two choices for this. Firstly you can buy a domain from Shopify and it will be added to your store automatically. This saves you time, especially if you have no knowledge of hosting a website. These domains typically cost 750-1500 INR per year. Your second option is to purchase a domain from a third party such as GoDaddy, BigRock etc. These domains start from 500 INR a year. The downside is that you'll have to redirect the DNS records yourself which can seem daunting at first.

If you're unable to come up with a good domain name, read my tips on how to choose a domain name.

Here are the steps to put your new Shopify store live on a third party domain name.

(i) **Add the new domain in Shopify:** In the Shopify admin, from the left hand navigation go to Settings and then Domains and add your domain name using the 'Add an existing domain' button.

(ii) **Update DNS records:** Login to your domain registrar and make the following changes to the DNS records:

❑ Replace the @ or main A record with the following IP address: 23.227.38.32

❑ Add or replace the www CNAME with storename.myshopify.com (i.e. your store Shopify link without the http bit, which you can see on the domains settings page)

(iii) **Remove any storefront passwords:** Otherwise no one will be able to access your site even once it's live.

(iv) **Set as primary if relevant:** Whilst in Settings > Domains, you can choose your main domain by using the dropdown at the top of the screen:

Primary domain

www.lifestyle-labs.com ⇕

☑ Redirect all traffic to this domain
This will redirect traffic from all your domains to the single primary domain.

Save

Ensure that you also check the 'Redirect all traffic to this domain'. This means that traffic to all other domains will be directed to your primary domain. This is crucial for good SEO.

(v) **Adding other domains:** You can repeat steps 1 and 2 with other domain names you own. All domain names will redirect to the 'Primary' domain, which you can change at any time with the 'Set as primary' option next to each domain name.

Note that the number of domain names you own has no influence on SEO.

5.14 Conclusion

And that is all there is to it. In theory you can have a great looking, unique and fully-functioning store in less than half an hour without having to be a web expert. This way you can spend most of your time marketing your product rather than having to maintain the site.

❏❏

Chapter 6: Alternatives for Shopify?

6.1 Introduction

I've been mainly using WordPress & WooCommerce combo (cheaper & easier), but Shopify can be a good alternative.

For further reading: Shopify vs. WordPress (WooCommerce)

Furthermore, you can actually build an ecommerce site with website builders, too. In regards to customisation, Shopify allows almost every aspect of their templates to be altered in some way. You can also change the functionality of most parts of your site. On top of this they also have the largest app store for added functionality. Comparatively, Volusion only has one template that can only have minor changes made to it.

The only real downside is not being able to fully customise your checkout. Shopify restricts access to this page for security reasons. However the checkout comes fully responsive, so it will work perfectly for customers shopping on mobile devices.

Your ready to use Shopify store will look like, though depending on your business and product line

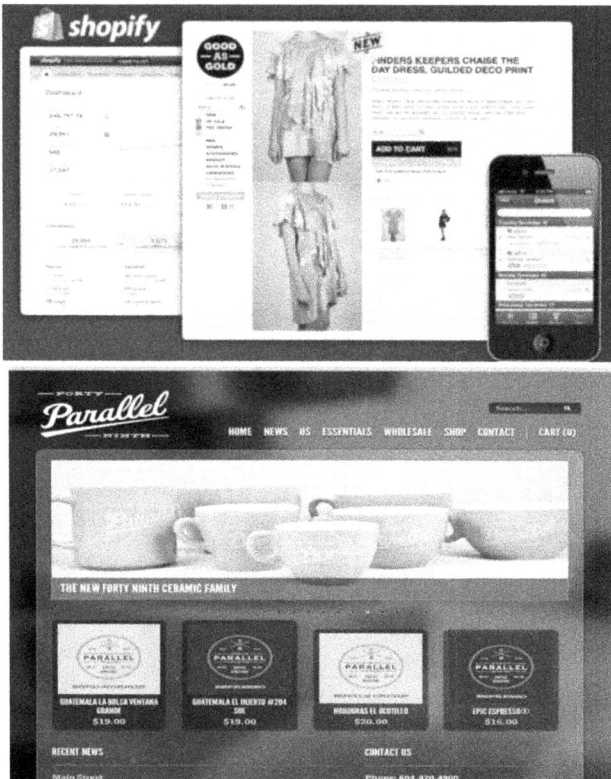

6.2 (Business Case- II with WooCommerce)

In this tutorial, I'll teach you how to set up an online store where you can list and sell physical products.

At the end of this tutorial, your e-commerce site should be something similar to this image at the right:

P.S. If you plan to sell services (instead of products), I recommend starting a business website (not online store). It can fetch you revenue and backed by a well versed strategy in place.

If you plan to sell more than 10 different products, keep reading.

Use WordPress + WooCommerce for online store (FREE)

In a sentence, WooCommerce is the best way to turn your WordPress website into a fully functional e-commerce store. Here are the specifics:

● Technically speaking, WooCommerce is a WordPress plugin. It needs to be installed and activated just like any other plugins in order to function.

● It's free and open source – just like WordPress – you don't need any licenses, things don't expire, no one comes asking for money at any point.

● It's the most popular e-commerce plugin for WordPress out there.

● It's (arguably) the most feature-rich such plugin too.

● You can set it up and configure it by yourself.

● The setup is fast. Usually just a matter of an afternoon.

● It works with any design/theme you currently have on your WordPress site = you don't need to ditch your current website design.

I could continue with the list above, but instead, let me just say that WooCommerce simply gives you all you could ever need to build a high-quality e-commerce store with WordPress.

What can you sell with WordPress + WooCommerce?

● digital products (e.g. software, downloads, eBooks),

● physical products,

● services,

● bookings (e.g. for appointments, or anything else that can be booked),

● subscriptions,

● other people's products – as an affiliate,

● Customizations (e.g. additional customizations on top of your product listings), and more.

In other words, you can make money with your website.

I would even risk saying that WooCommerce allows you to sell anything that can have a price tag assigned to it. On top of that, anyone can use it (if you've already managed to get a WordPress site launched, then you are also going to be able to handle WooCommerce).

How to build an online store with WordPress and WooCommerce

Note. The goal of this part of the guide is to show you the simplest method of building a functional e-commerce store on WordPress, so that you can get your store online as soon as possible. That is why I'm going to focus on just the essential things and skip the more advanced aspects.

STEP 1 Get a domain name and web hosting

In order to create an online store, or any other type of website, you're going to need to two things:

● Domain name is your store's unique address on the web. Something like YOURBUSINESS.com

● Web Hosting is basically a remote computer that stores your website and then serves it up to whoever wants to visit it.

There are hundreds of different hosting/domain providers, but I usually get both from Bluehost.com. They offer affordable web hosting, free domain name and reliability. They're also one of the few recommended (official) hosting providers by WordPress.org.

Total cost would be around INR 500/month To begin, you just need to go to Bluehost.com, or godaddy.com and click the "get started" button.

This will take you to a page where you can select a hosting plan for your store. You can get started with the cheapest option, labelled "basic":

	basic	plus most popular	prime
	normally $7.99	normally $10.99	normally $14.99
	$2.95* per month	**$5.45*** per month	**$5.45*** per month
websites	1	unlimited	unlimited
website space	50 GB	unmetered	unmetered
bandwidth	unmetered	unmetered	unmetered
performance	Standard	Standard	Standard
included domains	1	1	1
parked domains	5	unlimited	unlimited
sub domains	25	unlimited	unlimited
email accounts	5	unlimited	unlimited
email storage	100 MB per account	unlimited	unlimited
marketing offers	---	$200 included	$200 included
		over $24/yr in extras	over $80/yr in extras
		1 SpamExperts	1 SpamExperts
			1 Domain Privacy
			SiteBackup Pro

The next step is all about picking a domain name for your new online store.

This requires some brainstorming. But in general, you want your domain name to be unique, easy to remember and catchy. Also, if you already have a business entity set up for your store, then you should perhaps go with that as your domain name.

Once you make your domain choice, you can finalize the setup and pay the initial hosting fee.

Great! You've just got yourself a domain name and a hosting plan to go along with it.

STEP 2 Install WordPress (FREE)

The next step officially marks the start of your adventure with WordPress – you're going to install WordPress on your hosting account.

This might sound difficult, but it's actually not. All you do is go to your Bluehost user panel (Bluehost will send you a link to it in the confirmation email) – usually available at my.bluehost.com.

Once there, scroll down until you see an icon labelled "Install WordPress":

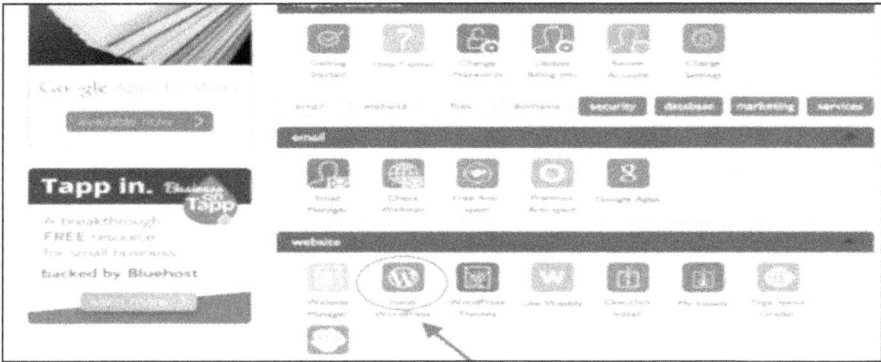

Click it and follow the on-screen instructions. You will be taken through the whole process step by step, so there's nothing to worry about.

At this point, you should have a blank WordPress website installed.

● You can see it by going to your main domain name (e.g., YOURSTORE.com)

● You can log in to the admin panel by going to YOURSTORE.com/wp-admin

Now it's time to turn that blank WordPress website into a fully-functional e-commerce store built with the excellent WooCommerce plugin.

STEP 3 Install WooCommerce Plugin (FREE)

Like with all WordPress plugins, the fun starts by navigating to your WordPress Dashboard / Plugins / Add New. Once there, type "WooCommerce" in the search field. You'll see WooCommerce as the first search result:

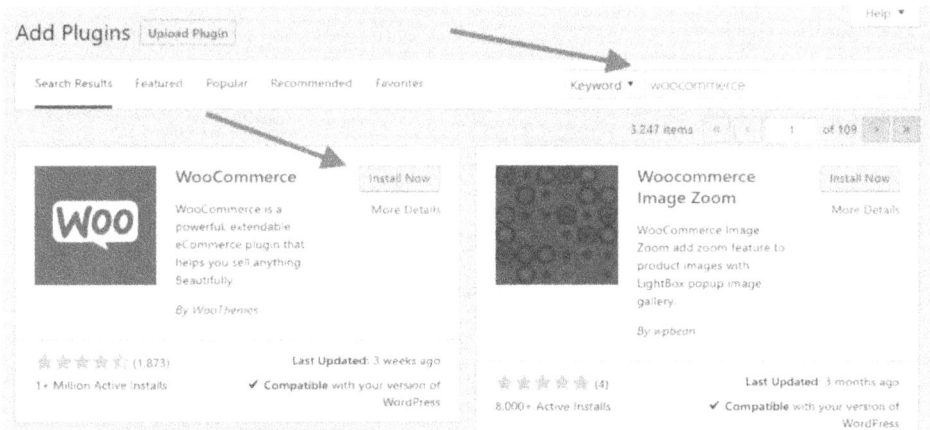

Just click the "Install Now" button next to the plugin.

After a couple of seconds, the text on the button will change to "Activate." Go ahead and click it.

WooCommerce

Activate

WooCommerce is a powerful, extendable eCommerce plugin that helps you sell anything. Beautifully.

More Details

By WooThemes

At this stage, you'll see WooCommerce's on-screen launch/setup wizard. This thing makes the process uber-easy and takes you by the hand through everything. To begin, click "Let's Go!"

WOO COMMERCE

Page Setup — Store Locale — Shipping & Tax — Payments — Ready!

Welcome to the world of WooCommerce!

Thank you for choosing WooCommerce to power your online store! This quick setup wizard will help you configure the basic settings. **It's completely optional and shouldn't take longer than five minutes.**

No time right now? If you don't want to go through the wizard, you can skip and return to the WordPress dashboard. Come back anytime if you change your mind!

Not right now   Let's Go!

Get the essential store pages created

Online stores are a particular kind of website, and they do need some particular pages to function properly. The first step in the WooCommerce wizard is about creating these pages for you:

- "Shop" – this is where your products are going to be displayed.

- "Cart" – this is the shopping cart where your customers can go to adjust their order before proceeding to checkout.

- "Checkout" – this is where the customers get to pick the shipping/delivery method and pay for whatever they've bought.

- "My Account" – a kind of a profile page for registered customers (they will be able to view their past orders there and manage other details).

All you need to do at this stage of the WooCommerce wizard is click the "Continue" button. WooCommerce will set up those pages for you.

Set up locale

The locale is a truly crucial part of your store setup. Those few parameters define your business origin, currency, and preferred units:

Once you're done, click "Continue" again.

Understand Sales Tax

Tax is by far the least exciting part of running an e-commerce store, but it's also something we can't disregard, sadly.

Anyway, you're going to be pleased to see that WooCommerce helps you with this part too.

First, you can select if you're going to be shipping physical goods or not. If you check the box, WooCommerce will pre-set the remaining shipping-related details in the settings.

> Will you be shipping products?   ☑ Yes, I will be shipping physical goods to customers

Next is tax. WooCommerce has a very neat tax module, and the best thing about it is that it helps you figure out the tax rates based on your store location (the thing you've set in the previous step).

So, if you're going to be charging sales tax (in most cases you are), just check the main tax box. As soon as you do this, a new set of boxes will appear and inform you of what's going to happen next.

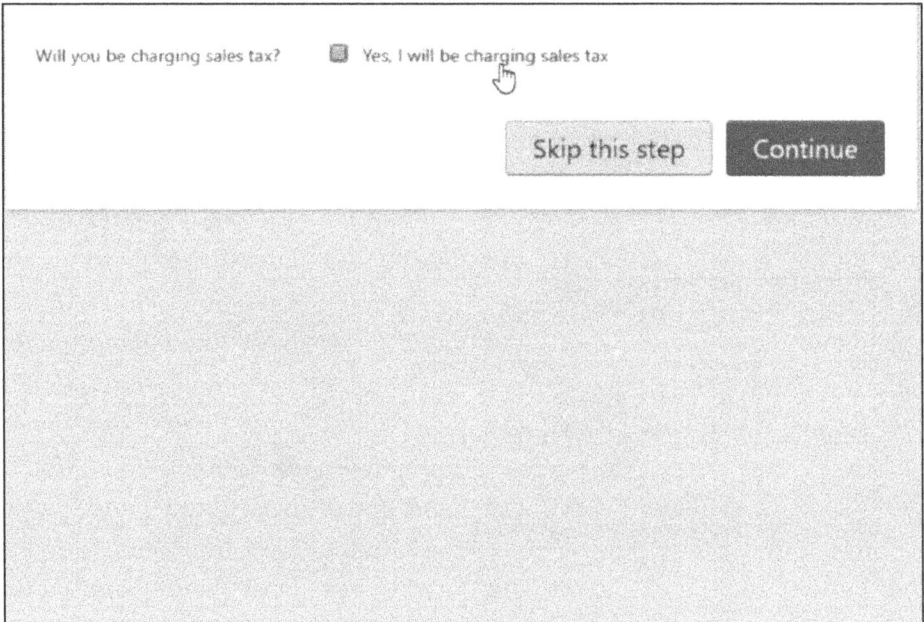

Will you be charging sales tax?   ☐ Yes, I will be charging sales tax

Skip this step   Continue

Note. Even though WooCommerce will pre-fill the tax settings for you, you still need to double-check with your local authorities what the actual current taxation rules are, especially if you're not in the US. You can change everything later on, so don't worry if you're not sure about the rules right now.

Click "Continue."

Pick a Payment Method (PayPal as an example)

Being able to accept online payments is at the core of any e-commerce store, and WooCommerce really offers a lot in terms of the available solutions.

Here's what you get to choose from during setup:

Payments

WooCommerce can accept both online and offline payments. Additional payment methods can be installed later and managed from the checkout settings screen.

☐ **P PayPal**

Safe and secure payments using credit cards or your customer's PayPal account. Learn more about PayPal.

☐ **stripe**

A modern and robust way to accept credit card payments on your store. Learn more about Stripe.

☐ **PayPal Standard**

Accept payments via PayPal using account balance or credit card.

☐ **Check Payments**

A simple offline gateway that lets you accept a check as method of payment.

☐ **Bank Transfer (BACS) Payments**

A simple offline gateway that lets you accept BACS payment.

☐ **Cash on Delivery**

A simple offline gateway that lets you accept cash on delivery.

Skip this step **Continue**

Two of the most popular payment options are at the very top – PayPal and Stripe – and it's highly recommended that you integrate your site with both. Just click their corresponding checkboxes.

You can also select other payment methods that seem to make sense, plus there's going to be even more options available later on in your WooCommerce settings panel.

Note. In order to make online payments work, you need to sign up with either PayPal or Stripe separately. The settings in WooCommerce are only for integrating your existing PayPal and Stripe accounts with your new e-commerce website.

Again, click "Continue" when done.

The next step is just a confirmation screen that everything went well. At this stage, your basic site setup is done – as in; you've just built a blank e-commerce store with WooCommerce!

The next step is adding products to it. Here's how:

STEP 4 Add your first product

To truly be able to call your store operational, you need some products in the database (or services, or downloads, or whatever it is that you want to sell).

To start working with products, go to your dashboard and then to Products / Add Product:

What you're going to see is a classic WordPress content editing screen. Here's what's going on:

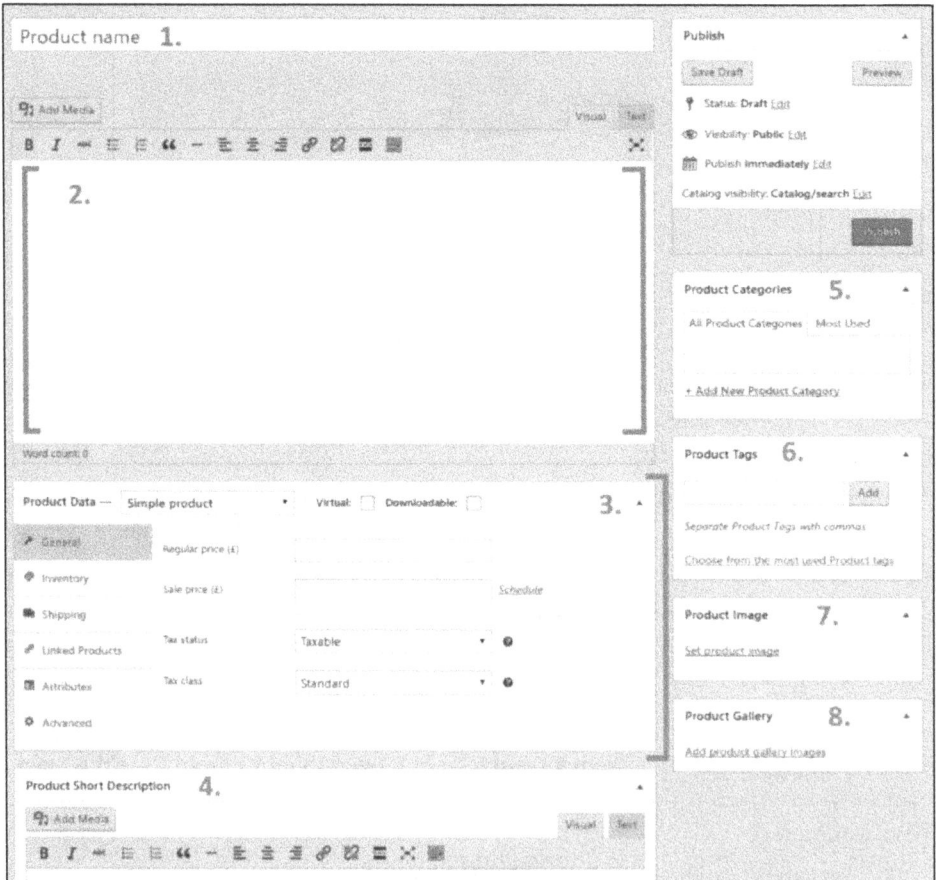

1. Product name.

2. **The main product description.** This large field allows you to enter as much info about the product as you wish. And since this is WordPress, you can put not

only simple text there but also images, columns, headings, even videos and other media. Basically, whatever you see fit.

3. **The central product data section.** This one is where you get to set the type of product that you're adding, and whether it's a downloadable or virtual product (services are considered virtual products too). As part of this central section, you also get tabs for various parameters of the product:

   a. General. This is where you get to set the pricing and taxes.

   b. Inventory. WooCommerce allows you to manage stock levels.

   c. Shipping. Set the weight, dimensions, and the cost of shipping.

   d. Linked Products. Great for setting things like upsells and cross-sales. (Think, "Customers who bought this also bought that.")

   e. Attributes. Set custom product attributes here. E.g., if you're selling shirts, you can set alternative colors here.

   f. Advanced. Additional settings. Non-essential.

4. **Short Description.** This is the text that gets displayed on the product page under the name. Works best as a short summary of what the product is.

5. **Product Categories.** Set those to group similar products together. E.g., "hats." Works just like standard WordPress categories.

6. **Product Tags.** Additional way to help you organize your database of products. Works just like standard WordPress tags.

7. **Product Image.** The main product image.

8. **Product Gallery.** Additional product images to showcase its awesomeness.

Also, the first time you visit this panel, WooCommerce will display some handy tooltips to explain what is the purpose of each field displaying their relevance.

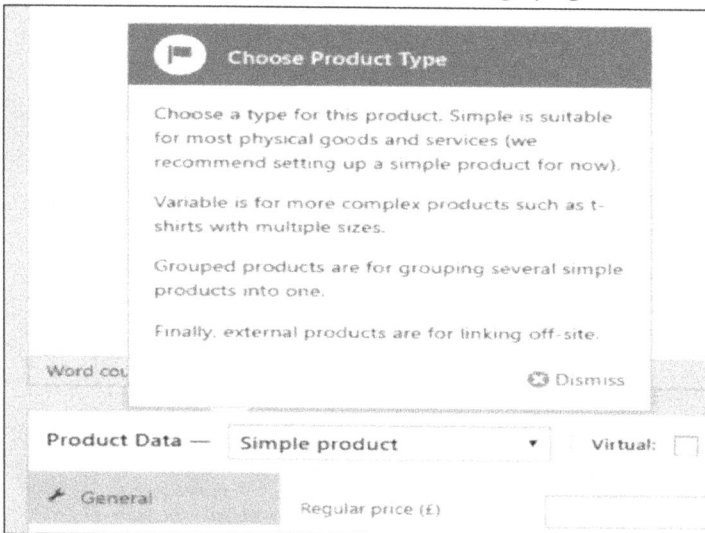

Once you're done setting all of the above, just click the big Publish button, and your first product has just been added!

After adding a handful of goods to your database, the products section in the dashboard should look something like this:

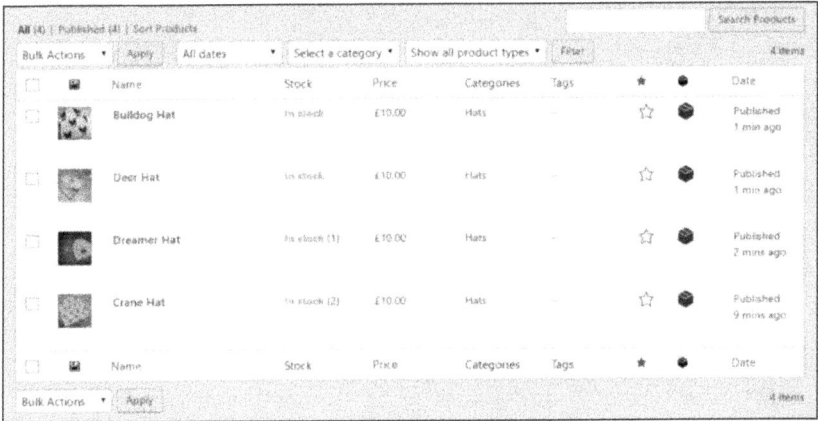

STEP 5 Choose a theme for your online store (FREE)

There's a very good reason why I first covered how to add products to your store, before discussing the visual appearance of the entire thing.

Quite frankly, without any products in the database, you wouldn't be able to see the individual pages of the store in any representative form, so you wouldn't be able to make sure that everything looks right.

But now that you do have most of your products added, we can make sure that things are in order from a purely visual standpoint.

WooCommerce vs your current theme

By default, WooCommerce works with any WordPress theme. This is great news especially if you've already picked your design and you want to stick with it.

Alternatively, you can go with special WooCommerce-optimized themes. Those themes come with pre-set styles that make all WooCommerce elements look great.

Here's my recommendation:

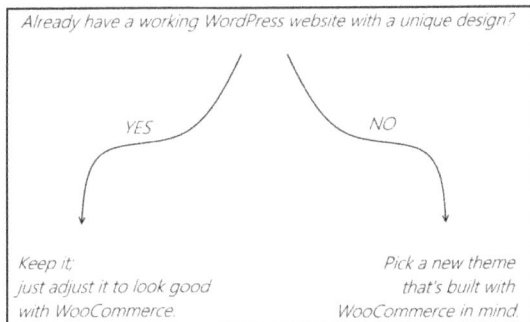

The official WooCommerce theme – and the one that's the most likely to work properly – is called Storefront. The default version is free, and it should be enough to get you going.

Alternatively, you can visit the e-commerce section at Theme Forest – the biggest directory of premium WordPress themes on the web.

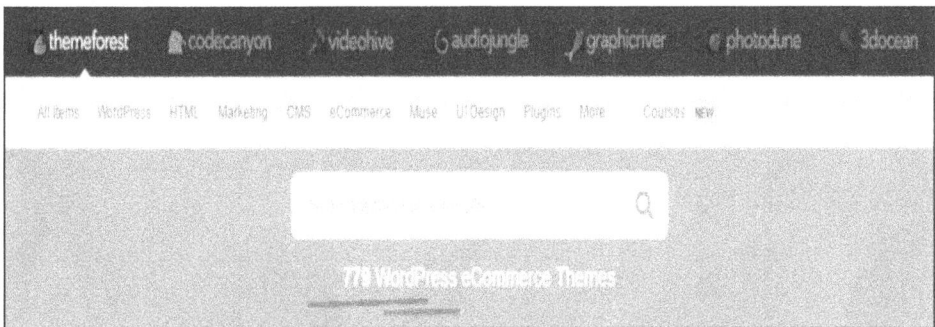

Regardless if you've decided to stick with your current theme or have gone for something new and WooCommerce-optimized, what you need to do next is make sure that the individual pages of the store look properly good. Let's do that now:

The rules of e-commerce store design

Let's discuss a handful of important points first, before we get into the nitty-gritty.

Mainly, what makes an e-commerce store design good (read: profitable)? Here are the most crucial parameters:

- The design needs to be clear and not confusing in any way. A visitor who's confused won't buy anything.

- The center content block needs to grab the visitor's attention right after they come to the site. That center block is where the products will be displayed.

- **Adjustable sidebars.** You need to be able to select how many sidebars you need, and also disable the sidebar altogether for some pages (more on that later).

- **Responsive and mobile-optimized.** Research indicates [2] that around 80% of people on the internet own a smartphone. And according to another research [3], 61% of your mobile visitors will leave immediately and go to your competitors if they have a frustrating mobile browsing experience. In other words, making sure that your website is optimized for mobile is crucial.

- **Good navigation structure.** You want clear menus that are easy to grasp – just so your visitors can find the page they're looking for.

Having the above in mind, here's what you can do with the individual pages of the store:

Your shop page

This is where the main listing of your products can be found. If you've gone through the WooCommerce setup wizard then this page can be found at YOURDOMAIN. com/shop

This is a standard WordPress page – you can edit it via WordPress dashboard / Pages.

The things that are worth doing:

- Add some copy that will encourage your visitors to shop with you.

- Decide if you want to have the sidebar on the page. This is done through your theme's own page templates. For instance, Storefront allows me to go full-width, which I will do:

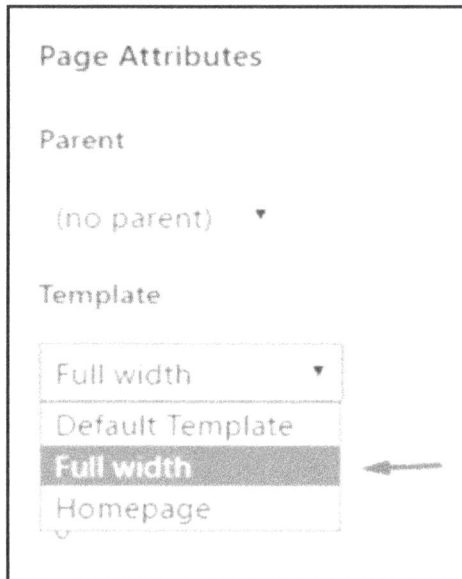

The main trait of the Shop page is that right below the standard content; it features a custom part where it displays your product listings. This is what it looks like on the Storefront theme:

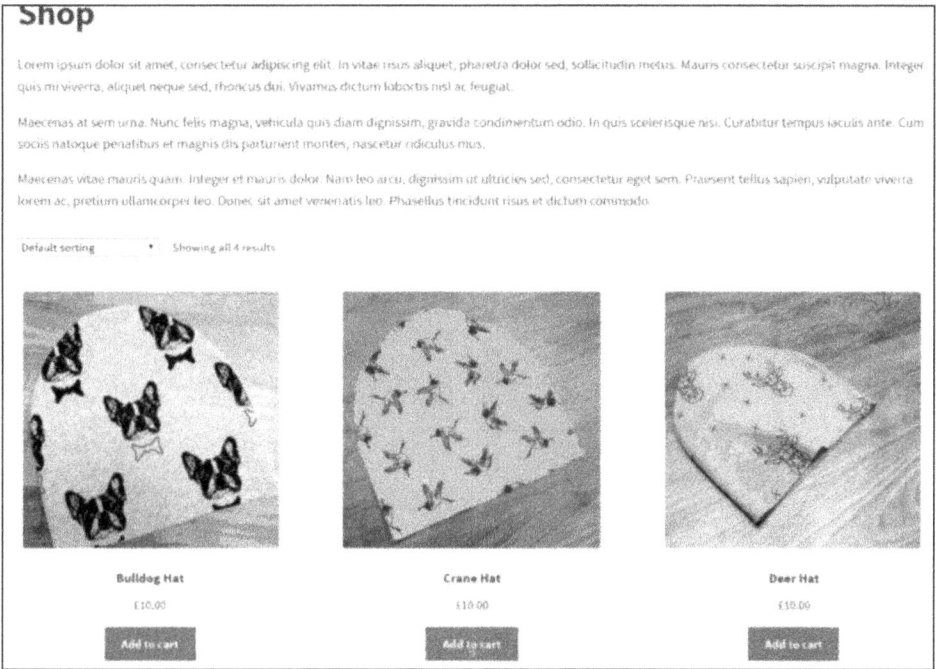

As you can see, nice product images are key, and this is the first thing that you should get right. In other words, you should probably work on your product images more than on anything else.

WooCommerce also enables you to display your products in alternative ways on this page. When you go to WordPress dashboard / WooCommerce / Settings / Products and then the Display section:

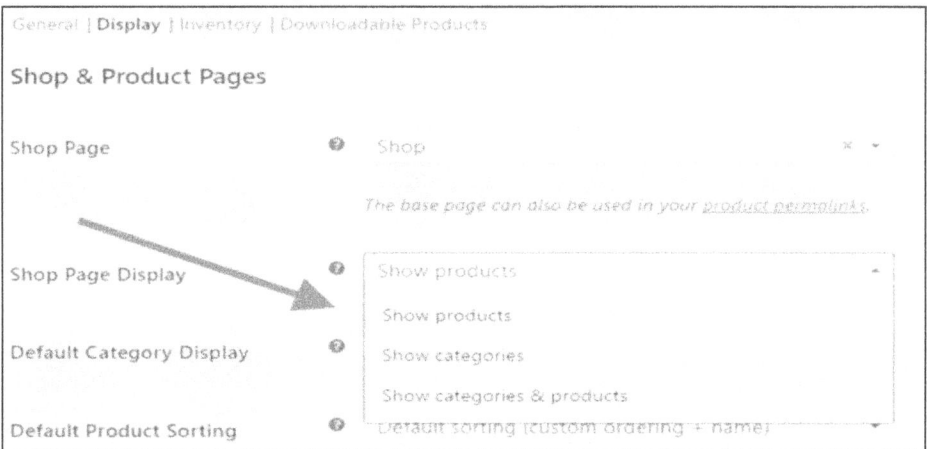

You can choose whether you want to display individual products or product categories on the Shop page. Select whatever makes the most sense for you, and save settings.

Individual product pages

In order to see those, just click on any product listing from the Shop page.

If you're using a quality theme, you shouldn't experience any difficulties on this particular page. Basically, the only thing you can do is adjust the amount of text that you're using for individual product descriptions, just to make sure that everything fits visually and that there are no blank spots that could confuse the buyer.

Here's my example with the Storefront theme (no additional customizations done):

Shopping cart

Another crucial page that can be adjusted through Dashboard / Pages

The one thing I would recommend here is to go for the full-width layout. You don't want to give the buyer too many options on this page, apart from proceeding to checkout.

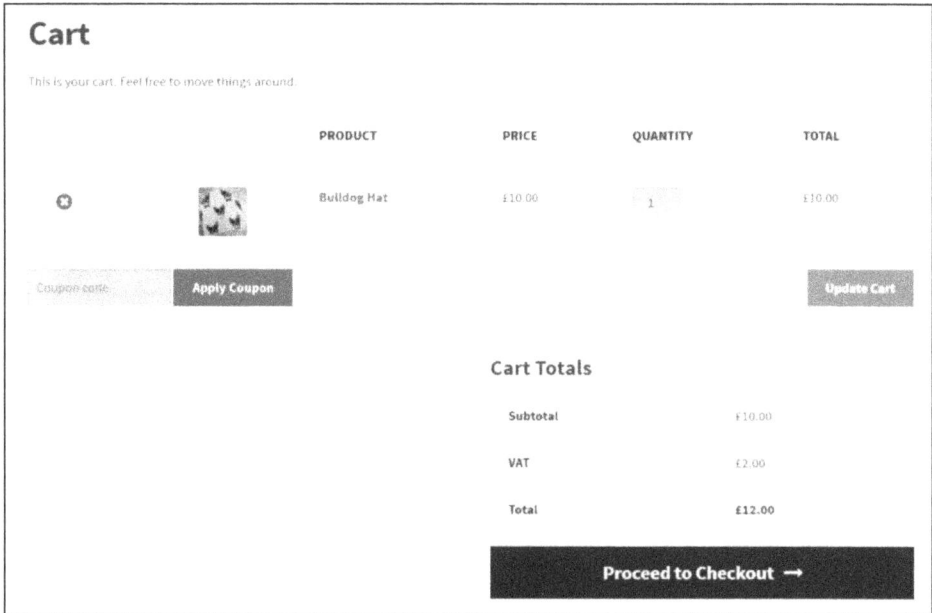

Checkout

Checkout is perhaps the most important page of them all. It's where your buyers get to finalize their orders and make the payments.

I don't actually encourage you to do any tweaks to that page apart from one:

The Checkout page absolutely needs to be full-width. The only acceptable way out of the page for the buyer should be to finalize their order, and not get distracted by the things available in the sidebar.

Again, you can do this via Dashboard / Pages (just repeat the process you went through with the Shop page).

Apart from that, the default look of the Checkout page is great:

Checkout

Have a coupon? **Click here to enter your code**

Billing Details

First Name *

Last Name *

Company Name

Email Address *

Phone *

Country *
United Kingdom (UK)

Address *

Street address

Apartment, suite, unit etc. (optional)

Town / City *

County

Postcode *

Additional Information

Order Notes

Notes about your order, e.g. special notes for delivery.

Your order

PRODUCT	TOTAL
Bulldog Hat × 1	£10.00
Subtotal	£10.00
VAT	£2.00
Total	£12.00

Place order

At this stage, you are basically done with adjusting your store design; now let's look into the possibilities to extend the store's functionality.

STEP 6 Extending WooCommerce – how to

One more thing that makes WooCommerce such an impressive e-commerce solution is that there are tens or even hundreds of extensions and plugins available for it.

Let's list some of the most useful ones here:

WooCommerce extensions

Let's start with the extensions – the official add-ons that have been approved by the WooCommerce team.

That catalogue is truly impressive and vast. But I don't want you to feel intimidated by it. You certainly don't need all of those extensions. Just treat that list as a buffet of sorts – pick whatever seems cool.

Some of the more worthy mentions:

- **Payment gateways.** These extensions allow you to accept more payment methods on top of just the standard PayPal. In general, the more methods of payment you can afford to accept (those gateways are often paid), the better.

- **Shipping extensions.** These are going to be handy if you want to automatically integrate your store with the official shipping rates from companies such as UPS or FedEx.

- **Accounting extensions.** Integrate your WooCommerce store with the accounting tool of your choice.

- **WooCommerce Bookings.** Allow customers to book appointments for services without leaving your site.

- **WooCommerce Subscriptions.** Let customers subscribe to your products or services and pay a weekly, monthly or annual fee.

- **GST Number.** For those operating within India.

Alternatively, if you don't want to spend any money on new extensions, you can browse around in the free category. There's more than enough stuff there to keep you occupied.

Plugins that supercharge your e-commerce store

Setting the extensions aside, you can also use other WordPress plugins to further supercharge your store. Here's what you should get:

- **Yoast SEO.** Improve the SEO of your whole website.

- **Yoast WooCommerce SEO plugin.** Improve the SEO of your products and other areas of your e-commerce store.

- **WooCommerce Multilingual.** Run a fully multilingual WooCommerce site.

- **Contact Form 7.** Let your site visitors contact you directly.

- **UpdraftPlus.** Back up all your site content, including your products and other store data.

- **Social Share Buttons by GetSocial.** Let your buyers share your products with their friends and family through social media.

- **MonsterInsights.** Integrate your site with Google Analytics.

- **IThemes Security.** Security presets for your website.

- **W3 Total Cache.** Speed up your website through caching.

Creating an Online Store in Nutshell

As you can see, the degree of difficulty when it comes to creating your own e-commerce store with WordPress isn't too high, but it will still take you a while to get through all of the steps above ... probably one afternoon or so.

But that's still incredible considering that just, say, five years ago you would need to hire a developer and pay them north of $5,000 to get something similar created. Now, you can do everything on your own.

Anyway, to help you get through all the tasks required, here's a cut-out-'n-keep checklist:

Before you begin

- Get a domain name, sign up for web hosting; get a working WordPress install running.
- Make sure that your new blank WordPress site works properly (no obvious errors popping up, etc.).

Installing WooCommerce

- Install and activate the main WooCommerce plugin.
- Go through the WooCommerce setup wizard, paying close attention to:
  - ❖ Getting the four required pages created (Shop, Cart, Checkout, My Account).
  - ❖ Setting up the store locale.
  - ❖ Setting up sales tax and shipping.
  - ❖ Picking initial payment methods.

Products

- Add most (or all) of your products or product categories to the store.

Design

- Select the right WordPress theme for your e-commerce store. Go either with your existing theme, or browse through the other possibilities. Review the rules of e-commerce store design when doing so.
- Adjust your Shop page.
- Adjust individual product pages.
- Adjust the Cart page.
- Adjust the Checkout page.

Extensions

- Install the payment gateways that you want to use.
- Consider some of the shipping extensions.
- Consider an accounting extension.
- Browse through other extensions, and also the free category

Plugins

- Consider installing all of the plugins that will supercharge your e-commerce store:
  - ❖ Yoast SEO
  - ❖ Yoast WooCommerce SEO
  - ❖ WooCommerce Multilingual
  - ❖ Contact Form 7
  - ❖ Updraft Plus

- ❖ Social Share Buttons by GetSocial
- ❖ Monster Insights
- ❖ iThemes Security
- ❖ W3 Total Cache.

Your ready to use WooCommerce store will look like, though depending on your business and product line

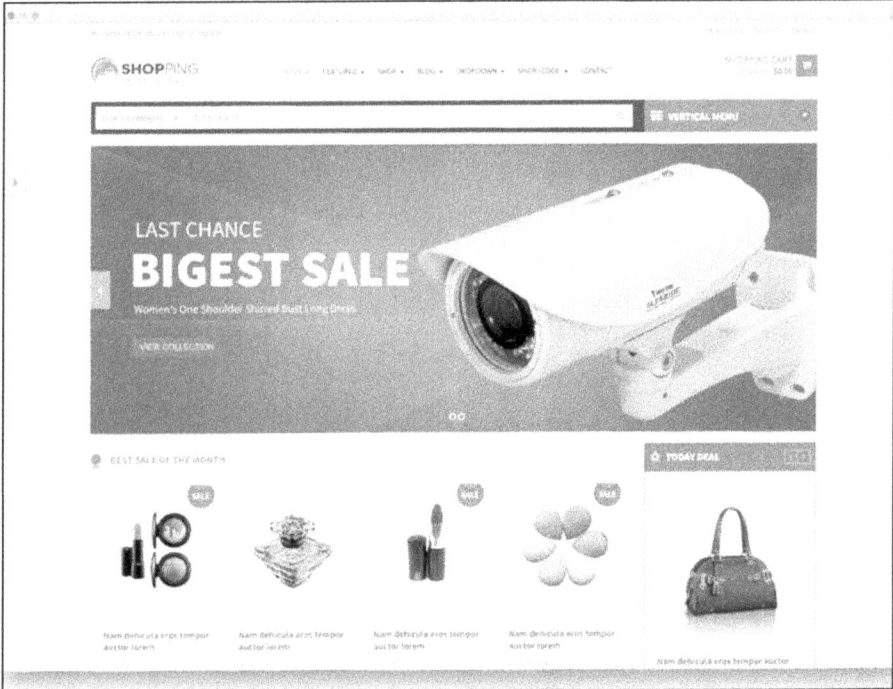

References and courtesy

- www.simplilearn.com
- www.kaushik.net
- www.websitesetup.org
- https://en.wikipedia.org/wiki/Digital_marketing
- https://images.google.com/
- www.slideshare.net
- https://www.smallbusiness.chron.com
- https://en.wikipedia.org/wiki/Copywriting
- https://blog.hubspot.com/marketing/beginner-inbound-lead-generation-guide
- http://www.awaionline.com/what-is-copywriting/

Abbreviation

1. **SEO:** Search Engine Optimization
2. **Web Design:** Website Design
3. **HTML:** Hypertext Markup Language
4. **CSS:** Cascading Style Sheets
5. **CGI:** Common gateway interface
6. **AJAX;** Asynchronous JavaScript and XML
7. **SEM:** Search Engine Marketing
8. **SMM:** Social Media Marketing
9. **e-Commerce:** Electronic Commerce
10. **eBook:** Electronic Book
11. **BFSI:** Banking Financial Services & insurance
12. **RoI:** Return on Investment
13. **RoR:** Rate of return
14. **Omni Channel:** Multi-communication channel
15. **App:** Application
16. **OTP:** One Time Password
17. **ASO:** App Store Optimization
18. **CAPEX:** Capital Expenditure
19. **OPEX:** Operational Expenditure
20. **CAGR:** Cumulative Annual Growth Rate
21. **PPS:** Pay-per-sale
22. **PPC:** Pay per Click
23. **OMP:** Online marketing platform
24. **CRM:** Customer Relationship Management
25. **CMS:** Content Management System
26. **CPM:** Cost per mille
27. **CPC:** Cost per click
28. **CPE:** cost per engagement
29. **CPV:** cost per view
30. **CPA:** Cost per Acquisition
31. **CPI:** Cost per install
32. **PPP:** Pay per Performance
33. **vCPM:** Cost per thousand viewable impression

34. **ROAS:** Return-on-AD-spend
35. **ECPC:** Enhanced cost-per-click
36. **Ad/s:** Advertisement/s
37. **LL:** Local Listing
38. **TM:** Traditional Marketing
39. **DM;** Digital Marketing
40. **SMS:** Short Message Service
41. **OIM:** Online identity management
42. **PRM:** Personal reputation management
43. **Web Analytics:** Website Analytics
44. **KPI:** Key Performing Indicators
45. **eWOM:** Electronic Word of mouth
46. **SCRM:** Social Customer Relationship management
47. **AI:** Artificial Intelligence
48. **CTA:** Call-to-Action
49. **eMarketer:** Electronic Marketers